The Meaning of Mourning

The Meaning of Mourning

Perspectives on Death, Loss, and Grief

Edited by Mikołaj Sławkowski-Rode

LEXINGTON BOOKS
Lanham • Boulder • New York • London

Rowman & Littlefield
Bloomsbury Publishing Inc, 1359 Broadway, New York, NY 10018, USA
Bloomsbury Publishing Plc, 50 Bedford Square, London, WC1B 3DP, UK
Bloomsbury Publishing Ireland, 29 Earlsfort Terrace, Dublin 2, D02 AY28, Ireland
www.bloomsbury.com

Published by Lexington Books
An imprint of The Rowman & Littlefield Publishing Group, Inc.
4501 Forbes Boulevard, Suite 200, Lanham, Maryland 20706
www.rowman.com
86-90 Paul Street, London EC2A 4NE

Copyright © 2023 by The Rowman & Littlefield Publishing Group, Inc.

All rights reserved. No part of this publication may be: i) reproduced or transmitted in any form, electronic or mechanical, including photocopying, recording or by means of any information storage or retrieval system without prior permission in writing from the publishers; or ii) used or reproduced in any way for the training, development or operation of artificial intelligence (AI) technologies, including generative AI technologies. The rights holders expressly reserve this publication from the text and data mining exception as per Article 4(3) of the Digital Single Market Directive (EU) 2019/790.

British Library Cataloguing in Publication Information available

Library of Congress Cataloging-in-Publication Data

Names: Sławkowski-Rode, Mikołaj, editor.
Title: The meaning of mourning : perspectives on death, loss, and grief / edited by Mikołaj Sławkowski-Rode.
Description: Lanham, Maryland : Lexington Books, an imprint of The Rowman & Littlefield Publishing Group, Inc., [2023] | Includes bibliographical references and index.
Identifiers: LCCN 2022044343 (print) | LCCN 2022044344 (ebook) | ISBN 9781666908923 (cloth) | ISBN 9781666908930 (ebook)
Subjects: LCSH: Bereavement. | Grief.
Classification: LCC BF575.G7 M439 2023 (print) | LCC BF575.G7 (ebook) | DDC 155.9/37—dc23/eng/20221021
LC record available at https://lccn.loc.gov/2022044343
LC ebook record available at https://lccn.loc.gov/2022044344

Contents

Acknowledgments		vii
Introduction *Mikołaj Sławkowski-Rode*		1
1	Hume and Doctor Johnson on Death *Jerry Valberg*	7
2	The Problem of Mourning *Eleonore Stump*	19
3	What Can the Roman Catholic Liturgies of the Dead Offer Mourners: Solidarity with the Deceased and Hopeful Protest? *Richard Conrad, OP*	33
4	Toward a Philosophical Theology of Pregnancy Loss *Amber L. Griffioen*	57
5	Mourning: A Phenomenology *Balázs M. Mezei*	77
6	Mourning and the Recognition of Value *Cathy Mason and Matt Dougherty*	93
7	Grieving and Mourning: The Psychology of Bereavement *Colin Murray Parkes*	107
8	Bereavement, Grief, and Mourning *John Cottingham*	119

9	Mourning and the Second-Person Perspective Mikołaj Sławkowski-Rode	131
10	Mourning Academic Mentors and Mentees Douglas J. Davies	149
11	Mourning and Memory, Private and Public Dimensions Anthony O'Hear	171
12	The Work of Mourning Roger Scruton	183
13	Sidgwick's Dilemma Lesley Chamberlain	193
14	"Israel but the Grave . . .": The Art and Architecture of Mourning Alexander Stoddart	203
15	The Difficult Art of Outliving Raymond Tallis	221
Index		239
About the Contributors		251

Acknowledgements

The idea for this collection originated with a colloquium at Blackfriars Hall, University of Oxford jointly organized by the Humane Philosophy Society and the Aquinas Institute. As the collection grew several persons and institutions have supported this project, and helped to bring it to completion. In particular thanks are owed to Andrew Pinsent and the Ian Ramsey Centre for Science and Religion at Oxford for guidance and support. Ralph Weir and Samuel Hughes, friends of the editor, and both implicated in the Humane Philosophy Society, have provided greatly appreciated advice and indispensable encouragement. Simon Mussell has been of immense help as a proofreader in preparing the manuscript. Special thanks are due to Jana Hodges-Kluck at Rowman and Littlefield who was responsible for overseeing the publication, and with whom it was a pleasure to work. This project has also received support from the John Templeton Foundation grant New Horizons for Science and Religion in Central and Eastern Europe. I am indebted to Blackfriars Hall, University of Oxford, and the Faculty of Philosophy, University of Warsaw, not only for their generous support of the event, which germinated the project, but also for making provision for me to devote time to the volume while working at both institutions. I would also like to take this opportunity to express my gratitude to Roger Scruton for the many years of mentorship and inspiration which have shaped my thinking about these and many other topics, and which continue through his work. Finally, I would like to thank all of the contributors for their patience with the process, and for believing in this project.

Introduction
Mikołaj Sławkowski-Rode

Grief is a universal human response to death and loss. Mourning is an equally universally observable practice in which grief is expressed and whereby the bereaved can come to terms with the reality of loss. Yet, despite their prevalence, there is no unified understanding of the nature and meaning of grief and mourning. There are important ethnic differences in how grief is experienced and a variety of forms that mourning can take across cultures and religions. Likewise, there is a wide range of approaches to what the desired ends of mourning are, or what a resolution of grief might consist in. Across literary traditions, poetic responses to grief and death range from the elegiac to the defiant. Grief and mourning have been a subject of interest to thinkers representing all of the world's major intellectual traditions, from Platonism to Daoism. These perspectives have typically been critical, suggesting that too great a preoccupation with death and loss undermines human self-sufficiency and rational self-control. Conversely, in most religious traditions, the remembrance of and continued relationships with the dead constitute an important part of individual and community life.

In recent years, a number of disciplines have made important contributions to our understanding of mourning including experimental psychology, cognitive neuroscience, and social anthropology. These approaches explore aspects of the emotional and spiritual turbulence caused by loss, and the corresponding paths to the resolution of grief, that represent, on the one hand, our evolution as biological and social beings, where the disruption of bonds caused by death affects our chances of survival, and, on the other hand, our individual constitution as conscious subjects, where our sense of personal and collective identity may be disrupted by the loss of a close relationship. Recent scientific work on loss, grief, and mourning has also promoted renewed philosophical and theological interest.

The present volume brings together fifteen original contributions from diverse disciplines addressing the topics of death, grief, and mourning from a variety of angles. While the collection is not designed to serve as a comprehensive study or companion, it assumes a holistic, interdisciplinary approach to the theme of mourning that combines philosophy, theology, psychology, medical science, and the arts. The volume provides a survey of the rich topography of methodologies, problems, approaches, and disciplines in light of which the issues surrounding loss and our responses to it may be viewed. The title of this collection therefore invokes the idea of mourning in a broad sense, which goes beyond the public display of grief caused by the loss of a loved one. The chapters are organized in such a way as to guide the reader through the spectrum of perspectives represented by the contributors, highlighting the connections and discontinuities between them.

The collection begins with four chapters that consider the metaphysics of death and the theology of loss, including expressions of these ideas in ritual form and their implications for concrete experiences, like reproductive loss. This set of issues leads into two chapters which analyze the relationship between mourning and the recognition of value, and the role hope plays in the experience of loss. There follow four chapters exploring themes in the psychology of loss and the psychological roots of grief in early childhood, psychological vulnerability to loss in later life when opportunities for rebuilding meaning are diminished, and the interpersonal phenomenology of loss. A particular case of the latter is considered in the form of the loss of academic mentors and mentees, and the forms that mourning in those cases may take. This also provides a transition to a set of issues connected with public and cultural aspects of mourning which are discussed in the next three chapters. Community mourning and the need for public commemoration is considered, and how these may become complicated by cultural or historical factors. Differing attitudes to the loss of an idea are contrasted, and how mourning can be expressed in the rethinking of intellectual heritage of a culture. The collection ends with a discussion of the cultural role of sepulchral art, and a meditation on the necessity of living with loss.

In Chapter 1, Jerry Valberg considers the ancient problem of whether death is bad for us. Valberg analyzes this problem in terms famously adopted in the dispute between Hume and Doctor Johnson. An important part of the meaning of loss in its interpersonal context is connected to the fact that we believe death to be bad for those we lose to it. The thought that this belief is mistaken can be consoling, but it may also impoverish our understanding of loss, and of the relationships it threatens. Valberg attempts to justify our belief in the badness of death even if it is followed by nothingness, as Hume insists.

In Chapter 2, Eleonore Stump considers a closely related question: Is death an evil if the Christian picture of redemption in the afterlife is true? If there is nothing that is left unredeemed in the larger perspective of a theodicy, then grief and mourning seem less justified. Stump argues that this is not the case and considers grief and mourning to be phenomena unaccounted for by traditional theodicies. Her contribution is a new development in her seminal work on the problem of evil.

In Chapter 3, Richard Conrad discusses the same theme in the context of the Catholic Office of the Dead. Conrad compares the Old and New Liturgies, showing how they differ in their respective approaches to death and mourning. The author defends the perspective implicit in the Old Liturgy in which the reality of death and the pain connected with loss are emphasized. Conrad argues that even if we accept universal redemption and resurrection, we are still justified in feeling outrage and anguish when we are bereaved. He defends this claim by suggesting that God does not demand of us that we joyfully accept his will in all cases, and indeed that conforming to God's will in some circumstances might mean willing something different from God.

In Chapter 4, Amber Leigh Griffioen takes the argument of the foregoing chapters a step further. Griffioen focuses not merely on how to philosophically and theologically justify the grief and lamentation expressed in the Christian tradition, but on how to broaden this tradition to make space for the expression of previously unacknowledged grief: that connected with reproductive loss. Griffioen argues, echoing Stump's reasoning in the second chapter, that a theology of reproductive loss that justifies grief and the mourning it prompts must be grounded in the metaphysics of the afterlife, and a resulting anthropology and ethics. For Griffioen, the development of grieving rituals for pregnancy loss that are philosophically adequate and theologically fitting requires a novel conception of God. Griffioen also notes that in the Christian context, grief for an unborn child is often connected to the hope of being able to be reunited despite the premature loss.

In Chapter 5, Balázs Mezei takes up this important theme of hope and considers how it relates to grief and mourning in a broader context of death and loss which undermine the meanings and values around which we organize our lives. Mezei uses the example of World War II concentration camps to argue that mourning is not merely an expression of an attitude taken towards a senseless loss, but a search for meaning which is guided by hope for the reconciliation of human values with even the most traumatic of experiences.

Chapter 6 focuses on the closely related topic of mourning as a form of recognition of value. It takes up the problem of the limits of mourning and sorrow in light of inestimable loss. The authors Cathy Mason and Matthew Dougherty consider the question of how it might be appropriate or even desirable to move on, and continue one's life, if mourning is proportional to the value of what has been lost. They argue that ceasing to mourn can be a fitting response to the object of love, which may represent its value in our life better than unending mourning.

In Chapter 7, Colin Murray Parkes takes a wider view of the issues surrounding the psychology of mourning and bereavement, arguing that human responses to loss are rooted in behaviors that have survival value in early childhood. In particular, this includes the disorientation and distress experienced due to the absence of a caregiver. The way that the relationship with caregivers in early childhood develops shapes later responses to loss in adult life, which in turn may require different therapeutic approaches that are sensitive to those early experiences, and not merely to facts about the suffered loss. The chapter also serves as a new introduction to Parkes's seminal work on this topic.

Chapter 8 discusses the disorientation and distress suffered as a consequence of the death of someone close as a result of the social distancing and disruption of the familiar in the wake of the coronavirus pandemic. John Cottingham argues that although grief and mourning are usually associated with the loss of some clearly definable good, this does not exhaust the phenomenology of loss. The chapter considers examples of this in poetical and religious accounts of loss, including those of Dante, Horatius, Keats, Housman, Manley Hopkins, as well as Eleonore Stump's seminal work, and Biblical accounts ranging from the Psalms to the Gospel of Luke. Cottingham then returns to the theme of hope as a guiding principle for grief that prevents it from slipping into depression and mourning collapsinginto despair.

Chapter 9, written by the editor, analyzes the phenomenology of loss and considers the connection between the interpersonal dimension of grief and the sense of disorientation caused by the radical change in how the world is experienced after loss. The author argues that an important part of this experience is constituted by sharing the world with others. With the loss of others, it is not merely that an element of the world we inhabit is removed, but rather that the whole world is radically altered. The chapter proposes a second-personal account of this phenomenon and suggests that grief and mourning are an attempt at rebuilding—to the extent that this is possible—the shared world.

In Chapter 10, Douglas Davies considers a particular case of mourning that could be seen as an example of how loss might threaten the way we view the world. Davies focuses on loss in a relationship between an academic mentor and mentee. The chapter considers how idea-generation is aligned with emotions and how it confers a sense of identity, which is threatened by loss. Davies observes that, because grief connected with this loss lies outside of the usually recognized circles of personal bereavement, it seldom finds public recognition. Yet, by applying the theoretical notion of "dividual" rather than individual personhood, he explores how shared knowledge contributes to identity formation, and how, through a process of mourning, this "dividual" identity may persist. The contribution is an important new addition to Davies's seminal work on the themes of loss, mourning, and grief.

Chapter 11 considers the relationship between public and private aspects of recognizing and coming to terms with loss. Anthony O'Hear argues that given the universality of human mourning, public commemoration and mourning rituals play an important role in this process, which cannot be reduced to overcoming the psychological trauma of private grief. The chapter looks in particular at the consequences of death being left unmourned, becoming problematic and at times tragic, and impeding personal healing and the restoration of communities affected by the loss. O'Hear claims that public commemorations can often have the opposite effect of simply opening up old wounds, and that, in fact, by recognizing those previously deprived of recognition may help with both private and public healing. The chapter develops themes that are present in some of O'Hear's most important works, including *The Landscape of Humanity: Art, Culture and Society* (2008) and *The Element of Fire: Science, Art and the Human World* (republished 2013).

In Chapter 12, Roger Scruton examines a case of mourning that is complicated for the community by historical and cultural factors. Scruton begins by considering the mourning for a devastated culture which was made impossible in the German experience by the appropriation of the German cultural heritage under the Nazi dictatorship. A complete repudiation of the values which we feel have been compromised by being employed in disgraceful contexts creates a conflict, Scruton argues, as it contradicts the obligation of piety we have towards our ancestors. He suggests we have a duty towards the dead, and that leaving this duty unfulfilled in the end makes it impossible to accept loss and move on. This contribution was written shortly before the author died and it is, as far as the editor is aware, the final piece that he completed before his death.

Chapter 13 combines the approaches of the three preceding pieces and considers an interesting case of mourning for an idea. Lesley Chamberlain looks at what she calls a "minimalist British version of 'The Death of God.'" Chamberlain compares two responses to Henry Sidgwick's skepticism towards moral realism. She contrasts Bernard Williams's enthusiasm with Alasdair MacIntyre's sorrowful acknowledgment of the loss. The chapter analyzes how these two attitudes influence the prospects for the reconstitution of value in human moral life.

Chapter 14 explores another important context of the public dimension of human responses to lossin the form of sepulchral architecture. Alexander Stoddart focuses on the Necropolis of Glasgow, which houses an impressive collection of sepulchral forms that commemorate the dead and at the same time address the living. The author considers the role of the tomb as an enduring testament to death and a sign of personal grief, which in time becomes a reminder of the bonds that account for the endurance of the community. Stoddart argues that Classicism is the architectural style that is best suited for the purpose of housing the dead. This is because, he claims, Classicism embodies those aspects of our relationship with the dead that are most difficult to represent, and for that reason are the most disturbing.

In Chapter 15, Raymond Tallis offers a meditation on enduring in the face of the loss which permeates our lives. "The art of outliving," Tallis observes, is "more pertinent the longer we live as this implies outliving many persons and things that in different periods were important to if not constitutive of our lives." He associates the ability to outlive with the capacity for personal growth, albeit this may often seem like a betrayal of those we have lost, and of ourselves. In what is at times a very personal account, Tallis's contribution connects with the opening chapter on the badness of death, and argues that living is itself outliving, just as growing up is growing away.

While each of the chapters can be read individually, the reader will benefit from reading the contributions in the suggested order, which emphasizes a movement from the reality of loss to the need to accept it in our lives through a detailed consideration of its metaphysical, psychological, interpersonal, cultural, and moral dimensions.

1

Hume and Doctor Johnson on Death

Jerry Valberg

SECTION 1

Boswell, in his famous biography, describes an occasion on which he relates to Johnson a conversation with Hume wherein the latter expresses a view about death.

> Boswell: When we were alone, I introduced the subject of death, and endeavoured to maintain that the fear of it might be got over. I told him that David Hume said to me, he was no more uneasy that he should *not be* after this life, than that he *had not been* before he began to exist.
>
> Johnson: "Sir, if he really thinks so, his perceptions are disturbed; he is mad: if he does not think so, he lies. He may tell you he holds his finger in the flame of a candle, without feeling pain; would you believe him? When he dies, he at least gives up all he has."[1]

On reading the above passage, many (most?) people, I reckon, will more or less agree with Johnson's negative attitude toward death (though not necessarily with his assessment of Hume). However, as we'll see, there is a simple line of reasoning that supports Hume's attitude and places the onus on those who side with Johnson to justify their reaction.

Hume compares the period of time before he was born with that after he dies. For each of us there is such a pair of times. What is it like for us during these times? An odd question. The only answer would seem to be that there is *nothing* which it is like for us. It is not like being in darkness, or bored, or feeling empty. It is not like anything. In both cases, one might say there is "nothingness" for us.

SECTION 2

We shall begin by attempting to formulate the (or at any rate, an) issue between Hume and Johnson. In this regard it is important to ensure we identify the assumptions that will guide our discussion.

Some may immediately wish to object that whereas there is nothingness for us before we are born, the non-bodily conscious part of us continues after we die. I believe (like lots of people these days) that we know enough about the dependence of consciousness on the brain, and about what happens to the brain after death, to reject such a view. In any case, we shall in the present chapter simply assume that with death there is nothingness for us—just as there was nothingness for us before we were born.

For each of us, then, there is a pre-birth and a post-death nothingness (the nothingness of death). The former nothingness has an end but no beginning, the latter a beginning but no end. Thus, each in its own way is temporally infinite. Moreover, since neither has any qualitative features, neither has any such features the other does not have; hence, the two nothingnesses are qualitatively identical.

A nothingness is always somebody's nothingness: it has a subject. The subject is the one "for whom" there is nothingness (not the one who experiences it; there is no such thing as experiencing nothingness).

Once a subject exists, we can assert of him that, before he existed, there was nothingness for him. Before he existed, however, we could not have made this assertion. At that time there was no relevant subject of whom we might have asserted that there is nothingness for him.

When a subject dies, and in that sense ceases to exist, he remains a possible object of reference.[2] Thus, after his death, it remains possible and in fact true to assert of him that now—that is, now that he has ceased to exist—there is nothingness for him; it is also true of him that, prior to the time he began to exist, there was nothingness for him. And both times (periods of time), both the time before and the time after his existence, are infinite.

If we reflect on the fact of the infinite nothingness which preceded our birth, it may give us a peculiar feeling; but that the fact should upset or disturb us seems like a form of mental illness. Hume, like most of us, is not troubled by the fact of his past (pre-birth) nothingness. But, unlike many of us, he is, or claims to be, equally untroubled by the fact of his future nothingness.

Given the qualitative identity of his past and future nothingnesses, Hume finds no more reason to have a negative attitude toward his future nothingness than toward his past, pre-birth, nothingness. That is, he finds no reason to have a negative attitude toward his past nothingness, and therefore, since his future nothingness seems indistinguishable from his past, he finds no reason to be negatively disposed toward his future nothingness—no reason, then, to be troubled by the nothingness of death.

Does not the same hold for all of us? Yet the fact is, like Johnson, we—at least many people (some more than others)—*are* troubled by the prospect of our future nothingness: by the fact that in the not hugely distant future (of course, it partly depends on where we are in life) nothingness will arrive in our case. Thus, while acknowledging the soundness of Hume's reasoning, many would admit to sharing Johnson's negative reaction to the prospect of their future nothingness. Hume, I suspect, would charge those who have such a reaction with irrationality.

Is it irrational? We shall take this question to be the same as the question of whether we are justified in our (let us assume) negative attitude toward the nothingness of death. If such an attitude is justified, it is rational, otherwise irrational; and if it is rational, it is justified. We may conceive of the issue between Johnson and Hume in these terms. Johnson thinks that it is rational of us to have a negative attitude toward our future nothingness, that such an attitude is justified; Hume thinks it is not justified, that it is not rational.

SECTION 3

Most people, as we said, will probably side with Johnson in this regard. On the other hand, Hume's view is supported by a simple argument:

(H1) There is nothing in our post-death nothingness to distinguish it from our pre-birth nothingness;

(H2) There is nothing in our pre-birth nothingness that justifies our being troubled by it.

(H3) Therefore, there is nothing in our post-death nothingness that justifies our being troubled by it.

What shall we say about Hume's Argument? (H2) seems unproblematic. Also, it seems obvious that (H3) follows from (H1) and (H2). It looks, then, as if everything hangs on the truth of (H1).

As a preliminary, note that if (H1) is true—if there is no difference between the two nothingnesses—there would seem to be no way of justifying a difference in our attitudes toward them, in which case Hume is right. Might there not, however, be a difference between them which fails to justify the difference in our attitude? But then Hume would still be right. In order that Johnson is right, there must not only be a difference between the two nothingnesses, it must be a difference which justifies the difference in our attitudes toward them. It must in this sense be a "justifying difference."

OK. It should be clear that the relevant justifying difference cannot be a qualitative difference between the nothingnesses. (By hypothesis, the nothingnesses are qualitatively identical.) On the other hand, might there not be a *non*-qualitative difference which justifies the difference in our attitudes?

Henceforth, we shall understand (though will not keep making it explicit) our question to be: Is there a non-qualitative justifying difference between our past and future nothingness: more particularly, a non-qualitative difference that justifies our being negatively disposed toward the nothingness that lies in our future while more or less indifferent toward that which precedes our birth? We may regard Hume's Argument as challenging us to identify such a difference (Hume's Challenge).[3]

SECTION 4

We ought at this point to stress that we are weighting the Challenge toward our future nothingness. That is, we are assuming that, in contrast to our negative attitude toward our future nothingness, our indifference toward our past nothingness does not require justification. We shall say more about this below; anyway, the assumption should be easy to accept.

Some may wish to claim that Hume's Challenge rests on a misconception. Contrary to what is presupposed by the Challenge, our negative attitude toward our future nothingness is not, in the first place, *open* to justification. It is neither justified nor unjustified, rational nor irrational. Questions about justification and reasons are out of place here.

Behind this claim is the thought that our negative attitude toward our future nothingness has more to do with biology than reason. Consider, say, the case of fear. In experiencing fear, the subject's pulse and galvanic skin response change; but there is no question of justifying such changes. They are not open to justification. Would not the same be true of the physiological reactions (whatever they are) that we have in contemplating our future nothingness?

Yes, but our negative attitude toward our future nothingness is no more exhausted by the associated physiology than is fear on our part.[4] In both cases we are concerned with emotions, and emotions, quite apart from their physiology, have a phenomenology—which involves an "object." In the case of fear, the object is, typically, something that the subject regards as a threat. In the case of death, the object is the nothingness that will replace our consciousness. In each case, justification evaluates the emotion in light of its object: our fear in light of the relevant threat; our negative attitude toward death (toward our future nothingness) in light of what this nothingness holds up or means to us.

SECTION 5

Is there, once again, a non-qualitative justifying difference between our past and future nothingness, that is, a difference which justifies us in being negatively disposed toward the nothingness that lies in our future while more or less indifferent toward the nothingness which precedes our birth? This is Hume's Challenge.

It may occur to the reader that the answer is contained in the Challenge itself. Our past nothingness is past, our future nothingness is future. Is it not the case that, quite generally, our attitude toward the future is fundamentally different from our attitude toward what is past?

But while this might justify us in maintaining different attitudes toward the two nothingnesses, the fact of its futurity versus pastness would not justify the negativity of our attitude toward our future nothingness. After all, we often look forward in a positive way to what lies in the future. By itself, the futurity of an event is compatible with our having toward it either a positive or negative attitude. (The same holds for the pastness of past events.)

SECTION 6

Let us reflect on our situation before the advent of nothingness. Except in extreme circumstances, we value the fact that we exist (though to speak of our "valuing" the fact of our existence may seem like an odd understatement). Thus, our future nothingness entails the absence of something we value: the fact of our existence. Does that not justify a negative attitude toward our future nothingness?

We are forgetting about Hume's Argument. True, once the nothingness of death arrives, our existence will no longer be a fact; it will have been replaced by the fact of our non-existence. Yet our non-existence was also a fact before we were born—and this does not seem to justify a negative attitude toward our past nothingness.

Nevertheless, it is difficult to deny that our negative attitude toward our future nothingness has something to do with the fact that it entails our non-existence. But what, exactly?

It has to do, I think, not with the entailed fact of our future non-existence *as such*, but with the fact that, given that we now exist, our future nothingness and hence non-existence entails that we will *cease* to exist. It is the fact that we will cease to exist, a fact entailed by our future but not our past nothingness, that gets to us. Hence, while both our past and future nothingnesses entail our non-existence, only our future nothingness evokes a negative attitude on our part.

The negative attitude might be described by saying that the fact that we will cease to exist strikes us—or may strike us—as *awful*.[5] Insofar then as the fact of our future nothingness entails our ceasing to exist, it may strike us this way: as awful.

There is here an obvious contrast with the case of our past nothingness. Something cannot cease to exist unless it already exists. Since at the time of our past nothingness, we did not yet exist, there was at that time no possibility of our ceasing to exist. Hence our past nothingness does not strike us in the same way as our future nothingness, that is, as awful.[6]

SECTION 7

However, these simple-minded reflections only highlight the real question. Our ceasing to exist is (we are supposing) awful; given that our future versus past nothingness entails our ceasing to exist, our future versus past nothingness is awful. But now, of course, we will want to ask, about our ceasing to exist, what makes *it* awful. In other words, in what does its awfulness consist?

One idea here relates to the fact that our ceasing to exist cannot be reversed. When we cease to exist, that's it—we cease to exist forever. We cannot begin to exist again. This is an instance of a general metaphysical truth about the existence of objects. Assume that, at time t, an object X ceases to exist. It cannot be true that, at a later time t+1, an object Y begins to exist and that Y = X. Otherwise it would be true of one and the same object that it existed and did not exist at the same time.[7]

It follows that the nothingness of death—unlike, say, the nothingness of deep sleep or anesthesia—has no end and, in that sense, is infinite. What faces us in death is a nothingness which never ends. This may—not so?—strike us as awful.

Yet, we know, in its own way our pre-birth nothingness is also infinite: there is no time that is the first time of this nothingness. (If the nothingness of death has no end, our pre-birth nothingness has no beginning.) With respect to infinitude, there is a kind of parity. Why is it then that we react with equanimity to our pre-birth (past) nothingness, while we (some, at any rate) tend to find our future nothingness awful?

It may be thought the difference is that our future nothingness is something we actually have to deal with. Not so, obviously, in the case of our past nothingness: when our past nothingness was actual, we were not yet there to deal with anything.

One might counter that when our future nothingness becomes actual, we will cease to exist and thus will not be there to deal with it either. But do we not have to deal with it before it arrives—in fact, all our lives? The response might be that we have to deal, as well, all our lives with our past nothingness.

Or will you now say that in this case there is nothing to "deal" with, that in contrast to our future nothingness, our past nothingness does not present us with anything which is difficult for us to take on board or come to terms with? This is true. But it simply draws attention to the very asymmetry that gives rise to Hume's Challenge. We are back where we started.

SECTION 8

So, let us start again. Following a new tack, it might be of interest to form a hypothesis about what lies behind Hume's relaxed attitude toward his ceasing to exist.

Hume, I suspect, is under the influence of what we might call an "external" picture of his (our) life. This is a perfectly legitimate way to conceive of one's life. It is, however, important not to overlook the possibility of a different kind of picture.

The picture implicit in the quote from Boswell, the external picture which appears to be influencing Hume, is one wherein our lives are neatly sandwiched between two nothingnesses. There is perfect symmetry: our lives in the middle; on either side a nothingness of temporally infinite extent. Insofar as the nothingnesses cannot be distinguished qualitatively, the picture would seem to contain nothing which might justify a difference in our attitudes toward them, hence nothing that might justify a negative attitude on our part toward our future versus our past nothingness.

In Hume's picture, our life plays out between two infinite nothingnesses, each of which serves as a limit on it. Crucially, such a picture provides no clue as to how things look from within the life that thus plays out. It should be clear, however, that if we seek insight into the awfulness with which we are confronted by our future versus past nothingness, and thus into the difference in what these two nothingnesses mean to us, we must adopt the other perspective: we must look not to an external picture like Hume's, but to how the two nothingnesses actually figure with us, that is to say, to how they figure from within our life.

Considered from within our life, our pre-birth nothingness exists in our past, whereas our post-death nothingness is yet to exist and thus is always in our future (until it arrives, and we cease to have a future).

In contrast, externally (from the perspective of Hume's picture), the nothingnesses are neither past nor future but simply outside our lives—two empty and therefore qualitatively identical spaces which mark its limits. Given this perspective, it is easy to miss the fact that, notwithstanding their qualitative identity, the nothingnesses differ profoundly in what they mean to us: that while we are not especially concerned about our past nothingness, that which awaits us in the future may loom as something awful.

It is as if Hume, in the thrall of the external picture, were not open to how things look from within his own life. Hence, he passes by what to one degree or another preoccupies many of his fellows—the awfulness of his own future nothingness.

SECTION 9

We have yet to say, though, what is supposed to make this nothingness awful (the question we raised but failed to answer in Section 7). In what, once again, does its awfulness consist?

Johnson invokes the idea of a "giving up" on our part. A giving up of what? Well, of everything we have. When a person dies (ceases to exist), Johnson tells us, "he [. . .] gives up all he has."

This constitutes an answer to the question of what makes our future versus past nothingness awful. At the time of our past nothingness, we did not exist; hence there was no possibility of our ceasing to exist. Now, we exist; so, the possibility is there. When it is realized, we will have to give up all that we have, which is what makes our ceasing to exist awful and thereby justifies our negative attitude toward our future versus past nothingness. Here we have Johnson's answer to Hume's Challenge.

Should we accept the answer? We can agree, giving up all that we have is awful. It is awful because, if we give up all that we have, we are left without anything. The question for us is not whether this is awful but whether its awfulness is the awfulness which confronts us in the prospect of our future nothingness.

It would seem that it is not. The awfulness for the subject who must give up all he has, is, as we just said, that he is left without anything. He has then to get along with nothing; hence his situation is awful. But, evidently, this assumes that he continues to exist, that he is there to endure the loss. The survival of the subject, however, is just what cannot be assumed in the case of the awfulness that confronts us with the nothingness of death. In this case, there is nothing which the subject will have to get along without—not because he will then have everything, but because he will no longer be there to have anything. He will no longer be there to get along in any way at all. He will simply not be there. Anywhere.

The problem with Johnson's conception of what makes the prospect of our future nothingness awful is that it implies our continued existence. Thus, it implies that after the nothingness of death arrives in my case, I will still be around to deal with its consequences. This is incoherent.[8]

SECTION 10

Then in what does the awfulness of our (in each case, my) future nothingness consist? Not, I would say, in the giving up of something on our part, but in the *ending* of something. Of "something"? In a real sense, of *everything*—of all there is. What makes our (my) future nothingness awful is that its advent entails the ending of all there is, of everything. Thus, if one believes the advent of nothingness is for him close at hand, he might think: "This is it—all there is!"[9] Is that not awful? (Not painful or terrifying, but awful.)

It is awful. You could say that the ending of everything is the paradigm of awfulness. Indeed, the suggestion that my future nothingness entails the ending of everything is apt to provoke the complaint that in our attempt to capture the awfulness of death we have gone over the top. Do I really believe that the advent of nothingness in my case entails the ending of all there is? Of everything? That is to say, of unqualifiedly everything: of everything *full stop*—as if my death will involve some kind of cosmic event or universal catastrophe?

The truth seems more modest. My death entails the ending not of unqualifiedly everything, but of everything *for me*. What each of us face is not a universal catastrophe (how many universal catastrophes could there be?) but, as we might express it, a personal catastrophe.

SECTION 11

Right now, the world is there for me. With the advent of nothingness for me, this will no longer be the case. The world will continue to exist, all right, but, since I will have ceased to exist, there will no longer be such a fact as the fact of the world's being there for me. It will have been replaced by the fact of there being nothingness for me.

Which will otherwise leave everything as it is. What is entailed by the advent of nothingness for me is not the unqualified ending of everything—only a mad man could think that—but the ending of everything for me.

Note, what ends with the "ending of everything for me" is not a subset of the objects which would end with the ending of what philosophers call "the world": the totality of objects which exist independently of consciousness. What ends, rather, is the holding of a fact, namely, the fact of the world being there for me, that is to say, of there being such a thing as my consciousness of the world.

Yet someone who is genuinely struck by the fact of his future nothingness may feel that in qualifying it as the ending of everything "for me" we lose something of what our future nothingness means to us, and thereby diminish the full impact of what it means. Thus, recognizing that what it means is not the unqualified ending of everything but the ending for me of everything, he may wish to add that, in a sense, "it might as well be" the unqualified ending of everything.

No difference could be greater, however, than the difference between the ending of everything for me and the ending of everything full stop; that is, between the catastrophe that I (all of us) face, which is a personal catastrophe, and the unthinkable madness of a universal catastrophe. In what sense, then, could it be true that, as we just put it, the ending that I face "might as well be" the unqualified ending, the ending of everything full stop?

SECTION 12

Imagine you are in a light-proof space and that the light in your space is extinguished. It thus ends. Compare this with the case in which you are in your light-proof space and light is extinguished everywhere. (God says, "Let there be no light.") Although the two endings are in themselves vastly different, and you grasp the difference, would they not from the standpoint of your light-proof space seem exactly the same? We might say that, while the endings would be different in themselves, from your standpoint they would be experientially equivalent.

My thought in this regard is that, similarly, while the unqualified ending of everything and the ending of everything for me are in themselves vastly different, from my standpoint, despite my grasping the difference between them, the endings would seem exactly the same. They are, as we just put it, experientially equivalent endings.

The advent of nothingness in my case, the ending of everything for me—the ending which is my death—is, experientially, as radical as any ending could be for me. (There is, experientially, no way of upping the ante.) This is—returning to the point raised at the end of the previous section—the sense in which the ending for me that is my death "might as well be" the unqualified ending of everything.

SECTION 13

Hume's Challenge asks us, in light of their qualitative identity, to justify the asymmetry in our attitudes toward our future versus past nothingness. While we are more or less indifferent toward our past nothingness, we tend to be negatively disposed toward the nothingness which lies in our future; we tend to find it awful. What is it about our future nothingness, in contrast to our past nothingness, that makes it awful? In what does its awfulness consist? If we can answer this question, we will have justified the attitudinal asymmetry on our part toward the two nothingnesses and in doing so will have answered Hume's Challenge.

The points required to answer the question have, I venture, emerged in the course of or discussion. They are three. First, the unqualified ending of all there is, of everything full stop, is the paradigm of awfulness (Section 10). Second, our future versus past nothingness entails, for each of us, the ending of all there is for me (Section 11). Third, the ending of all there is for me is experientially equivalent to the unqualified ending of all there is, and thus is, experientially, as radical or extreme as an ending could possibly be (Section 12).

For each of us, then, our future nothingness entails something experientially equivalent to the paradigm of awfulness. Therein consists its awfulness which, since it has no counterpart in the case of our pre-birth nothingness, justifies the asymmetry in our attitude toward the two nothingnesses. This, it would seem, answers Hume's Challenge.

NOTES

1. James Boswell, *The Life of Johnson* (London: Penguin Books, 1979 [1791]), p. 148.
2. Our persistence as a possible object of reference is (I would say) as close as we get to immortality.
3. The "challenge," which goes back to the ancients (Lucretius), is sometimes referred to as the "symmetry argument."
4. It is worth pointing out that the appropriate attitude toward the nothingness of death is not (as many seem to assume) fear. Of course, there are certain, no longer widely believed, conceptions of what happens after death—such as that illustrated by the fate of the denizens of Dante's *Inferno*—toward which fear would be appropriate. If our death were followed by a future in Dante's hell, we would face endless suffering, whereas what we actually face is not endless suffering but endless nothingness. Given the advent of nothingness in our case, there will be for us no possibility of suffering (we will not be there to suffer).
5. I use the term "awful" in this context hoping to retain something both of its usual negative overtones (e.g., when we speak of a book or film or a person's behavior as "awful") as well as its use of something which is regarded as arousing awe (e.g., when the god of the Old Testament is described as "awful"). But if someone wants to insist that the nothingness of death is not awful, I do not know how to prove that it is awful. Lots of people seem to find it awful, and we are assuming that it is. Remember, though, agreeing that it is awful does not entail being worried or bothered by it. In principle, you might recognize the awfulness of death without its prospect giving rise to any negative feeling.

6. This is why it seems correct to weight Hume's Challenge toward our future nothingness (see the first paragraph of section 4).

7. Assume, as in the text above, that X begins to exist at t and that, at a later time, t+1, X ceases to exist; assume, further, that Y begins to exist at t+2, and, finally, that Y=X. Insofar as Y begins to exist at t+2, at t+1 it, Y, does not exist; however, given that Y=X and X exists at t1, Y exists at t+1. It follows that, at t+1, Y both exists and does not exist. Cf. John Locke's judicious remark that "the much inquired after *principium individuationis* is existence itself, which determines a being of any sort to particular time and place"; John Locke, *An Essay Concerning Human Understanding* (New York: Dover Books, 1959), Chapter XXVII, Section 4.

8. It would be similarly incoherent to suggest, say, that the awfulness of death consists in our having to leave behind everyone we love, everything we value. Certainly, that is awful. Why? Normally, the awfulness of leaving people etc. behind consists in having to suffer their absence. But again, this assumes our continued existence, which is just what cannot be assumed in the case of our death.

9. One might address the same words to a small child who has finished his plate of ice cream and looks up hopefully for more. We get used to running out of things in life, but not to running out of life itself.

BIBLIOGRAPHY

Boswell, James. *The Life of Johnson*. London: Penguin Books, 1979 [1791].

Locke, John. *An Essay Concerning Human Understanding*. New York: Dover Books, 1959 [1689].

2

✝

The Problem of Mourning

Eleonore Stump

The problem of evil is so perennial a topic in philosophy that it sometimes seems an icon for philosophical puzzles that cannot be solved. Only the most tendentious would deny that there is suffering in the world. Even if we turn our eyes away from the destruction of the earth, and even if we make ourselves oblivious to the afflictions of the beasts, there is the undeniable suffering of human beings. No dramatic list of the kinds of human suffering, no heart-wrenching Dostoevskian narratives of particular sufferers, does justice to the overwhelming suffering of human beings in all times and places. How is this suffering to be explained? How could it possibly be compatible with the existence of the kind of God embraced by the Abrahamic religions? How could there be an omnipotent, omniscient, perfectly good God in this world, given this vast panorama of human suffering?

In addition, although the panoply of human suffering typically elicits complaints about the apparent incompatibility of the existence of this suffering with the existence of God, in fact this spectacle is also a mirror for us. It ought to evoke some insight into the depth of human evil. Certainly, at the very least, it is undeniably true that human beings have a significant role in the destruction of the earth and the afflictions of beasts; and even if we confine our view just to the suffering of human beings, the great array of human suffering demonstrates abundantly the viciousness of human beings to one another. By far the largest part of the human suffering which is showcased in discussions of the problem of evil is directly or indirectly attributable to human evil. But according to the Abrahamic religions, human beings are God's idea. That is, it is God's doing that human beings exist at all. Why is this theological claim alone not enough to raise the problem of evil?

From the ancient story of Job to the most recent efforts at theodicy, there have been many varying attempts to come to grips with these questions. In other work, I myself have tried to delineate a successful defense against the argument from evil.[1] But what is much less noticed in connection with the problem of evil is what would be left still unexplained if any of the attempts at theodicy were successful.

As the story is told in Judaism and Christianity,[2] in the beginning God created everything that there is in the world; and when he had finished creating it, he saw and said that all of it was very good. In the beginning, in other words, there was only innocence and harmony within all of creation, which was not only very good but even beautiful. The point of this part of the common theological story is to make clear that God is not the creator of human beings as they are now. As God created them, in the beginning, in their origin, human beings were like God in being perfectly good. They hurt nothing, at least not willingly; and they were lovely in all that they did. According to the story, the fact that human beings are no longer what they were when God created them is their own fault.

The doctrine of original sin is the theological doctrine that is intended to explain this claim.[3] The human beings God created broke their relationship with their Creator, fell from their original righteousness, and in consequence changed their own nature. They turned themselves into something like gremlins, creatures with dispositions to will and to do what is harmful or unjust to others. Furthermore, the new gremlin-like nature of these fallen human beings was transmissible and so was reproduced in all their descendants. From this Fall, there arose all the misery in the world as we now know it, everything from the lamentable tendency to evil lurking in every human being to the actual horrors perpetrated on what is vulnerable or otherwise open to oppression and depredation. On the doctrine of original sin, then, the current condition of human beings is attributable to human beings, not to God.

Nonetheless, on Christian theological doctrine, contrary to what one might suppose, God does well to allow this change in his original creation. That is because the Fall and its resultant suffering are not the end of the story of the creation or of human beings and their relation to their Creator. In his goodness, mercy, and love, God finds a way to save human beings from their evil and its consequences, including the liability to shame, guilt, and suffering. Through the life, passion, and death of Christ, God saves human beings from their post-Fall human condition and brings them to union with himself, so that the human part of creation is not irretrievably ruined. In fact, it is part of the same story that in the end, the final end of the story of creation, there will be a new heaven and a new earth, so that all creation will somehow be restored to the condition of beauty and goodness that was part of God's original plan for creation.

Now suppose, just for the sake of argument, that this entire theological story of creation, original sin, theodicy, redemption, and the restoration of a new heaven and earth is true. That is a lot to suppose, of course. But here is the point of the exercise. Even if this whole story is true, why does it not simply raise the problem of evil in a new form? Why does it not leave something that should be mourned?

In this chapter, my aim is to raise this form of the problem of evil—the problem of mourning—but not to attempt to solve it. In my view, a solution would require an extensive investigation of the nature of a human being's true self, and such an investigation is too much for a short chapter. Consequently, I will concentrate on illuminating the problem and then only gesture at the form an attempted solution might take.

THIS FORM OF THE PROBLEM OF EVIL

To see this problem of mourning, consider the story of the post-Fall world from the perspective of the creator in the story, who first pronounced his creation very good. It may be that the creator can redeem this history, so that in the end it is restored to the creator's original plan for it. But why should the creator not see the whole story—with the human horrors in the middle between the good beginning of creation and the redeemed end of it—as a damaged version of what the creator had in mind when he originally created heaven and earth? Why should the creator not find his creation, even redeemed and restored, something worthy of lament?

Or think about the question this way. The biblical book of Revelation predicts an end time of great peace and beauty and joy when God creates a new heaven and a new earth. But this time comes after the apocalyptic destruction of the earth and the great suffering of human beings during the end time. Even if it is possible to show successfully that such destruction and suffering are defeated by the good of the new heaven and the new earth, would it not have been better if the first heaven and earth had remained in their original goodness, if there had not been the intervening apocalypse?

We can focus in from the extended mural of human history to the details of particular human lives and raise an analogous question with respect to individual human beings. Take, for example, Harriet Tubman. In other work, I have argued that her suffering was defeated for her in the luminous excellence of her life; through her suffering she became the person so many people, me included, are now glad to honor.[4] To say that her suffering was defeated for her is to say that, given the nature of post-Fall human beings, there was a benefit from her suffering, that that benefit came primarily to her, that it would not have come without her suffering, and that it significantly outweighed her suffering. Suppose just for the sake of the argument that this complex claim is correct. Then it will be true that, given the post-Fall human world, God was justified in allowing Tubman's suffering and that she herself would have had reason to think so if she had known the whole story of creation.

But consider what remains sorrowful about her life even so. The suffering of Tubman's early life under the abuse of her slave masters lived on in her memory. More to the point perhaps, it also lived on in the wounds on her body and in her psyche. And then there are the consequences of the deprivations she endured. She was not allowed any education in her formative years, for example. A deprivation of nurture for the mind is also a lasting suffering. What might she have been if she had learned to read as a child? What is it like to know that those around you whom you admire have a power of mind derived from education that is permanently lost to you because of the great injustices done to you by your oppressors?

Even if Harriet Tubman's suffering was defeated in the gloriousness of her life, the wounds and scars of that suffering remain, in her psyche for as long as she lives, and in fact everlastingly in her life's story. Because the past is permanent, the past injuries are permanent also; and so her life narrative includes the wounds and scars of those injuries forever.

As far as that goes, there is biblical warrant for supposing that Christian theology must be committed to the view that even the physical wounds and scars remain in the afterlife in the resurrected body. Consider in this connection the only set of stories in the New Testament that give detailed information about a resurrected human body. These are the stories about Christ during his earthly life after his resurrection. In these stories, the resurrected body of Jesus has still the wounds of the crucifixion; and the wound in the side of his resurrected body is large enough that an adult human hand can be put into it. In the Gospel of John, the resurrected Jesus shows Thomas the wounds of his crucifixion and says to him, "Bring your hand here and put it into my side, and be not faithless but believing" (John 20:27). If the resurrected body of the incarnate Christ keeps its wounds, then it seems that, a fortiori, Christian theology is committed to the claim that the wounds and scars of the bodies of all other human beings also remain in the resurrection of the afterlife.

So, why is it not the case that there is something disappointing, something worth mourning, about God's creation with the Fall and all the subsequent suffering in the story? Why is there not something sad at best or devastating at worst about the lives of human persons in the post-Fall world, even if those persons are redeemed and restored in the end? Why is it not the case that every human life is a depressing or distressing variation on the beautiful thing it might it have been, or even (in some cases) a deplorable monstrosity by comparison with the life that it could have been? Why should one not conclude that the whole story of the world is a broken version of what the original creation was supposed to be, on Christian doctrine? And an analogous question arises for individual human lives: would it not have been better for Tubman if she had lived the sort of life she could have had if she had been part of the creation as, on Christian doctrine, it was originally intended to be by the creator?

In the book of Lamentations, the prophet says, "My eyes fail with tears, my heart is in turmoil, my soul[5] is poured out on the earth, because of the destruction of the daughter of my people" (Lamentations 2:11). The prophet is mourning the sufferings of his people, which is described in heartbreaking detail in that biblical book, and which most certainly merits such mourning. How much more, then, does the suffering of the whole post-Fall world warrant intense sorrow? And perhaps for many people their own enduring wounds, incurred through life in the post-Fall world, will prompt such intense lamentation too. Why is this lamentation not an indictment of the created world?

For these reasons, even if it is possible to justify God's allowing the suffering of post-Fall human beings, something still remains to wonder about. How is a theological story intelligible if it posits an omnipotent, omniscient, perfectly good God whose creation turns out to be a defective version of what God intended it to be? How is it to be understood if even a redeemed and restored creation still merits grief?

Consequently, although it has been largely unnoticed in contemporary discussion, there would be something leftover of the problem of evil, there would be something to mourn, even if there were a successful theodicy.

THE *FELIX CULPA* VIEW

What is surprising to see is that the Christian tradition has taken just the opposite view of the matter. It reads the story of creation this way: the creation with Adam's Fall in it and all the suffering which the Fall brought into the world made God's creation better, more glorious, than it would otherwise have been. That is, the story of creation with the Fall in it is more of a success for God than the story would have been had there been no Fall and no evil in the world. I will call this claim "the *felix culpa* view" after an early liturgical text, the *Exultet,* which uses this phrase to summarize the Christian view in question. Speaking of the fall of Adam, with theological audaciousness, the text of the *Exultet* puts the view this way:

> O truly necessary sin of Adam,
> destroyed completely by the death of Christ!
>
> O happy fault (*felix culpa*) that earned for us
> so great, so glorious a Redeemer!⁶

The same perplexingly bold attitude towards the story of the world with the Fall included can be found centuries before the appearance of the *Exultet*. In fact, it is evident from the earliest days of Christianity. To take just one example, in the New Testament book of Acts, when some of the apostles are imprisoned and then beaten for bearing witness to the events of Christ's life and death, the text says that they came away from this suffering rejoicing, with a sense of having been honored in being allowed to endure that suffering. In their view, their suffering was something to celebrate (Acts 5:41).

In the Patristic period, it is not hard to find expressions of this view. An attitude like that of the *felix culpa* kind can be found, for example, in the letters of John Chrysostom to his friend and companion Olympias. When Chrysostom was sent into exile by the empress, who was angry at him, Olympias had a hard time enduring her separation from him and her worry about him as he was marched by soldiers through rough territory in challenging circumstances. We have a number of his letters to her written while he was on that march; and the overarching theme of those letters is his attempt to persuade her to something like the attitude underlying the *felix culpa* view. In his letters to her, he is concerned that Olympias see the suffering caused both of them by Chrysostom's exile as a kind of gift of God's to his more trusted and advanced people. To take just one of many examples that might be given, Chrysostom writes to her,

> I would like to speak about something else that may seem paradoxical but is true. If someone accomplishes a good thing, great and noble, but without having pain or danger or sufferings, his reward will not be very large . . . For this reason, [the apostle] Paul, when he boasted, did not boast only of the noble acts of virtue that he had done, but also of the evils that he had suffered. . . . He did not say, "I preached the gospel to such and such people," but rather, leaving aside his acts of virtue, he enumerated the evils that he had suffered, saying, "in toils more exceeding abundant, in stripes beyond measure, in prisons more frequently, in danger of death often . . . " Do you see this series of sufferings, and the occasion for his boasting? Then he adds to these his works of virtue—but again, the sufferings have the greater importance, not the virtuous acts.⁷

Clearly, the Christian *felix culpa* view is evident here.

And if we fast-forward centuries to the scholastic period, we can find Aquinas explicitly affirming this same view. In the *Summa theologiae*, for example, Aquinas actually cites the *Exultet*; and he explains the line in the *Exultet* about Adam's Fall as a *felix culpa* by saying that God allows the evils of this post-Fall world to occur in order to bring out of them an even greater good.[8]

From its inception, then, and through much of its history, there is ample evidence that Christian communities and influential Christian writers held the *felix culpa* view, which supposes not that the story of God's creation with the Fall and its subsequent suffering is a disappointment for God but that, on the contrary, the world with its history of sin and suffering is better and more glorious than the world would have been if there had been no Fall.

It is worth noticing that the *felix culpa* view has a small-scale analogue in the contemporary disability rights pride movement, although it is much more audacious than that analogue. The disability rights movement wants to celebrate what others have generally pitied or disrespected as the suffering of misfortune. It wants others to see that those with disabilities are not among life's losers, or even among life's heroic overcomers of the tragic. Instead, the disability rights movement holds disability pride parades. Here is an excerpt from a text by Sarah Triano, the founder of the Chicago Disability Pride parade (as cited in Elizabeth Barnes's *The Minority Body*):

> The sad sack, the brave overcomer, and the incapable are worn-out stereotypes the parade refutes by giving us a time and space to celebrate ourselves as we are. First, we want to show the world the incredible joy that exists in our lives. We are part of the richness and diversity of this country and the world. The Parade is an international celebration of our continued and continuing survival. We also, by marching in this parade, are giving the world a chance to express pride in us, too![9]

Here the sense is that there is nothing, or at least very little, to sorrow over in disability. There is only joy in the good of the lives of those with disabilities.

This is a view of disability that has struck many as highly counterintuitive. But the *felix culpa* view takes such counterintuitiveness to an extreme, it seems, because it wants to accept that the consequences of the Fall are worth great mourning and yet that the world which contains those consequences is nonetheless better, more worth celebrating, than the world would have been without them.

It is one thing to note that Christianity adopted such a view early on and stayed largely committed to it. It is another thing entirely to try to understand why. How could the world with all the evil in it be somehow greater, more beautiful or more worth having, than the world would have been if it had gone as God originally intended? How could the life of a human person such as Harriet Tubman be better, more glorious, than it would have been in a world without the Fall? If wounds and scars remain even in the resurrected body of Christ, why would a resurrected human body not be more beautiful without them?

THE TRUE SELF

The issue highlighted by these questions is in fact a corollary of a more fundamental issue, namely, the nature of the true self of a human person. Think about the matter this way. If on the *felix culpa* view a human person such as Tubman is more glorious in the post-Fall world than she would have been in the world without the Fall, then what is it to be glorious as a human being? Or if, as the story about Christ's resurrected body implies, a resurrected body even with wounds is more perfected than it would have been had there been no Fall, what is it that is supposed to be perfected in the resurrection in the afterlife? On Christian doctrine, *you* are able to be made glorious and perfected in the afterlife. But what exactly are *you*?

Consider in this connection an otherwise perplexing claim made by the apostle Paul in Romans. There Paul says,

> what I would, that do I not; but what I hate, that do I. . . . For the good that I would I do not: but the evil which I would not, that I do. Now if I do that I would not, it is no more I that do it, but sin that dwells in me.[10]

It would be possible—but obtuse—to read Paul's words as trying to disclaim moral responsibility or even agency for his own moral wrongdoing. Clearly, the metaphysical entity that is Paul is the agent who does the evil that Paul "would not," and so it is also that entity who is morally responsible for that evil.

But in these lines in Romans, Paul is evincing a global second-order will for a will that wills the good; and he is here identifying himself with something characterized by that higher-order will. He concedes that his first-order will is divided against itself. Sometimes his first-order will is in harmony with that global second-order will of his, and sometimes it is in opposition to it. Nonetheless, as Paul sees it, his true self is characterized by the higher-order will for the good. That is why Paul repudiates as alien to himself—alien to his *true* self—his own first-order volitions that are discordant with that second-order will. Insofar as the true self of Paul is characterized by his global second-order will for a will that wills the good, then in Paul's view his true self wills the good. And that is the sense in which it seems to him correct to say, "it is not I who do [the evil that I would not]." As he sees it, even in his internally fragmented state, the self that wants to will what is good is his true self.

But what, then, is the true self? More significantly, what is it for the true self of a person to be glorious or perfected? Are the wounds and scars of post-Fall human life compatible with the perfection of a person's true self, or even somehow crucial to it? Is it possible for those wounds to add to the perfection of the person who has them? And, on Christian doctrine, what is the role of suffering in eliciting the true self in the process that brings a human person to be made glorious and perfected in this life and then ultimately in the resurrected state in heaven?

The serious puzzle raised by the *felix culpa* view cannot be examined properly without some careful consideration of these and related questions.

There are multiple theories that might be thought to explain the notion of the true self of a human being; but in the end, I think that the notion of the true self can be understood best by delineating the nature of suffering and then, as it were, reverse-engineering the notion of the true self from the nature of suffering.

We can begin by noting that suffering cannot be adequately glossed just as pain, as a little reflection shows. On the contrary, pain is neither necessary nor sufficient for human suffering. Instead, as I have argued in detail elsewhere, suffering is a function of what a person cares about.[11]

Every human person has some care about what kind of person she is and about her being what she ought to be, where what she ought to be is something like thriving as a good specimen of the species *human being*.[12] Consequently, part of what it is for a human being to suffer is for her to be kept, to one degree or another, from thriving, in this broad sense. What makes a human person thrive, however, is an objective matter. And so, there is an objective element in human suffering.

On the other hand, what human beings care about has a subjective element too, which does not have to do just with thriving. This subjective element is something to which a person is committed but which need not be essential to her thriving and which may not even be compatible with it.[13] This is a matter of the desires of the heart. It is not easy to give a crisp formulation of the notion of the desires of the heart. But we can say that a desire of the heart for a human being is a particular kind of commitment to a person or project which matters greatly to her apart from her own thriving.

Consequently, if we take suffering to be a function of what a person cares about, then suffering can be understood this way: a human being suffers when she fails to thrive, or she fails to have the desires of her heart, or both.

We can use this view of suffering as the basis on which to sketch an account of the true self. If in heaven a human being is her true self in its perfected state, and if in heaven she does not suffer, then in heaven she has, harmoniously ordered, both thriving and heart's desires. She has the convergence of what she cares about on both an objective and a subjective scale of value.

We can think of the true self of a person, then, as the emergent condition of that person when she has what she most cares about in both an objective and a subjective sense and when her deepest heart's desire converges with her thriving. The true self of any human being thus has both an objective component which is the same for all human beings, namely, thriving as a human being, and also a subjective component, which will vary in some respects from one human being to another. Furthermore, the true self will not be a sum of the objective and subjective components. Rather, it will be what emerges from the interweaving of a human being's thriving with the fulfillment of her heart's desires. Consequently, the perfected version of a person's true self, the condition of a person in the afterlife in heaven, is what she is when what she most cares about, in both an objective and a subjective sense, converge in her and in her life.

We can fill out this delineation of the true self by considering that, on Christian doctrine, human beings are made in the image of God. The perfection of a human person's true self will thus also be the fulfillment of that image in her. But something is an image of something else in virtue of somehow resembling it. To be in the image of God, then, is to resemble God in one way or another. The perfection of a human being's true self will therefore also be an intensification of that resemblance in her.

We can think of the resemblance between a human being and God in different ways because, on Christian doctrine, God is triune. That is, God is one and only one deity; and yet there are also three persons in that one God. So, a human being can be considered to be made in the image of God in virtue of resembling somehow the nature of the one Deity; or, on the other hand, a human being can be supposed to resemble God in virtue of somehow resembling the three persons in their loving interactions. Both of these ways of thinking about the image of God in human beings are well represented in Christian theological thought.

But there is yet one other way to think about the image of God in human beings. On Christian doctrine, God is also incarnate in Christ. On the Chalcedonian formula for the incarnate Christ, Christ is one person, the second person of the Trinity, with two natures, one fully divine and one fully human. The things predicated of Christ in his human nature are predicated of the second person of the Trinity; and since each person of the Trinity is God, the things predicated of Christ in his human nature are also predicated of God. That is why, on Christian doctrine, it is true to claim that God suffers, even though in his divine nature it is not possible for God to suffer. So, yet another way to think about the image of God in human beings is to consider the resemblance between a human being and Christ in his human nature.

As evident in the Gospel of John, there is biblical warrant for the Christian claim that the incarnate Christ is most glorious in his crucifixion; that is the explanation typically given for why the wounds of the crucifixion remain in Christ's resurrected body. In fact, on Christian doctrine, the nature of God is most manifest in the crucified Christ. That is because the only divine attribute picked out in the New Testament as expressive of God's nature is love: "God is love" (I John 4:8). In addition, there is also biblical warrant for the claim that there is no greater love than the love of a person who lays down his life for the sake of another (John 15:13). On this way of thinking about the matter, then, the nature of God is most evident in Christ's crucifixion because love is greatest and most evident there.

Consequently, it is possible to see a third way of identifying the image of God in human beings. If it is the image of God in human beings that perfects the true self of a human being, and if the nature of the love that is God is most evident in the crucified Christ, then there may be some way in which the wounds of human suffering could intensify the image of God in a human being too. In the Epistle to the Colossians, the apostle Paul says, "I rejoice in my sufferings for you, and fill up that which is wanting in the afflictions of Christ" (Col. 1:24). And in the Epistle to the Romans, he says, "we are the children of God; and if children, then heirs; heirs of God, and heirs with Christ if we suffer with [Christ] that we may be glorified with [Christ]" (Rom. 8:17).

If these suggestive lines can be suitably explained, then it may be possible to see a way in which the wounds of a person's suffering could become for that person an image of Christ. On this way of thinking about the perfection of the true self of a human person, what makes a human person glorious and perfected is her resemblance to the incarnate Christ when the love of God is most manifest in him.

CONCLUSION: THE TRUE SELF AND THE *FELIX CULPA* VIEW

In this chapter, I have presented a version of the problem of evil—the problem of mourning—and then made a breathless dash through the lineaments of a solution to it. I have argued that there is a perplexing problem of evil which remains even if there is a successful theodicy, and I have tried to show that the traditional Christian resolution of this problem of mourning is the *felix culpa* view. This is the view that the post-Fall world with all its sufferings is better than the world would have been if it had been what God originally created it to be and there had never been a Fall.

This claim implies a comparative evaluation of worlds; and, like the comparison of whole worldviews, a comparative evaluation of worlds is difficult to assess. But it can be approached more easily by considering the smaller-scale comparative evaluation of human lives that it implies. On the *felix culpa* view, it is possible for a human being in his true self to be more glorious than he would have been in a world without a Fall, that is, without the moral evil and the suffering of the post-Fall world.[14]

This smaller-scale comparative evaluation requires some understanding of what is being compared. Evaluating the *felix culpa* view thus requires some insight into the nature of the true self of a human being. On Christian doctrine, the true self of a human being is the emergent condition that results from the convergence of his thriving and his deepest heart's desire. When this emergent condition is perfected, the image of God which, on Christian doctrine, is in human beings is also completed.

With this much elucidation of the nature of a human being's true self and its perfection on Christian doctrine, there is then some clue about how the *felix culpa* view could be defended. If the love that is God's nature is most evident in the wounds of the incarnate Christ and if the wounds of human suffering could be suitably connected to Christ, then there is a basis for an argument that the wounds of a post-Fall human being can render him more in the image of God than he would have been had there been no suffering in the world. In that case, on Christian doctrine there would be something more glorious about redeemed human beings with wounds than there would have been had there been no Fall, no suffering, and no wounds and scars. On this view, it is the image of love incarnate that makes a wounded post-Fall human person more glorious in his true self than he would otherwise have been, and the image of love incarnate in the true self of a human person would have been less in a world without a Fall.

In the end, then, the last perplexing part of the problem of evil, the problem of mourning, which remains even if there is a successful theodicy, is inextricably interwoven with the notion of the true self of a human being and with an understanding of God as love. If the true self of a human being is perfected when the image of God is most fulfilled in him, and if the nature of God is most manifest in the love of God, then we may be able to see how the *felix culpa* view might be defended and this form of the problem of evil might find a resolution.[15]

But to say so is only to highlight the problem of mourning and to suggest one way to approach the evaluation of the traditional Christian solution to it. A full examination of both the problem and the elements of a possible solution to it require the extended treatment only a whole book enables.

NOTES

1. See my *Wandering in Darkness: Narrative and the Problem of Suffering* (Oxford: Oxford University Press, 2010).

2. From this point onwards, I will say little about Judaism and nothing about Islam, since my expertise lies primarily in Christian theological doctrine.

3. For some discussion of the question whether the doctrine of original sin can itself be squared with the existence of an omnipotent, omniscient, perfectly good God, see my *Wandering in Darkness*, Chapter 8.

4. Eleonore Stump, *Atonement* (Oxford: Oxford University Press, 2018), Chapter 9.

5. The Hebrew term actually signifies the liver, and the phrase is usually translated as "my liver is poured out on the ground," or "my bile is poured out on the ground." But in English these phrases make little or no sense. In the ancient world, the liver was sometimes taken as the seat of the soul or as the seat of the most powerful emotions. So, I have translated the Hebrew word for liver as "soul" in order to make the English version of the phrase convey more nearly what it seems to me that the Hebrew is expressing.

6. In its form in the *Exultet*, the thought is that the good of having God incarnate as Christ is so great a good that it defeats the suffering incurred by the Fall (the fault) of Adam, and that is why the Fall is a *felix culpa*. But this cannot be quite the right way to explain the *felix culpa* view. Explained this way, the view is evidently not true. That is because for the incarnation to defeat the suffering incurred by the Fall, it would have to be true not only that the good of the incarnation significantly outweighed all that suffering, but also that the good in question could not have been gotten without the Fall. But plainly this latter claim is false. The incarnation of God as Christ could have happened even without a Fall. On Christian theology, there is nothing to prevent God's adding to God an assumed human nature even without a Fall and without a need for human redemption. God might have done so simply for companionship with human beings, for example. So, the incarnation might have occurred even without the fall of Adam; and for that reason, the incarnation does not defeat the evil of the Fall. For this reason, the incarnation is not by itself sufficient to explain why the *culpa* of Adam should be considered *felix*.

7. Saint John Chrysostom, *Letters to Saint Olympia*, trans. by David C. Ford (New York: St. Vladimir's Press, 2016), Letter 10, pp. 110–11.

8. Thomas Aquinas, *Summa theologiae* (ST) III q.1 a.3 ad 3. Aquinas is here affirming a claim much like that made by Augustine. Augustine says that God judged it better to bring evil out of good than to prevent evil from occurring (cf. *Enchiridion* VIII.27). I like and therefore generally use the translation of the *Summa theologiae* by the Dominican Fathers of the English Province, which is readily available on the internet; but I have felt free to modify it in those few cases where I thought I could do better.

9. Elizabeth Barnes, *The Minority Body: A Theory of Disability* (Oxford: Oxford University Press, 2016), Chapter 6; the excerpt from the quotation appears on p. 185.

10. Romans 7:15–20. I cite the passage in the King James translation since it is familiar to many people.

11. See Stump, *Wandering in Darkness*, Chapter 1.

12. For further discussion of this issue, see Stump, *Atonement*, Chapter 9.

13. Marilyn Adams makes a distinction which is at least related to the distinction I am after here. She says, "the value of a person's life may be assessed from the inside (in relation to that person's own goals, ideals, and choices) and from the outside (in relation to the aims, tastes, values, and preferences of others). My notion is that for a person's life to be a great good to him/her on the whole, the external point of view (even if it is God's) is not sufficient"; Marilyn Adams, *Horrendous Evils and the Goodness of God* (Ithaca, NY: Cornell University Press, 1999), p. 145.

14. The claim has to be put in this hedged way because of human free will. The *felix culpa* view implies only that it is open to every post-Fall human being to have a life better than that person's life would have been had there never been a Fall. It does not imply that every post-Fall human person actually does have such a better life.

15. This chapter is a precis of a book: Eleonore Stump, *The Image of God: The Problem of Evil and the Problem of Mourning* (Oxford: Oxford University Press, 2022).

BIBLIOGRAPHY

Adams, Marilyn. *Horrendous Evils and the Goodness of God.* Ithaca, NY: Cornell University Press, 1999.

Barnes, Elizabeth. *The Minority Body: A Theory of Disability.* Oxford: Oxford University Press, 2016.

Saint John Chrysostom. *Letters to Saint Olympia.* Translated by David C. Ford. New York: St. Vladimir's Press, 2016.

Stump, Eleonore. *Atonement.* Oxford: Oxford University Press, 2018.

Stump, Eleonore. *Wandering in Darkness: Narrative and the Problem of Suffering.* Oxford: Oxford University Press, 2010.

Stump, Eleonore. *The Image of God: The Problem of Evil and the Problem of Mourning.* Oxford: Oxford University Press, 2022.

3

What Can the Roman Catholic Liturgies of the Dead Offer Mourners

Solidarity with the Deceased and Hopeful Protest?

Richard Conrad, OP

INTRODUCTION

My purpose is to explore something of what Roman Catholic Liturgies of the Dead,[1] stand to offer mourners. My reflection, largely theological, draws on some experience of officiating at funerals and on a basic familiarity with the stages of grief identified by psychologists.[2]

The Catholic doctrine and theology that inform these Liturgies can be summarized as follows:

- The human being is created in the image of the Triune God, for eternal communion with God.
- As social beings, who live in time, we are to *journey* towards this communion, empowered by faith, hope, and the God-given love we call charity.
- The human soul (the human form of life) is immortal; but it naturally animates a body. Hence if *whole human beings* are to be fulfilled the body must be raised to glory.
- The first human beings were granted immunity from sickness and death, but lost those gifts by turning from God's friendship. Their descendants thus inherited a natural vulnerability, plus a moral neediness.

- Christ liberated humanity from sin and death, not by putting the clock back, but by *passing through death* and rising to a life of glory we hope to share, making himself the Way for us to journey to it.
- To belong to Christ explicitly one must take on the Christian Faith in Baptism, committing to participate in the Church's life centered on the Eucharist, to express hope by prayer, and to practice charity.
- To die in a state of charity involves (at least implicitly) giving oneself into God's hands in union with Christ.
- Someone who refuses charity at the time of death cannot enjoy God's eternal company, because (at least implicitly) he or she does not want it. But God can convert people to himself even at the last moment.
- The souls of those who die in charity journey into the Vision of God, which we call Heaven, where they await the resurrection of their bodies and intercede for those still on earth and in Purgatory.
- Many who die in charity still cling to small faults and imperfections. Before entering Heaven their souls undergo Purgatory, where they complete their dying with Christ.
- The souls in Purgatory form one Body with the Church on earth, which prays for them, and celebrates the Eucharist ("offers Mass") to channel to them the liberating effects of Christ's Sacrifice.
- Thus celebrating the Funeral Liturgy and offering Mass for the dead is an act of hope, and a prayer made in love for their speedy enjoyment of God's vision.

By expressing this Faith, the Liturgy of the Dead locates the mourners' grief within a larger context than merely philosophical reflections offer: *a hope-filled* context. Thus, it can help them journey through the stages of grief. I propose it does this most effectively if, besides affirming (or awakening) Christian *hope*, it also acknowledges a *legitimate grieving process* which may involve *anger and protest*.

I begin by asking whether—in some sense—we should accept death as God's will. Besides Scripture, I employ the thought of Thomas Aquinas, whose theology the Catholic Church commends, and whose account of the human psyche drew on the Aristotelian tradition. In my second section I explore what the Catholic Liturgy of the Dead stands to offer mourners. Finally, I examine elements of the Liturgies of the Dead as they developed during the Middle Ages, to argue that they appropriately voiced *anger and protest*.

In the High Middle Ages, the Catholic Liturgies of the Dead settled into the pattern summarized in Section 2. There was significant local variation in the prayers for taking the body to the church and to burial, much less in the Mass and Office of the Dead. The seventeenth-century *Rituale Romanum* drew on late Medieval and sixteenth-century developments; its shorter prayers for taking the body to the church and to burial became the norm for most Catholics as various local uses disappeared,[3] but, for instance, the Dominican Order retained a Funeral Liturgy close to the Sarum version of Medieval England, which itself preserved many prayers already found in the eighth-century *"Gelasian" Sacramentary*. For convenience, I use "Medieval Liturgies of the Dead" to cover *all* the forms celebrated until 1969, given the strong continuities between the Medieval and post-Tridentine Liturgies. Histories of Liturgy identify an increasing note of fear in the late Medieval Liturgies of the Dead,[4] and the *Rituale Romanum (Roman Ritual)* did, proportionally, contain more on judgment than the Sarum Use, which retained many prayers with a more positive tone. The Church revised her Liturgy after Vatican II, promulgating *Ordo Exsequiarum* ("Rite of Funerals") in 1969[5] (after which Bishops' Conferences promulgated local variants), and the revised Office of the Dead (as part of *Liturgia Horarum*)[6] in 1971. I refer to all this as the "current" Liturgy of the Dead.

1. IN WHAT SENSE MUST WE ACCEPT DEATH AS "GOD'S WILL"?

Death as an Evil

Funeral orders of service are sometimes headed: "A Service of Thanksgiving for the Life of N."[7]—never "for the Death of N." Yet the Burial of the Dead in *The Book of Common Prayer* says, "Almighty God . . . We give thee hearty thanks, for that it hath pleased thee to deliver this our *brother* out of the miseries of this sinful world . . ." The *Alternative Service Book* contains no such formula, for it seems odd to *give thanks* for a death even in cases when some mourners whisper, "Death was a blessèd release." Mourners sometimes ask for texts or songs that give the impression that "Death is nothing at all."[8] Eamon Duffy argues that this seems plausible only in modern Western culture.[9] Liturgical formulae such as, "your servant whom you have summoned out of this world,"[10] can give the impression that God willed the death. We must examine whether death is not particularly bad, and whether in any sense God wills it.

Scripture acknowledges death's reality,[11] but as an evil from which we ask rescue.[12] Wisdom 1:13 (RSV) declares: "God did not make death, and he does not delight in the death of the living." Jesus raised the dead. The first time a devout Christian died a natural death, the disciples' reaction was that something had gone wrong; in response, Peter recalled her to life.[13] Christians came to acknowledge the ongoing fact of death, but as "the last enemy to be destroyed."[14]

For Aquinas, "To live is to be,"[15] and insofar as things *exist*, they are *good*.[16] Evil, in itself, has no being; it is the absence of a good that should be there.[17] Thus life is *good*, the loss of life *evil*. Nevertheless, when asking whether human death is natural or unnatural, Aquinas gives a nuanced reply: as rational, the human soul is both immortal, and has to "form" a highly sensitive body on which we rely for acquiring and using concepts.[18] Such a body is naturally mortal.[19] This tension calls out for remedy, especially since our soul's uniquely close relationship with the body implies that, for human beings, death is more repugnant than for other animals.[20] Aquinas holds that the first humans were granted immunity from disease and death.[21] Had they not sinned, their descendants would have inherited these gifts.[22] By turning from God's friendship, they forfeited these gifts for their family; hence our vulnerability is both natural, and a penalty for sin.[23] This raises the question whether death, though an evil, might in some way be willed by God.

How and Why Might God Will Death?

The *absence* of being does not need to be held in being, hence Aquinas holds that God—whose creative will *causes* being—cannot will evil directly.[24] However, Aquinas distinguishes evil *committed* (*malum culpae*) from evil *suffered* (*malum poenae*).[25] While no good intrinsically attaches to the former—God "permits" it—evil suffered involves one good driving out another. By willing one good directly, God *"indirectly"* wills its flip side, for example, by willing the lion's life, God *indirectly* wills the lamb's death.[26]

Malum poenae can be indirectly willed as *punishment* by human or divine authority; in such cases justice is the annexed good.[27] Aquinas accepts straightforwardly the Scriptural passages about eternal punishment for those who refuse God's love.[28] This raises questions beyond our scope;[29] the following points belong here.

First, Aquinas locates his theology within the overall shape of God's plan, which is for us eternally to enjoy God's *friendship*.[30] Thus, Aquinas insists, we *must hope*, hence work and pray *with confidence*, for eternal bliss, for ourselves and others.[31] Hope's certainty is not *absolute*,[32] and the Liturgy suggests death can prompt salutary fear: "Let us improve for the better . . . lest suddenly overtaken by the day of death we seek the opportunity to repent, and are not able to find it."[33] Since God can attract people to repent even at the last minute, we pray in hope for *everyone's* salvation.

Secondly, Christ's Sacrifice far outweighs all evil.[34] Because of it, our journey into bliss, though harder than if humanity had not fallen, is more glorious. In his Commentary on the Book of Job, Aquinas never presents Job's sufferings as a punishment for Adam's sin; they were permitted by

God as tests, as opportunities for virtue, and for Job's ultimate renown. In his Summa Aquinas brings out how the "poenalitates" (penalties? pains?) of our present life serve as ways of sharing more personally in Christ's Passion so as to share his glorious Victory.[35] In this vein, one text in the current Roman Missal reads: "Our death has been redeemed by [Christ's] Death,"[36] implying that our death is not wasted, but has become the route to eternal life in solidarity with Jesus' Passing Over.

Thirdly, another text thanks God "at whose command we are freed from the rule of sin in the earth . . . and . . . redeemed by your Son's Death . . . are awakened . . . to the glory of his Resurrection."[37] This presents death as remedying the compulsion to sin by being a stage in God's refashioning of the body.

In sum, death is a natural necessity but not a good; it is an enemy to be defeated. But it is *indirectly* willed by God, in a small way as penalty and sobering fact, in a more positive way for solidarity with Christ's victorious journey through death and as a stage in our liberation to glory. The current Liturgy of the Dead seeks to emphasize how being patterned on Jesus' Death leads to being patterned on his Resurrection.[38]

Should We Accept Our Own Death as God's Will?

Since Jesus taught us to say, "Thy will be done,"[39] we expect Aquinas to argue that the human will should "be conformed to the divine will." He does so, but in a *general* way: we must make God our chief Goal, and this relativizes everything else.[40]

Aquinas' account of human willing is subtle,[41] and the way he analyses Christ's human will, especially as exercised in Gethsemane, is instructive.[42] Besides "sense appetite" (*roughly* speaking, "emotions"), human nature includes *will*, the ability to be attracted by the rationally-perceived good. This has two dynamics, for which Aquinas employs the Greek terms of John Damascene:

1. *thelesis*, an attraction to what is good in itself, as a goal;
2. *boulesis*, a free choice made, in interaction with reason, for *means* to an end. Jesus' *thelesis* desired his Father's glory and our salvation. Like his sense appetite, it also, *naturally*, repudiated whatever damages human nature, especially death. Rather as we sometimes make rational choices *against* natural inclinations and *for* means to important ends (choosing a painful medical procedure, risking death in battle), so Jesus, by *boulesis*, translated his permanent commitment to his Father's will into a choice, here and now, to hand himself over to his Passion.

A Martyr makes the same choice. But Jesus calls *all* to share his self-giving daily; St. Paul urges us to "die with Christ."[43] The traditional commendation of a departing soul encourages the dying person to say, with Jesus and the Proto-Martyr, "Into your hands, Lord, I commend my spirit; Lord Jesus Christ, receive my spirit."[44] Herbert McCabe sees *everyone* facing death as called to a form of martyrdom, and practices of mortification as preparation for dying.[45] But if *Jesus* went through a struggle involving prayer and help in Gethsemane,[46] it is not surprising if others come to terms with approaching death through a demanding—a *grieving*—process for which they need support. Besides the comfort provided by the Church's Sacraments and prayers, the Middle Ages produced *Ars Moriendi* treatises;[47] this tradition has been continued by, for example, The Centre for the Art of Dying Well at St Mary's University.[48]

Should We Accept the Death of a Loved One as God's Will?

If all are called to come to accept their own death as God's (indirect) will, how should we view the death of those we love? Aquinas asks whether our will should conform to God's *in a particular matter*.[49] His nuanced answer employs this analogy: a judge wants a criminal executed for the common good; his wife wants him spared. Both judge and wife rightly want what their roles present to them as *good*. Aquinas implies a *direct conflict of will* would arise only if the wife helped her husband escape, contravening the common good that she must acknowledge. Analogously, we must acknowledge God's wise plan as "the common good" of the cosmos. But each of us belongs in a network of relationships, and *it is God's will* (a) that we respect our natural inclinations towards the good of ourselves and those who belong to us, and (b) that we love them by charity, wanting, working and praying for their natural good and, even more, for them to share God's happiness.[50] Thus, paradoxically, someone is conformed to God's will by wanting the life and salvation of those who belong to her, *even if this means she wills something different from God*, as happens in the case when God allows her husband, say, to die, or even (Aquinas envisages) to choose hell.[51]

Therefore, we are *not* asked to will, and *not* meant to see as good, the suffering and death of those we love, even when God does—indirectly—will these. We must accept God's will only in two senses. Firstly, by not rebelling against him, giving up neither faith in his Wisdom nor hope for eternal communion with him. Although Job complained about his bereavement, he did not sin by doing so, for he persisted in worshipping God, and refused to curse God.[52] We need not repeat his words, "The Lord gave, the Lord has taken away; blessed be the Name of the Lord," in a way that bypasses natural affections, natural grief.

Secondly, the bereaved fulfill God's will by going through the grieving process *humanely*, without getting stuck in an unhealthy way. Thus, the Old Testament forbids mourning rituals that (literally) leave a permanent scar:[53] it is God's will that life go on. The Liturgy of the Dead can assist the process—but should not suppress the legitimate voice that execrates a loved one's death.

2. WHAT CAN THE CATHOLIC LITURGY OF THE DEAD OFFER MOURNERS?

The Liturgy of the Dead

With the variants noted, the Liturgy that follows death developed into the elements listed below, although only Cathedrals, religious communities, and close-knit parishes served by several priests would usually have managed them all. Until recent times, burial followed soon after death; the precise order was adapted to the time at which death occurred. The family of the "average" contemporary Catholic who dies in hospital participate in elements (i), (iv), (vii)–(x), (xiii) and (xiv) in the list; the "month's mind" (element [xii]) remains popular in certain areas. Elements (ii), (iii) and (xi) are now very rare, at least in Britain, as is (vi) outside monastic contexts. The Church celebrates a daily round of "Offices," and an Office of the Dead developed, comprising elements (v), (vi) and (xv). It was not meant as a stand-alone Office,[54] but as an addition to the day's own Office; partly for that reason it comprised fewer elements than standard Offices: only Vespers, Matins and Lauds, comprising Psalms, other Scriptural poetry, prayers and, at Matins, readings and responsories. The difference from normal also fitted a pattern whereby the Liturgy for somber occasions retained primitive features. For well over a century, it has been difficult to maintain the public singing of the Office, except in monastic settings and in Cathedrals and similar important churches;[55] hence a public Office of the Dead has not been part of the "average" Catholic funeral for a long time. The full list of elements is as follows:

  i. Prayers for the person who has just died.
  ii. Psalms and prayers accompanying the laying-out of the body.[56]
  iii. A service held at home by the body, which is then formally carried to the church.
  iv. A solemn reception of the body at the church.[57]
  v. Vespers of the Dead.
  vi. A night vigil kept by the body in the church, incorporating Matins and Lauds of the Dead.

vii. The Funeral Mass,[58] including a sermon/homily (which into the 1960s followed the Mass).
viii. The "Absolution," now called "Final Commendation and Farewell."
ix. Taking the body to the cemetery or (nowadays) to a crematorium.
x. Committing the body to burial or cremation.
xi. Further Masses for the deceased on the third and seventh days.
xii. A further Mass for the deceased on the thirtieth day.
xiii. After cremation the burial of ashes; after burial, the blessing of a headstone.
xiv. A further Mass for the deceased on the first anniversary of death.
xv. Perhaps also the Office of the Dead on the third, seventh and thirtieth days, and on the first anniversary.

Contemporary constraints often mean the whole Funeral is conducted at a crematorium, in which case (iv), (viii) and (x) are combined with readings, homily and (usually) hymns. Unless a crematorium offers a generous time slot, or the family books a double slot, this can generate a sense of haste; it also prevents Mass being offered as part of the Funeral,[59] although a separate Requiem Mass can be organized.[60]

Stages of Mourning, Moments of Closure

Elisabeth Kübler-Ross famously recognized the need for a *process* of grieving. This need has arguably been implicit in traditional formal periods of mourning, and rituals of "closure" which help the bereaved "move on." By enshrining beliefs about what becomes of the dead, traditional rituals also offer perspectives from which to interpret what has happened.

Where funerals usually take place fairly soon after death,[61] distant family members cannot always attend, but (in close-knit communities) local people gather in support. The month's mind provides an opportunity for distant family and friends to gather, while defining a period after which an element of closure is felt normal. In England funerals now often take place two, even three, weeks after death. This allows a greater number of relatives and friends to gather; it means the funeral can be planned carefully and can "close" the first stage of the grieving process.

Supplementary moments of closure, and further opportunities for friends and family to gather in support, are provided by the blessing of a headstone or burial of ashes, and a first anniversary Mass—anniversaries, especially the first, often reawaken a sense of loss. Such rituals offer the bereaved well-defined goals that can be part of their "coping strategy"; arranging them with the clergy evokes a sense of being accompanied by the "official Church."

If a funeral is severely delayed, for example, because an inquest is needed, family and friends often feel unable to close a stage of mourning. Restrictions on attending funerals due to COVID-19 have caused widespread sadness, a sense of unfinished business in people unable to attend, and a feeling that the deceased has been denied "a proper send-off." This can partly be remedied by a Requiem Mass once restrictions are lifted; it manifests the natural concern to "do the right thing" by the deceased.

"Doing the Right Thing"

"The right thing" comprises several elements, including:

1. Showing reverence towards a body that was a temple of God[62] and is destined to rise.
2. Paying tribute to the deceased (especially in the case of a public figure) and giving thanks for his or her life.
3. Respecting the wishes of the deceased and of close family and friends.
4. Observing cultural expectations.
5. Praying for the deceased. For Catholics, this is the chief component of "doing the right thing" by them.

The current Funeral Liturgy gives a Christian dimension to (2) by thanking God for blessings given to the deceased and for what they have meant to us. *Order of Christian Funerals* allows a relative or friend to give a brief recollection between the Funeral Mass and the Final Commendation, an option often taken up.

Regarding (3) and (4), the failure to respect wishes and customs can cause lasting hurt. *Ordo Exsequiarum* speaks of "endeavoring" (*nitantur*) to transform customs contrary to the Gospel,[63] implying tact. For example, in England, relatives and colleagues may want a flag or insignia on the coffin of a serviceman or woman, especially one who died in the line of duty. If this is deemed inappropriate,[64] the minister might allow the coffin to be borne in in the flag, which is then replaced by a pall as a sign that we come before God simply as baptized Christians; the flag can be restored after the Commendation to acknowledge a contribution the deceased made to society.

Arousing Hope

Besides providing moments of closure and paying tribute, a Christian Funeral offers *a hope-filled perspective* within which mourners can begin to make some sense of the death. Most fundamentally, it presents Christ's

Death and Resurrection as the interpretative pattern. With the nuances proposed in Section 1, death must be accepted as a stage in our conformity to Christ, who leads us through it to a life patterned on his Resurrection. The Medieval Liturgies prayed for the resurrection of the deceased[65]; "passing-over with Christ" was, arguably, *implicit* in the journey motif mentioned below, and in the Mass as sacramental re-presentation of Christ's Sacrifice. In the current Liturgy, this theme is *explicit* in many prayers, including those that accompany symbols[66] like the holy water traditionally sprinkled in memory of the Baptism in which the deceased began dying and rising with Christ.

The homily should let "the love of God manifested in Christ crucified and risen enliven faith, hope and charity," and by affirming "belief in eternal life and the communion of the saints" bring "consolation to those who grieve"; it should offer "the proper perspective of life on earth as a pilgrimage . . . Avoid[ing] the form and style of a eulogy," the preacher should "keep in mind . . . the identity of the deceased."[67] To my mind, *some* reminiscences belong in the homily, so that it is not "impersonal" but brings out how the deceased manifested Faith, and finds signs of grace in his or her journey.[68] This brings hope into the recollections *this* family and *these* friends have. A preacher who did not know the deceased must seek reminiscences from family and friends. This greatly assists their own journey through grief. It can be combined with inviting them to help plan the Funeral, which evokes a sense of empowerment and helps remedy feelings of being out of control.

The preacher should show concern for attendees who are not practicing Catholics[69]—not by proselytizing a captive audience, but by weaving his knowledge of the deceased into his message so as to *accompany* them as their memories of the deceased and participation in the funeral become part of a journey in which faith may reawaken or fresh perspectives open.

Praying for the Dead

Ordo Exsequiarum[70] begins by saying the Church celebrates Christ's Paschal Mystery[71] at funerals, chiefly by offering Mass for them, so that Christ's members may pass with him through death to life, their souls—once purified—entering heaven and their bodies awaiting resurrection; she offers further prayers for the dead so that what benefits some of her members may console others. The longer introduction in the *Order of Christian Funerals*[72] emphasizes the ongoing communion between dead and living and the elements of proclamation of faith, giving thanks, and bringing hope and consolation to the living—for in a post-Christian society it is necessary to refresh Christian Faith and Hope—but gives proportionately less weight to praying for the dead, and only *implies* that their souls need purification and that Mass is offered for this purpose. In fact, *explicitly to emphasize praying for the dead* is a highly effective way of proclaiming hope and consoling those who mourn, for the following reasons:

   a. Praying for the dead expresses the conviction that their souls are not extinguished, and the hope that they are journeying into glory.
   b. It enacts an ongoing union of love in which we help them and, their journey completed, they help us.
   c. It engages the human instinct to care for the dead,[73] in fact the conviction that we have a *duty* to do so.
   d. Offering Mass *for* the dead *enacts the real power* of Christ's Death and Resurrection to *cause* both the resurrection of the body, and "grace," the soul's share in God's own life and love.[74]
   e. The opportunity to benefit the deceased by prayer is consoling if a death leaves unfinished business (e.g., the bereaved had no chance for a farewell or for reconciliation after an estrangement) or if the bereaved feels (rightly or wrongly) he or she failed the deceased in some way.
   f. If the bereaved has been wronged by the deceased, prayer for his or her soul is an act of forgiveness; if the bereaved finds forgiveness difficult, the Church's prayer can "carry" them until the hurt has been worked through.
   g. If the bereaved is anxious about some real or perceived fault of the deceased, praying for his or her soul can allay the anxiety.
   h. "Bargaining" is a common stage in the grieving process, and one which the mourner has to grow beyond by accepting that death cannot be reversed. The opportunity to intercede for the deceased can gather up the instinct to bargain into the ongoing journey *forwards* of both mourner and deceased.

The current Funeral Liturgy does effectively enable the mourners to pray for the dead by its wide selection of prayers asking God to forgive the sins of the deceased, to welcome him or her into his presence, and to raise him or her to glory on the Last Day. Some *almost* match the eloquence of the ancient prayers which included phrases such as, "we implore you courteously and gently to receive the soul of our beloved N. as it returns to you who personally gave it him," and, "clothe her with a heavenly garment, wash her in the holy fountain of eternal life, so that she may rejoice among the joyful, be wise among the wise, be crowned and enthroned among the martyrs . . . and among the angels and archangels see God's glory . . ."[75]

A dramatic motif in some old prayers is that of the soul's *journey*.[76] This survives in chants of the current Liturgy, such as, "Saints of God, come to her aid; come to meet her, Angels of the Lord: receive her soul and present it in the presence of the Most High."[77] These arouse a powerful sense of *accompanying* the soul of the deceased. Any hints that the journey is perilous[78] have almost completely disappeared from the current Liturgy, perhaps because notes of fear seem inappropriate in a post-Christian society when persevering in the Faith is a strong sign that one dies in God's love.

It is the Office of the Dead that has changed most radically. The Medieval forms were, through and through, a prayer for the dead, ending each Psalm with, "Eternal rest grant unto them, O Lord, and let perpetual light shine upon them." The current form has been forced into a standard mold: the Psalms end with "Glory be to the Father . . ." Hymns have been added—which, like some intercessions, focus chiefly on the needs of the *living*. This diminishes the opportunity to pray, in the Church's name, for the dead. When the Divine Office was being revised, it was hoped that many lay people would participate in it. Devout lay people do often participate in Lauds and Vespers, but rarely in the Office of Readings (previously "Matins"), which is chiefly recited by priests and religious, who may be presumed to be least in need of a didactic Office. Since many of them are engaged in pastoral care, the readings, focused on resurrection, can inspire their preaching; the one from Braulio of Saragossa encourages them to acknowledge grief. I argue below that the current readings fail to encourage them to acknowledge the *anger* many people feel when grieving.

Acknowledging Grief

Ordo Exsequiarum urges clergy to be attentive to mourners' grief.[79] The current Funeral Liturgy includes sensitive prayers for the mourners. This has most profoundly affected children's funerals. *Rituale Romanum*,[80] certain of the salvation of baptized infants, did not pray for them, since they need no Purgatory. It prayed that we may safely join them in Heaven— but made no mention of the grief of the parents and wider family.[81] The current Liturgy acknowledges their grief and integrates their ongoing concern for the child with the certainty of his or her salvation. It is important to plan such funerals with pastoral care, taking account of whether, for example, the death was unexpected, or due to an illness in which the parents accompanied the child and carefully made the difficult decisions necessary concerning medical treatment.

At an adult's funeral, it is possible to nurture hope without importing an unrealistic joyfulness. The current Liturgy's flexibility[82] allows clergy to accompany the mourners in adapting the Funeral to the wishes of the deceased and their own, while the guidelines it provides can "hold" people numb with grief. A Sarum prayer began, "Pierced by a new, fell wound, and almost sick at heart, we implore your mercy with tearful voices, Redeemer of the world . . ."[83] Nothing quite matches this in the current Rite, though bidding prayers (ad lib intercessions) provide an opportunity to incorporate such sentiments.

3. ACKNOWLEDGING ANGER, ANSWERING PROTEST

Feelings of anger are common in the grieving process. They may be directed at the deceased, at someone suspected of responsibility for the death, or (especially if death was tragic, painful, or followed a long period of sad decline) at *God*. Bewilderment may reinforce anger: why has God allowed a death he could have prevented? Christians angry with God may feel guilty. They can be reassured that such anger is a *legitimate* part of the grieving process, for Scripture contains *God-given* words expressing anger. The Medieval Office of the Dead employed some of them, offering, I propose, a model for working through that stage of grief. The current Liturgy of the Dead does not do this.

The Genre of the Medieval Liturgy of the Dead

The assumption seems widespread that, like Doom paintings, the Medieval Liturgies of the Dead intended to strike fear in the *living*.[84] A *few* texts render this plausible, such as "While I sinned daily, and did not repent, the fear of death shook me."[85] However, some liturgical books ordered certain Psalms to be said *in persona defuncti*,[86] and many texts are best interpreted that way.[87] The dead cannot speak; the living must take on their role, lend them their voices, and pray *in solidarity with the dead*. Some texts clearly work this way, such as, "Before I was born, you knew me, and, Lord, you formed me to your image; now I am giving back my soul to you my Creator."[88]

The famous *Dies irae*,[89] originally a meditation on judgment, came into the Requiem Mass, I suggest, as the prayer *of the one who has just died*, and in Christ's presence is discovering his or her state of soul. While voicing anxiety,[90] at its heart it claims mercy: "Remember, loving Jesus, that your Way [of the Cross] was for *me*: do not lose me on that Day. You sat down, tired, in search of *me*,[91] you redeemed *me* by undergoing the Cross; do not let such labor be in vain."

Read this way, the Medieval Liturgies of the Dead are *for the dead*; but the living pray not just *for*, but *in solidarity with* the dead. They have a further dynamic: a sense of transcending time.[92] Some prayers of the Funeral Liturgy spoke of "the soul . . . whom you have commanded to journey from this world *today*."[93] Thus the living share any anxiety the deceased may have felt when approaching death, for people do experience fear in the face of death, and, despite the Church's Sacraments, may not be entirely at peace by the time they die. The living accompanies the soul as she goes to face the Judge and discover what will be revealed publicly on the Last Day. In the present moment, the bereaved call to the God who transcends time, reach back to support the deceased in a period of anxiety now past, ask that grace may have ensured the soul has met Christ with love, and pray in hope for the Judge to make this grace manifest at the End.

If someone died during the day, Vespers of the Dead was typically recited before or after taking the body to the church. The Medieval form began with Psalm 116: "The pangs of death surrounded me. . . . He has delivered my soul from death . . . I will enjoy the Lord's pleasure in the land of the living." In context, this is the prayer of one who has died and is confident of liberation from death and life in God's presence.[94] Other texts expressed similar hopes. In principle, Matins and Lauds followed later; the Funeral Mass was celebrated the morning after death. To their dynamic we now turn.

Medieval Matins of the Dead: Angry Protest

Matins comprised nine Psalms and nine readings, each reading with a responsory. The readings all came to be taken from Job.[95] Apart from the well-known "I know that my Redeemer liveth," it seems odd to read them *to* a congregation; they make sense only as *a prayer*—better still, *a protest*—*in persona defuncti*. They come from the long debate in which Job replies to his "comforters," who tell him he must have deserved his suffering. He knows this is not true, and demands an explanation from God, while realizing he cannot force God. God *does* answer, but by emphasizing his greatness—which Job is already well aware of! Job says, basically, "Oops, I shouldn't have spoken," but it's the *comforters* God rebukes, who "have not spoken of me what is right, as my servant Job has."[96] Their neat explanations did not match reality; Job was *not* wrong to protest, his anger and bewilderment were no sin. He receives no clear answer; but he gets *God's personal attention*, which somehow satisfies.[97]

Matins of the Dead did not claim innocence: "Alas for me, Lord! I have sinned . . . Where shall I fly but to you, my God?"[98] But, through Job's mouth, it expresses anger and bewilderment:

> I have sinned. What can I do to you, O watcher of men? . . . Why do you not take away my sin? . . . I will speak in the bitterness of my soul, and say to God: Do not condemn me; tell me why you judge me in this way! Does it seem good to you to censure, to suppress me, the work of your hands? . . . Man born of woman lives a brief time . . . and do you consider it right . . . to

call him before you for judgment? Who can make clean what was conceived from unclean seed? Surely you, who alone Exist? . . . You will call me, and I shall answer you; you will stretch out your right hand to the work of your hands.[99]

Job demands that the omnipotent Author of Life take merciful care of his frail creature. A full literary analysis of the Office would be a major task, but perhaps the hopeful texts in Vespers, and the first responsory, "I believe that my Redeemer lives . . ." have already set the scene for bewilderment that death still happens. Then the Matins readings imply that *death does not make sense*—less sense than did Job's suffering, for Christ has defeated both death and sin! On behalf of the deceased we say to God, "What are you up to, letting me die, and judging me strictly? This is wrong; do something about it." Thus, the bewilderment expressed *in persona defuncti*, as well as the demand that God grant rescue, resonates with any anger the bereaved feel.

Catharsis of Anger, Acceptance of Death

The eighth reading is confident that the demand will be met:

> My flesh has been consumed; my bones cling to my skin. . . . Who will grant me that my words be written? Who will arrange for me that they be inscribed as a record with an iron stylus in a lead plate, or engraved with a chisel in stone? For I know that my Redeemer lives, and that on the Last Day I shall rise from the earth and be clothed again with my skin, and in my flesh I shall see God my Savior. I myself will see him, and my eyes shall look upon him; it will not be some other being. This my hope lies deep in my heart.[100]

The Book of Job ends with him satisfied and vindicated, but leaves the reader puzzled. We can read it as "the Old Testament awaiting the New," demanding a fuller answer. Likewise, Matins ends on a question mark, for instead of coming from later in the Book of Job, the final reading is an earlier, deeply bitter, passage:

> Why did you bring me forth from the womb? . . . Surely the few days of my life can't be over so soon? Let me alone, therefore, that I may lament my sorrow a little before I go whence I shall not return, to the land that is dark and covered with the mist of death . . .[101]

The challenge thus laid down, that death surely cannot be the final word, is answered as the Liturgy unfolds.

Within the convention of which Scriptural passages to use, Lauds marshalled prophecies of resurrection: "The bones that have been humbled shall rejoice"; "you will pardon our transgressions. Blessed the one you have chosen and taken: he shall dwell in your courts"; "your right hand has raised me up."[102] From Isaiah 38:10–20 it included Hezekiah's protest at dying before his time, answered by his rescue from Hades; it quoted Jesus' "I am the resurrection and the life."[103]

The Requiem Mass began, "Eternal rest grant unto them, O Lord, and let perpetual light shine upon them." Once the *Dies irae* had been incorporated, a note of fear surfaced part way through the Mass—but at its center this chant *in persona defuncti* claimed mercy. The Offertory chant, taking up the journey motif, asked for the souls of the dead not to sink into Hades but to be carried by St. Michael into the promised light. The note of fear hardly surfaced again in earlier forms of the Sarum Use, which employed mostly positive chants at the Absolution, the point when imminent burial would arouse strong emotions: "You raised Lazarus from the tomb . . ." then, after "Alas for me, for I have sinned greatly . . . where shall I flee but to you, my God?," this chant to Christ who harrowed hell: "Deliver me, Lord, from journeying to hell, for you broke down the gates of bronze and visited hell to give light to those who were suffering darkness, that they might see you and cry out: You have come, our Redeemer." From the later Middle Ages onwards, the note of fear often resurfaced at the Absolution;[104] nevertheless, in most forms of the Funeral Rite, "May the Angels lead you into Paradise; as you arrive, may the Martyrs receive you and lead you into the Holy City, Jerusalem,"[105] was sung as the body was carried out, so that the final note was always positive.

Thus, without toning down the urgency of prayer or glossing over the reality of judgment, the Funeral Mass carried no hint of bewildered anger, giving the impression that it had been worked through. Somehow Job's question had been answered. Partly by the Scriptural readings at the Mass:[106] "I am the resurrection and the life . . ." and, "The dead in Christ shall rise . . ."—the prophecies of resurrection *are* being fulfilled. More powerfully, by *what the Mass represents and is*. God satisfied Job by his personal attention. Now he has given us more wondrous personal attention: God has become man, has become one of our family. In *friendship*, he still gives himself in Holy Communion; the deceased (hopefully) had received him just before death as Viaticum, Food for the journey. Moreover, the Eucharist is the Sacrament *of Jesus' Self-Sacrifice on the Cross*. That is what is New: God has died on the Cross.[107] He has not *explained* death in *words*—but has *shared* our death, or, better, allowed *us* to share *his*.

By praying for the remission of their sins we assist souls through Purgatory. However, no Liturgy uses the word "Purgatory," perhaps signaling that ensuring people die in charity is urgent, whereas souls in Purgatory are certain of Heaven, and because the Liturgy prefers to imply that in Purgatory we *complete our dying with Christ*;[108] we "joy to undergo the shadow of [Christ's] Cross sublime"[109] whose liberating power the

Requiem Mass applies to the souls there. The unfolding of Medieval Liturgies of the Dead paralleled the purgatorial journey, for up to and including Vespers they expressed the hope in which the deceased had died. Despite hope, Christians can struggle to accept death, and Matins, with its readings from Job, followed by Lauds and Mass, voiced an initial protest against death, gradually resolved by the great act of God's solidarity, his Sacrifice. By accompanying them through the scandal of death and, so to speak, coming in prayer to accept death on their behalf, the living helped the dead complete losing their lives in order to find them.[110]

In principle, wrestling with the scandal of death *in persona defuncti* could help the bereaved wrestle with any feelings of anger of their own. When burial followed soon after death, the Liturgy resolved anger within twenty-four hours. But the repetition of the Office of the Dead and Requiem Mass at, for example, the month's mind, allowed that the mourners might take longer; it allowed for an ongoing cathartic program within their discipleship of the Crucified.

In practice, few lay people would have participated in Matins; the clergy would have understood it in various ways, since from Liturgies that develop organically we can mine complementary meanings.[111] It is difficult, today, to voice anger in a Funeral Liturgy, for the Mass never voiced it (the homily can acknowledge it), and to recite the whole Medieval Office would be a major undertaking. However, if the body is received at the church the evening before the Funeral (item [iv] in the list), close family and friends often stay afterwards, for instance, to recite the Rosary. Conceivably, a service might be held at that point, condensed out of the Medieval Office, to voice negative emotions. At the least, this Office reminds those clergy who use it privately, and stands as a monument to remind *all* pastors, neither to dismiss, as illegitimate, anger at death, nor to expect mourners to work through anger easily. It may also suggest ways of helping them through this part of the grieving process.

CONCLUSION

Catholic doctrine sees death as an evil, which, however, we are called to undergo in solidarity with Christ, as part of being refashioned into sharers of his glory. The Church's Liturgy aids this journey by accompanying those facing death with Sacraments and prayers, and by praying for the dead and offering Mass for them. The Liturgy of the Dead can also help the bereaved through the grieving process, by providing moments of closure, by honoring the dead; more significantly, by presenting Christ's Passing Over as the hope-filled perspective from which to interpret death, and by enabling the bereaved to remain in a communion of loving prayer with the deceased. It does not require us to approve of the death of loved ones. The current Funeral Liturgy acknowledges grief as natural, and, in the case of children's funerals, does so better than the seventeenth-century *Rituale Romanum*. Its flexibility allows funerals to be arranged with pastoral sensitivity;[112] it says little about judgment, perhaps because persevering in Christian Faith in a post-Christian society is a sign of grace. The dramatic dynamic of the full Medieval Liturgy, especially in forms like the early Sarum, allowed the bereaved, retrospectively, to reach out in prayer to the deceased while he or she was in process of dying in the mixture of hope, anxiety and protest that is often experienced; it enabled the living prayerfully to accompany the deceased who, in Purgatory, is completing dying in conformity to Christ's Sacrifice, thus helping him or her journey into glory. This stood to legitimate any feelings of anger and protest on the part of the bereaved and, arguably, to help them work through them. The revisers of the Liturgy in the 1960s abandoned the genre of praying *in persona defuncti*, and silenced the voice of anger that had been heard in Matins of the Dead. The parts of the Funeral Liturgy normally experienced by the bereaved have never expressed protest and anger; but the Scripturally-inspired voice of Matins of the Dead as sung by the Church for over a millennium still validates such feelings, it reminds those who care pastorally for the bereaved to hear anger sympathetically and it may offer pointers towards its gradual resolution.

NOTES

1. The Liturgy of the Dead includes, but extends beyond, Funerals. See Section 2. Other Churches' Liturgies well deserve study, but I can only refer in passing to Anglican services. For a brief account of post-Reformation Liturgies, see Geoffrey Rowell, *The Liturgy of Christian Burial: An Introductory Survey of the Historical Development of Christian Burial Rites* (London: Alcuin Club, 1977), chapters 5 and 6.

2. I also draw on a talk I gave to the Association for Latin Liturgy in 2002, "Complaining to God or Soothing the Grief?—The Old and New Liturgies of the Dead Compared," itself inspired by Eamon Duffy, "An Apology for Grief, Fear and Anger," *Priests and People* 5 (1991): 397–401. I also draw on my paper "Thomas Aquinas on How Not to Resign Ourselves to God's Will," delivered at a Conference on Mourning jointly sponsored by the Humane Philosophy Project and Aquinas Institute, Oxford, 3 March 2016.

3. Richard Rutherford, CSC, with Tony Barr, *The Death of a Christian: The Order of Christian Funerals* (Collegeville: Liturgical Press, 1990), 75–89, 93–108.

4. E.g., Rutherford, *Death of a Christian*, 59–60, 62–64; p. 86 speaks of "an almost unhoped-for mercy."

5. On the preparation of *Ordo Exsequiarum*, see Annibale Bugnini, *The Reform of the Liturgy 1948–1975* (Collegeville: Liturgical Press, 1990), chapter 46.

6. Catholic Church, *Liturgia Horarum iuxta Ritum Romanum: Officium Divinum ex decreto Ss. Oecumenici Concilii Vaticani II instauratum* . . . (Vatican: Polyglot Press, 1971). The Office of the Dead is printed towards the end of each volume, after the Common Offices.

7. This is not a characteristically Catholic heading.

8. From a sermon "Death the King of Terrors," preached by Henry Scott-Holland while the body of King Edward VII lay in state.

9. "Apology for Grief," 401.

10. Catholic Church, *Order of Christian Funerals Approved for Use in the Dioceses of England and Wales, and Scotland* (London: Geoffrey Chapman, 1990) [henceforth *Order of Christian Funerals*], no. 580, prayer 3.

11. E.g., Psalm 89:47–48. I give the Psalm numbers of the Hebrew and most English versions; liturgical books normally use the numbering of the Septuagint and Vulgate. Unless otherwise noted, Scriptural translations are my own, from the Latin used in the Liturgy.

12. E.g., Psalm 13:3.

13. Acts 9:36–42.

14. E.g., 1 Thess. 4:13–18; 1 Cor. 15:26.

15. For a detailed analysis of this maxim, see Albert E. Wingell, "*Vivere Viventibus Est Esse* in Aristotle and St. Thomas," *The Modern Schoolman* XXXVIII (1960–61): 85–120.

16. *Summa Theologiae, Prima Pars*, Q. 5, a. 1. [Henceforth ST, followed by Part, Question, article.]

17. ST, I, 48, 1.

18. ST, I, 75, 2 and 6; 76, 1 and 5; 91, 3.

19. ST, I-II, 85, 6.

20. John Finley, "Man More Animal than Anything: The Unity in Human Agency," *New Blackfriars* 100 (2019): 696–9
7.

21. ST, I, 97, 1, 2 and 4.

22. ST, I, 100, 1. They would not have lived on earth forever, but transitioned to a heavenly life without the trauma of dying (ST, I, 102, 4).

23. ST, I-II, 85, 5; II-II, 164, 1. This is the Doctrine of Original Sin.

24. ST, I, 19, 9; 20, 2; 49.

25. ST, I, 48, 5.

26. ST, I, 19, 9; 49, 2. Cf. Herbert McCabe, "Evil," in *God Matters* (London: Geoffrey Chapman, 1987), 25–38.

27. ST, I, 49, 2

28. *Compendium Theologiae*, Part I, chapters 172–80.

29. But see Herbert McCabe, *The New Creation* (London: Continuum, 2010), 134–37.

30. Richard Conrad, "Humanity Created for Communion with the Trinity in Aquinas," in *A Transforming Vision: Knowing and Loving the Triune God*, ed. George Westhaver (London: SCM, 2018), 121–34.

31. ST, II-II, 17, 1–3; 21, 2; 22, 1.

32. ST, II-II, 18, 4.

33. Catholic Church, *Missale Romanum: Ex decreto Ss. Concilii Tridentini restitutum* . . . (Rome: Desclée, 1961) [henceforth *Tridentine Missal*], and: Catholic Church, *Missale Romanum: Ex decreto Ss. Oec. Concilii Vaticani II instauratum* . . . (Vatican: Polyglot Press, 2002) [henceforth *Missale Romanum*], responsory for Ash Wednesday. [All translations, and added emphases, are mine.] Cf. Psalm 90:12.

34. ST, III, 48, 2. Cf. 1, 2; 22, 3; 46, 3; 49, 1–2.

35. *Expositio super Iob ad litteram*, Prol.; Ch. 1, lessons 2, end, & 4; Ch. 2, lesson 1; ST, III, 69, 3.

36. Paschal Preface II.

37. *Missale Romanum*, Preface of the Dead, IV.

38. Catholic Church, *Ordo Exsequiarum: Rituale Romanum ex decreto Ss. Oec. Concilii Vaticani II instauratum* . . . (Vatican: Polyglot Press, 1969), *Decretum*; *Praenotanda*, 1. Cf. Romans 6:5.

39. Matthew 6:10.

40. ST, I-II, 19, 9.

41. ST, I, 80–83; I-II, 6 and 8–17.

42. ST, III, 18.

43. Luke 9:23–24; Rom. 6:6, 11–13; Col. 3:1–5.

44. Cf. Luke 23:46; Acts 7:59; Catholic Church, *Rituale Romanum Pauli V . . . jussu editum* . . . (Rome: Desclée, 1947), Titulus V, Chap. VIII; Catholic Church, *Pastoral Care of the Sick, Rites of Anointing and Viaticum* Approved for Use in the Dioceses of the United States of America (New Jersey: Catholic Book Publishing Corp., 1983), no. 217.

45. *The New Creation*, 125–31.

46. Luke 22:43–44.

47. David William Atkinson (ed.), *The English* ars moriendi (New York: Lang, 1992).

48. https://www.artofdyingwell.org/

49. ST, I-II, 19, 10.

50. ST, II-II, 25, 4 & 5; 26, 4, 6–9, 11 & 12.

51. ST, I-II, 19, 10, incl. ad 1, ad 2, & ad sed contra 1.

52. Job 1:20-22; 2:9–10; 42:7.

53. Lev. 19:28. Cf. Rutherford, *Death of a Christian*, 15–16 on the early Christian exclusion of pagan mourning rituals.

54. Under Benedict XV it came to be such on All Souls' Day.

55. Except that Sunday Vespers remained frequent in many parishes, and in many parishes some of the faithful gather regularly for Lauds and/or Vespers.

56. Absent from *Rituale Romanum*, these remained in Dominican books. *Ordo Exsequiarum* no. 31 and *Order of Christian Funerals* no. 62 provide for such prayers, but in the modern West undertakers usually prepare bodies for burial.

57. This is often done at the beginning of the Funeral Mass.

58. A Mass for the Dead is often called a "Requiem Mass" because it always began with the chant *Requiem aeternam*.

59. At least in the UK, crematoria are not set up for the celebration of Mass.

60. A separate Mass is also appropriate when no priest is available, and another minister conducts a Funeral of readings, prayers, homily, hymns and the Final Commendation.

61. In my experience, Scotland is one such society.

62. 1 Cor. 3:16
63. *Praenotanda* 2.
64. As by many clergy, and by *Order of Christian Funerals* no. 38.
65. More frequently in the Sarum Use than in *Rituale Romanum*.
66. Symbols often speak for themselves, and the prayers that accompany them usually explain ones that do not; any further explanations required can be incorporated into an order of service.
67. Congregation for Divine Worship and the Discipline of the Sacraments, *Homiletic Directory* (Vatican City: Libreria Editrice Vaticana, 2015), no. 155.
68. Cf. *Order of Christian Funerals* no. 27.
69. *Homiletic Directory* no. 156.
70. *Praenotanda* 1.
71. That is, his Death and Resurrection which fulfilled what the Passover Sacrifice had promised.
72. Nos. 1–7.
73. To argue for this instinct is beyond my present scope.
74. ST, I-II, 112, 1 ad 1; III, 48, 6; 56. While those in Purgatory died "in a state of grace," we can understand Purgatory as grace coming to pervade their souls completely.
75. Catholic Church, *Liber Sacramentorum Romanae Aeclesiae Ordinis Anni Circuli* (Rome: Herder, 1960) [henceforth *Gelasian Sacramentary*], nos. 1608, 1611; cf. Catholic Church, *The Sarum Missal Edited from Three Early Manuscripts* by J. Wickham Legg (Oxford: Clarendon Press, 1916), 428–430.
76. We must disentangle the truths the motif implies from out-of-date astronomical views. In fact, the early Christians did likewise, as well as exorcizing elements of pagan mythology.
77. *Rituale Romanum*, Titulus VI, Cap. III, no. 3; *Ordo Exsequiarum*, no. 47; *Order of Funerals*, no. 185, B (cf. *Sarum Missal*, 428; Catholic Church, *Manuale ad usum percelebris Ecclesie Sarisburiensis*, ed. A. Jefferies Collins (Henry Bradshaw Society Vol. XCI, 1960) [henceforth *Sarum Manual*], 123–24).
78. E.g., *Gelasian Sacramentary* no. 1609. Vincent Owusu, "Funeral Rites in Rome and the Non-Roman West," in *Handbook for Liturgical Studies*, Vol. IV: *Sacraments and Sacramentals*, ed. Anscar J. Chupungco (Collegeville: Liturgical Press, 2000), 361–62, arguably overstates the perception of peril and the exclusive focus on the soul, especially as regards the *Gelasian Sacramentary* and the Sarum and Dominican Uses.
79. *Praenotanda* 17–18; cf. *Order of Christian Funerals* nos. 4, 7–13, 16.
80. Titulus VI, Capp. VI and VII.
81. Rutherford, *Death of a Christian*, 90–92.
82. E.g. *Order of Christian Funerals* no. 580, provides sensitive prayers (prayers 42–45) for one who died suddenly, or by violence, or by suicide. Like that for a young person (prayer 27: we "mourn the loss of N., whose life has passed so quickly"), they avoid speaking of such deaths as "God's will."
83. *Sarum Missal*, 429; already found in *Gelasian Sacramentary* no. 1608.
84. E.g. Rutherford, *Death of a Christian*, 63.
85. Matins of Dead, responsory 7.
86. Rutherford, *Death of a Christian*, 71.

87. Noted by D. Sicard, "Christian Death," in *The Church at Prayer: An Introduction to the Liturgy*, ed. A. G. Martimort *et al.* Vol. III (New ed., Collegeville: Liturgical Press, 1988), p. 238; and by Owusu, "Funeral Rites," p. 360.

88. Order of Preachers, *Processionarium juxta ritum Sacri Ordinis Praedicatorum* (Rome: in hospitio Magistri Ordinis, 1930), *Officium Sepulturae Fratrum*, 2nd responsory for the Absolution.

89. For much detail: Mary Cecilia Hilferty, *The Domine Jesu Christe, Libera Me, and Dies Irae of the Requiem: A Historical and Literary Study* (Washington: Catholic University of America, 1973).

90. Many New Testament texts give grounds for such anxiety!

91. Cf. John 4:6.

92. This is typical of Liturgy because of (a) the theme of *anamnesis*, a recollection which *actualizes now* a great event of the past (F. A. Brunner, *New Catholic Encyclopedia* [1967], s.v. "Anamnesis"), and (b) each Sacrament symbolizing saving acts of past, present and future (ST, III, 60, 3).

93. *Missale Romanum* also allows for "today."

94. Following the idiom of the Hebrew, "He *has* delivered" indicates a *future* event certain to occur.

95. Except on All Souls' Day. The passages were: Job 7:16–21, 10:1–7, 10:8–12, 13:22–28, 14:1–6, 14:13–16, 17:1–3 & 11–15, 19:20–27, 10:18–22.

96. Job 38:1–42:9.

97. Eleonore Stump offers a helpful reading of Job: *Wandering in Darkness: Narrative and the Problem of Suffering* (Oxford: Clarendon Press, 2010), 177–226. Aquinas' *Expositio super Iob* presents Job as answering objections to God's providence, and repenting because he did not do so convincingly enough.

98. Responsory 4 (*Sarum Manual*, 138), or 5 (*Rituale Romanum,* Titulus VI, Cap. IV).

99. Job 7:20–21, 10:1–3, 14:1, 3–4, 15, from Readings 1, 2, 5 and 6.

100. Job 19:20, 23–27.

101. Job 10:18, 20–21.

102. Psalms 51:8 (Vulgate 50:10); 65:3–4; 63:8.

103. John 11:25.

104. Compare *Sarum Missal,* 446, based on thirteenth-to-fourteenth-century MSS, with *Sarum Manual*, 154, based on sixteenth-century MSS, which replaces the third of these chants with "Deliver me, Lord, from eternal death on that fearful day when the heavens and the earth shall be shaken, when you come to judge the world with fire," the ninth responsory of Matins. In *Rituale Romanum* (Titulus VI, Cap. III, 8) it became the sole chant for the Absolution at most funerals. To reintroduce a note of fear at this stage arguably ran counter to the earlier dynamic of the Funeral Liturgy.

105. *Rituale Romanum*, Titulus VI, Cap. III, no. 11; *Ordo Exsequiarum*, no. 50; *Order of Funerals*, no. 187 (cf. *Sarum Missal*, 447; *Sarum Manual*, 155).

106. 1 Thess. 4:13–18; John 11:21–27. Other readings were read at other Requiem Masses (*Tridentine Missal, In Anniversario Defunctorum* and *In Missis Cotidianis Defunctorum*; cf. *Sarum Missal*, 431–33).

107. Cf. Second Council of Constantinople, 553 AD, canon 10.

108. McCabe, *New Creation*, 132–34.

109. From John Henry Newman's hymn "Help, Lord, the souls that thou hast made."
110. Cf. Mark 8:35; John 12:24–26.
111. This parallels Scripture itself, and any great poetry or ritual.
112. Factors such as time constraints at crematoria may limit the possibilities.

BIBLIOGRAPHY

Aquinas, St. Thomas. *Compendium Theologiae*. [English translation: *Compendium of Theology*. Translated by R. J. Regan. Oxford: OUP, 2009.]

Aquinas, St. Thomas. *Expositio super Iob ad litteram*. [English translation: *Commentary on the Book of Job*. Lander, Wyoming: The Aquinas Institute for the Study of Sacred Doctrine, 2016.]

Aquinas, St. Thomas. *Summa Theologiae*.

Atkinson, David William (ed.) *The English* ars moriendi. New York: Lang, 1992.

Bugnini, Annibale. *The Reform of the Liturgy 1948–1975*. Collegeville: Liturgical Press, 1990.

Catholic Church. *Liber Sacramentorum Romanae Aeclesiae Ordinis Anni Circuli (Sacramentarium Gelasianum)*, edited by Leo Cunibert Mohlberg, OSB. Rome: Herder, 1960.

Catholic Church. *Liturgia Horarum iuxta Ritum Romanum: Officium Divinum ex decreto Ss. Oecumenici Concilii Vaticani II instauratum, auctoritate Pauli PP. VI promulgatum*. Vatican: Polyglot Press, 1971 (2nd (no superscript) edition 1985).

Catholic Church. *Manuale ad usum percelebris Ecclesie Sarisburiensis*, edited by A. Jefferies Collins. Henry Bradshaw Society Vol. XCI, 1958. [See pages 97–118 for Visitation of the Sick, Last Anointing, Commendation of a Departing Soul; 118–25,142–44, 152–62 for Funeral Rites; 125–42 for the Office of the Dead; 144–52 for Mass for the Dead.

Catholic Church. *Missale Romanum: Ex decreto Ss. Concilii Tridentini restitutum, Summorum Pontificum cura recognitum*. Rome: Desclée, 1961. [In all editions, Masses for the Dead appear towards the end, after Votive Masses.]

Catholic Church. *Missale Romanum: Ex decreto Ss. Oecumenici Concilii Vaticani II instauratum, auctoritate Pauli PP. VI promulgatum*. Vatican: Polyglot Press, 1970 (2nd ed. 1975; 3rd 2002). [In all editions, Masses for the Dead appear towards the end, after Votive Masses.]

Catholic Church. *Order of Christian Funerals Approved for Use in the Dioceses of England and Wales, and Scotland*. London: Geoffrey Chapman, 1990.

Catholic Church. *Ordo Exsequiarum: Rituale Romanum ex decreto Ss. Oec. Concilii Vaticani II instauratum, auctoritate Pauli PP. VI promulgatum*. Vatican: Polyglot Press, 1969.

Catholic Church. *Pastoral Care of the Sick, Rites of Anointing and Viaticum* Approved for Use in the Dioceses of the United States of America. New Jersey: Catholic Book Publishing Corp., 1983.

Catholic Church. *Rituale Romanum Pauli V Pontificis Maximi jussu editum*. Rome: Desclée, 1947.

Catholic Church. *The Sarum Missal Edited from Three Early Manuscripts* by J. Wickham Legg. Oxford: Clarendon Press, 1916. [See pages 419–28 for Viaticum, Last Anointing, Commendation of a Departing Soul; 428–31, 446–50 for Funeral Rites; 431–45 for Mass for the Dead.]

Congregation for Divine Worship and the Discipline of the Sacraments. *Homiletic Directory*. Vatican City: Libreria Editrice Vaticana, 2015.

Conrad, Richard. "Humanity Created for Communion with the Trinity in Aquinas." In *A Transforming Vision: Knowing and Loving the Triune God*, edited by George Westhaver, 121–34. London: SCM, 2018.

Duffy, Eamon. "An Apology for Grief, Fear and Anger." *Priests and People* 5 (1991): 397–401.

Finley, John. "Man More Animal than Anything: The Unity in Human Agency." *New Blackfriars* 100 (2019): 677–97.

Hilferty, Mary Cecilia. *The Domine Jesu Christe, Libera Me, and Dies Irae of the Requiem: A Historical and Literary Study*. Washington: Catholic University of America, 1973.

McCabe, Herbert. *God Matters*. London: Geoffrey Chapman, 1987.

McCabe, Herbert. *The New Creation*. London: Continuum, 2010. Chapter 9: "Life After Death" (Chapter 10 in some impressions of earlier edition).

Order of Preachers. *Processionarium juxta ritum Sacri Ordinis Praedicatorum*. Rome: in hospitio Magistri Ordinis, 1930.

Owusu, Vincent. "Funeral Rites in Rome and the Non-Roman West." In *Handbook for Liturgical Studies*. Vol. IV: *Sacraments and Sacramentals*, edited by Anscar J. Chupungco, 355–80. Collegeville: Liturgical Press, 2000.

Rowell, Geoffrey. *The Liturgy of Christian Burial: An Introductory Survey of the Historical Development of Christian Burial Rites*. London: Alcuin Club, 1977.

Rutherford, Richard, CSC, with Tony Barr. *The Death of a Christian: The Order of Christian Funerals*. Revised edition. Collegeville: Liturgical Press, 1990.

Sicard, D. "Christian Death." In *The Church at Prayer: An Introduction to the Liturgy*, edited by A. G. Martimort *et al.* New ed. Vol. III, 221–40. Collegeville: Liturgical Press, 1988.

Stump, Eleonore. *Wandering in Darkness: Narrative and the Problem of Suffering*. Oxford: Clarendon Press, 2010.

Wingell, Albert E. "*Vivere Viventibus Est Esse* in Aristotle and St. Thomas." *The Modern Schoolman* XXXVIII (1960-61): 85–120.

4

✢

Toward a Philosophical Theology of Pregnancy Loss

Amber L. Griffioen

CW: The following contains sometimes graphic descriptions of pregnancy and pregnancy loss.

SECTION 1: INTRODUCTION

Issues surrounding pregnancy loss are rarely addressed in philosophical or theological circles,[1] let alone in Christian philosophy. Yet a *modest* estimate based on the empirical and medical literature places the rate of pregnancy loss between fertilization and term at somewhere between 40–60 percent.[2] If miscarriage really is as common as the research gives us to believe, then it is also likely that a significant number of women in philosophy and theology have experienced the loss of one or more pregnancies in their sexually active lifetimes. And when we add spouses, partners, family, and friends, the number of those touched by pregnancy loss within these disciplines grows even larger.

So why the dearth of Christian philosophical and theological literature on miscarriage, stillbirth, and other forms of reproductive loss? For starters, the scholarly silence tracks a much larger cultural quietism surrounding pregnancy loss, one tied to social taboos concerning the open discussion of women's sexual and reproductive health more generally. This has led to widespread ignorance about miscarriage, particularly among men (whose voices still dominate Christian philosophy).[3] Some Christian subcultures augment this silence—especially those that place the injunction to "be fruitful and multiply" (Gen. 1:28) at the center of their discourse surrounding marriage, family, sexuality, and reproductive choice. The felt violation of such norms when a woman's pregnant body "malfunctions" often gives rise to feelings of shame, guilt, and self-betrayal—feelings amplified by neoliberal tendencies in both the religious and secular spheres to paint miscarriage as a *failure to (re)produce* for which the woman and her body are often made responsible.[4] This is underscored by the fact that metaphysical questions concerning pregnancy and reproductive loss in Anglo-American philosophy have been hijacked by the abortion debate, which, for all its good intentions, tends to implicitly reinforce the idea that a pregnancy which does not lead to the birth of a living human being is a *morally regrettable failure* on the part of the pregnant "caretaker" of the fetus.[5]

In what follows, then, I want to show how thinking more closely about pregnancy loss understood as a *grievable* (even if not always grieved) event can have a profound impact on the way we think about particular theoretical debates in Christian philosophy and provide opportunities for the discipline to put its skills to use in the development of helpful conceptual and hermeneutical resources for those grieving such losses.[6] However, this will require seeking out and taking seriously the testimony of those who have undergone pregnancy loss, as well as getting clearer on how best to conceptualize pregnancy and its loss in the first place. I will thus begin by addressing the appropriateness of taking first-personal subjective testimony as a basis for "care-ful(l)" and "consider-ate" philosophical theorizing (Section 2), and I will go on to discuss how paying closer attention to pregnancy itself can lay the groundwork for I am calling a "philosophical theology of pregnancy loss" (Section 3). I will then look at one domain in which such a philosophical theology is sorely needed—namely, for the development of grieving rituals for pregnancy loss that are conceptually informed by philosophically adequate and theologically fitting models of God (Section 4)—and I will discuss how Christian philosophy might go about constructing such models (Section 5). Finally, I will explore how one kind of alternative model of God in particular—what I call a "gestational" model—might use the loss inherent to all pregnancy to tease out new ways of thinking about standard philosophical approaches to God (Section 6) and how the "grievous" experience of miscarriage can give Christian philosophers a better way of approaching Trinitarian theology (Section 7).

Before proceeding, a few qualifications are in order. First, it is important to remember that emotional responses to pregnancy loss are not always negatively-valenced, even for those who undergo it. Although it often elicits feelings of sadness and grief, this is by no means always the case, nor is grief the only appropriate emotional response to such loss. Historically speaking, miscarriage may even have been the best way for some women to *survive* their pregnancies,[7] and (both then and now) such loss has sometimes been accompanied by feelings of relief or even a tempered joy.⁸ Therefore, a more comprehensive philosophical theology of reproductive loss than I can discuss here should be sensitive to the fact that such loss can involve many different kinds of responses.

Moreover, although I will sometimes refer to "women" or notions of "motherhood" as a basis for my reflections, I mean my thoughts to be inclusive of all persons capable of gestating a human being inside them. Likewise, I by no means intend to ignore the experience of non-pregnant persons whose concerns are relevantly tied to pregnant persons, though I will be focusing more closely on those bodies whose experience of loss is most immediate and "visceral." Finally, I will sometimes use more "clinical" terms like "embryo" or "fetus" and sometimes more "emotionally-charged" terms like "baby" to refer to what is lost. Different women characterize their losses in different ways, and the preferences of one need not reflect those of another. I will therefore use these terms as they feel right to me in context. I think it important to be permitted to speak personally in these matters, since if we who have lost pregnancies remain afraid to talk about our experiences and speak our losses back into being, we are unlikely to have an adequate testimonial basis from which to elucidate and critique scholarly reflections when it comes to pregnancy loss.

SECTION 2: SCHOLARLY "RIGOR," HARMFUL DISCOURSES, AND CARE-FUL(L) THINKING

To some, the relevance of pregnancy loss to philosophical theology may be obvious. Yet in my experience, topics perceived as involving more "pastoral" concerns are often thought to be of less speculative interest. Moreover, in some academic circles, scholarly reflections that make explicit reference to the subjective experiences and interests of those pursuing them are still treated with suspicion or dismissed as lacking in "objectivity" or "philosophical rigor."

On the one hand, I agree that, within the academic philosophical context, it is often necessary to abstract from particular cases, permissible to discuss hypotheticals that go beyond what is actual, and acceptable to defend views that have little potential for real-world application. On the other hand, those discourses that *do* appeal to autobiographical experience should not automatically be treated as less "rigorous" or "objective," merely because they are personal and particular.⁹ As I have argued elsewhere, considering various particular, experiential perspectives might actually lead to a *more* perspicuous and "objective" approach—a view from *somewhere*, as opposed to *nowhere*—that can serve as a more adequate starting point for theorizing.¹⁰

Additionally, there is sometimes an unfortunate failure in Christian philosophy to think carefully about the *perlocutionary effects* of particular discourses—that is, the actual consequences a discourse has or may have on those implicated in or affected by the discourse.[11] I think philosophers have a duty to try to avoid putting forward theories that are likely to cause epistemic or moral harm to others, especially when those harmed belong to marginalized or underrepresented groups whose lived experience partially constitutes the data set for those discourses. Therefore, when it comes to issues regarding which we cannot easily divorce the systematic from the pastoral, as scholars responsible to a wider public we have a duty to proceed with both *caution* and *care*.

Quite obviously, this is the case with issues that have direct relevance to the experience of pregnancy loss, especially where such loss is lamented, grieved, and potentially traumatic.[12] From an epistemic standpoint, this minimally means taking seriously the testimony of these subjects and treating it as relevantly authoritative for the discourse. Morally and practically, it means that the activity of theorizing about pregnancy loss must fundamentally involve concern for those whose bodies have been the subjects of such loss. In other words, if we care to consider pregnancy and pregnancy loss in philosophical theology, it must involve engaging in *care*-ful(l) and *consider*-ate thinking.

SECTION 3: THE GERMS OF AN ADEQUATE PHILOSOPHICAL THEOLOGY OF PREGNANCY LOSS

If we want to develop a both considered and *consider*-ate philosophical theology of pregnancy loss, we will need to think more closely about what we mean by terms like "pregnancy," "conception," "life," and "organism."

Take, for example, discussions concerning what happens to the "lost baby" in the afterlife. Many women speak of being "reunited" with their miscarried babies in heaven, but this seems to imply that there is some *independent entity* with which one could be reunited—one that is wholly distinct from the individual who gestates it. However, although many Christian scholars appear to treat it as such, a clear-cut distinction between the mother and the baby-in-utero is—whether from a phenomenological, metaphysical, or even biological standpoint—by no means a philosophical given. Certainly, sometimes part of what is mourned with respect to the loss of a pregnancy has to do with imagined counterfactual futures of a wholly independent (i.e., *birthed* and *living*) human subject and one's future parental relationship with that subject. However, to place the locus of a mother's grief solely on this aspect is to fail to make any distinction between the loss of a baby-in-utero and that of an infant, a child, or even the adult offspring of a parent. Indeed, despite all their similarities and the grief for lost futures that may accompany the death of any offspring, birthed or not, it is one thing to mourn the loss of something that was organically independent and already living outside of your own body and quite another to carry that death inside you in a way that involves the experience of a "loss of bodily integrity."[13] This "rupturing of the self," as Serene Jones puts it, results from the "radical dissolution of the bodily borders that [. . .] give the self a sense of internal coherence"[14]—a phenomenological blurring of the lines between self and other that, I would argue, is actually symptomatic of pregnancy itself. There is also a radical difference in experience when your own body is caused, in one way or another, to *expel* this "not-wholly-other" in an act of "birthing death."[15]

Phenomenological aspects aside, there might also be reason to suspect that independence claims regarding the fetus rest on a *metaphysical* confusion. For example, Elselijn Kingma has recently defended a *parthood* over a *containment* account of pregnancy. Arguing that a fetus is not only part of the internal environment of the gestating individual but also "hooked into" that individual metabolically, functionally, and topologically, Kingma claims this makes it more like a bodily part than a distinct and separate human being.[16] While I am inclined to think that something like the parthood view is right, nothing I say here hinges on this account being the correct one. The point is only that it is necessary to have this kind of metaphysical conversation if we want to develop a meaningful Christian philosophical approach to pregnancy loss. It can also influence how we might understand analogies to pregnancy and birthing when approaching what I will below call "gestational models" of God.

Importantly, merely having some metaphysical account or other of pregnancy and miscarriage will not suffice. We must also pay attention to how social expectations, values, and structures shape our intuitions about and experiences of pregnancy. For example, many attitudes and assumptions about pregnancy are intimately bound up with deeply engrained teleological attitudes about *nature and naturalness* with respect to the sexed female body. Indeed, in many contexts, both sacred and secular, the woman who does not produce live offspring is considered somehow "unnatural." In the Christian Bible, infertility is often not only understood as *un*natural but even as *super*natural—a kind of "absence of blessing" commonly explained in terms of God's having "closed" the womb of the woman in question.[17] Furthermore, these "barren" women or their spouses usually end up receiving promises from God that they will, in fact, be divinely "blessed" with children. Indeed, the Scriptures almost exclusively present contemporary women readers with instances in which a desire for children is ultimately *fulfilled*, not where it is thwarted. The miscarriages, stillbirths, and other losses that women like

Sarah, Rachel, Hannah, and Elizabeth likely endured are erased in favor of stories that narratively center the shame of not successfully producing male heirs. This ends up rendering the Christian script for miscarriage as largely co-extensive with a common Western neoliberal script that equates childbirth with output and productivity, at least insofar as it focuses its energies on the *possibility* of a "successful" future pregnancy while silencing the *reality* of the experienced badness of past and present losses (exceptions being made for attributions of blame on one or more parent, not seldomly the woman). Indeed, in both scripts, miscarriage becomes, as Alison Reiheld has put it, a kind of *non-event*, one that both "is, and is not."[18]

The view of pregnancy loss (and the woman who undergoes it) as an unnatural, dysteleological, non-event fails to see just how common miscarriage is and how much a normal part of the (remarkably inefficient) human gestational experience. For example, if we adopt the rather modest estimate that 40 percent of all pregnancies do not result in a live birth, those Christian philosophers who assume that human life begins at fertilization will be forced to admit that almost *100 million* unbirthed human lives are lost each year.[19] So perhaps we need to start thinking about pregnancy differently, in order to make room for the normalcy and naturalness of miscarriage. One example of how this can be done is provided by Jennifer Scuro in *The Pregnancy ≠ Childbearing Project*. Scuro rightly points out that although not all pregnancies carry the possibility of birth, they do all carry the possibility of miscarriage. When we understand pregnancy in light of the "the possibility of miscarriage *that follows all pregnancy*," we see that pregnancy is essentially tied up with *existential risk*.[20] Not only does a woman risk literally losing her life (given the dangers involved in both giving birth to another human being and miscarrying one), she also risks losing her identity—and her very *self*—to that with which she is physiologically and emotionally bound up. In this sense, the bodily *host* of a fetus—the one whose womb is supposed to be "hospitable" to it—is simultaneously a *hostage*, regardless of how positively or negatively the woman feels about her pregnancy.[21]

On Scuro's approach, which seeks to decouple our notion of pregnancy from that of childbirth, what is common to *all* instances of pregnancy is the fact that they all eventually involve the *loss* of something that was, for a time, inextricably tied up with the pregnant person's embodied self. That is, all humans who become pregnant will someday be postpartum, whether they have given birth to a live baby or not.[22] The event that is most "natural" to pregnancy, then, is not necessarily childbirth; it is loss, expulsion, an *emptying out*. However, although this loss is inevitable, it is not something with respect to which the birthing body is wholly passive: It is always a *labor*, an existentially risky activity—and something that, if we take the parthood view of pregnancy seriously, involves a kind of paradoxical (and perhaps, put in theological terms, *kenotic*) emptying out of one's own self. Yet, importantly, the "necessary labor" of this loss, or what Scuro fittingly calls *ontological griefwork*, "needs to be done and ought not be done by women alone."[23] The development of a philosophical theology of pregnancy loss must therefore be a *communal* effort—one not just left to women, but one that nevertheless privileges their experiences and perspectives. Additionally, given that miscarriage is an essentially *bodily* event, any philosophical theology of pregnancy loss must take embodiment seriously. Karen O'Donnell suggests, for example, acknowledging the woman's body itself as both a "grave site" and a "theological landmark."[24] As the former, the woman's body marks the site of the death of the baby and, in some cases, represents the only grave a baby will have.[25] As the latter, it is "the site of unanswered theological questions and an incomplete rite of passage."[26]

With these considerations in mind, I now want to turn to a concrete pastoral task for a philosophical theology of pregnancy loss, one intertwined with conceptual work that I think Christian philosophy is especially suited to undertake.

SECTION 4: A CHRISTIAN PHILOSOPHY FOR PREGNANCY LOSS: DEVELOPING INFORMED RITUALS

There are very few secular social scripts available to process pregnancy loss and even fewer religious ritual scripts available to those whose bodies have become gravesites. Addressing this lack is, I think, one of the main tasks for an embodied approach of the kind I envision. However, given that the experience of profound grief does not always track one's doxastic states, this might mean moving away from the overemphasis on belief and the cognitive in Christian philosophy. For example, Tasia Scrutton has noted that even though the content of our cognitive belief-set often changes when we experience the loss of something we care about, it is oftentimes difficult for individuals to really *feel* the reality of the situation and to epistemically, affectively, and volitionally orient themselves according to it.[27] In the case of miscarriage, a woman might cognitively register (and even believe with 100% certainty) that the human being growing inside her has died, but she may not be able to experience this proposition *as real* or to re-orient herself in the world accordingly. This is particularly common in pregnancy loss. Not only does the body continue to behave as though it were pregnant, but there is also no recognizable corpse to take leave of or to bury, perhaps because the fetus has become reabsorbed, or because the embryonic material is indistinguishable from the other material expelled by the woman during her miscarriage. Or, as in my own case, because the small clump of blood and tissue slipped too quickly into the irrecoverable depths of overly efficient German plumbing for me to fish it out of the toilet at 3 a.m.

Scrutton goes on to discuss how religious ritual—especially insofar as it can be sensorily rich, bodily, and embedded in narrative—can help to provide "experiential knowledge or understanding of the view of reality that truth claims [. . .] express more thinly."[28] Yet this requires that there actually *be* bodily, sensory, and narrative rituals that can be publicly accessed and performed. Some churches and religious communities do offer short prayers or ceremonies on the occasion of miscarriage. The Anglican Church, for example, has developed "A Rite for Mourning the Loss of a Pregnancy." Or, in Konstanz, where I live, the city cemetery contains a memorial grave remembering miscarried and stillborn babies, and an ecumenical memorial service is held there twice a year for parents who have lost pregnancies. However, these resources are few and far between, and most clergy "are either unaware, uncomfortable, or dismissive regarding the use of [the] minimal [liturgical] resources" that exist to address pregnancy loss.[29]

Given their unavailability within the church, many Christian women have had to improvise their own rituals. Serene Jones writes about digging a hole with her friend who had miscarried, in order to bury a handkerchief containing a small bit of bloody tissue, the only thing left of the miscarried embryo.[30] For my part, every time I came from an ultrasound during my subsequent pregnancy, I visited the Konstanz cathedral, lighting one candle in front of the "Man of Sorrows" for my embryo that died, one in front of the fifteenth-century Mary-and-child statue for the fetus that still lived in my womb, and one in front of the altar painting of Doubting Thomas in the hope of learning to fully trust my body (and the body of Christ) again. These rituals were meaningful for me because I could simultaneously do something with my body in a sensorially rich context in a space that carried *sacramental weight*, especially for me (as I was married there). Still, I had to do it alone, and it didn't feel like enough.

Can the development of more communally supportive mourning rituals be a task for Christian philosophy? I don't see why not, so long as philosophers remain in conversation with clergy and the religious community, and especially with those who have experienced pregnancy loss. The models and narratives offered in such ritual contexts need to be systematically and theologically fitting so as to be capable of giving women a coherent theological "compass" for existentially orienting themselves with respect to their losses. Christian philosophers and theologians can therefore further contribute to the constructive development of models of God that better speak to pregnancy loss and show women that their pain is not invisible, their experiences not non-events. In fact, they might be surprised to find their own doctrines of God transformed by engaging in such communal "griefwork."

In the remainder of this chapter, then, I want to briefly explore what such transformation might look like by focusing on what I call "gestational models" of God—that is, approaches that conceive of God as *pregnant*. However, instead of placing birthing at the center of these models, I want to build instead on Scuro's insight that all pregnancy involves loss. These types of models are thus intended not only to disrupt the masculinist and patriarchal characterizations of the divine often inherent in many Christian philosophical approaches but also to course-correct for feminist approaches to "Mother God" that implicitly suggest the woman who best "images" God is the one who "successfully" gives birth to a live, healthy human being. That is, I want to think about what it might mean to construct models of a pregnant God that make room for the naturalness of and grief involved in all pregnancy loss (whether via live birth or death)—and to situate them within the context of traditional approaches to God in Christian philosophy. I will suggest that such models are, for the most part, commensurate with these approaches and/or might even help us to better think them through to their logical conclusions.

SECTION 5: CONCEIVING ALTERNATIVE MODELS OF THE DIVINE

Just as in the natural sciences, which legitimately use models, idealizations, and other "felicitous falsehoods" to cultivate disciplinary understanding,[31] I maintain that models of God need not be strictly speaking *true* to be epistemically valuable. Furthermore, I think that when we shift our philosophical focus from merely showing how it is that theistic *belief* of a certain kind could, under certain conditions, if true, constitute religious *knowledge*—and we focus instead on the cultivation of deeper religious *understanding*—we might see how the construction, or even projection,[32] of non-factive models of God can be epistemically valuable, both for us as theorizers and for religious practitioners "on the ground."[33]

The theist, of course, is likely to hope that some models of God *do* point beyond themselves to some greater reality—and theologians can argue about which models do so better than others. Important for our purposes is merely the point that good models of the divine need not match up one-to-one with reality to do their epistemic work. They can, for example, speak to the lived experience of certain human beings in ways that create opportunities for increased *resonance* and *participation*, which can open up space for new understandings of the "God that may be."[34] They can also sometimes provide necessary *epistemic frictions*[35] for the status quo that can serve as a corrective for bias, hubris, or epistemic imperialism and make space for more fitting beliefs about God and our fellow human beings that standard approaches might occlude.[36] Even for those with more strongly realist intuitions than I who insist on the "metaphysical accuracy" of their models, there is still some reason to think that employing feminine-coded (or other kinds of non-masculine-coded) language about God is at least as metaphysically accurate as using masculine or patriarchal language[37] and potentially does less harm than its patriarchal counterparts.[38] Whatever the case, if our models of God are to reflect how it is that human beings are made *ad imaginem dei*, then we should hope that they speak to *various* facets of human experience, including those of gestational persons, who make up a large portion of the human population. I therefore think that gestational models are, at least in some contexts, both theologically and epistemically appropriate, perhaps even called for (though we should obviously not think that the *only* appropriate feminine-coded models of God are those having to do with pregnancy, birthing, mothering, and caretaking).

With this is mind, let us now explore how a gestational model might fare on a few traditional, analytically-favored approaches to God's creative activity—especially when we take into account Scuro's insights about the risk and loss inherent to pregnancy and Kingma's parthood approach to the metaphysics of pregnancy. I again want to insist that I am not maintaining that any particular gestational model discussed here is, strictly speaking, *true*, nor even that the accounts of pregnancy and loss on which they rest are *correct*. Instead, I simply want to show how changing the way we think about pregnancy and miscarriage can transform the way we think about God (and vice versa), even within contexts already familiar to Christian philosophers. A future project for Christian philosophy will be to discuss the appropriate parameters of such accounts, to see whether and how they can be used as a corrective for standard approaches to God that have traditionally marginalized women's experience, and to reflect on whether and how such models can helpfully speak to those who have undergone pregnancy loss.

SECTION 6: GESTATIONAL MODELS AND CHRISTIAN PHILOSOPHY

Let us begin with the favored approach of analytic philosophers of religion: classical "perfect-being" theism—which, in Christian philosophy, is usually shot through with a kind of (abstract) theistic personalism. On this approach, God possesses all the perfections—including agential traits like knowledge, power, and goodness—to an infinite or maximal degree. If we assume that risk is inherent to all pregnancy, then classical theism might appear *prima facie* hostile to gestational models of God, since God seems to risk virtually nothing by creating as they do: God knows how their creation would turn out were they to create, is powerful enough to bring that creation about, and cannot be changed or affected by anything that happens in it. Of course, although the classical view preserves what its proponents see as a "robust" sense of divine sovereignty, absolute dominion is not usually at the top of the list of divine attributes a feminist-friendly approach is concerned with preserving, given the problematic notions of power and submission that often accompany it, as well as the way it has been historically abused to justify and/or explain away all sorts of evils.[39]

Still, if we think about risk as simply involving the *possibility of loss*, there might be a real sense in which classical perfect-being theists might be able to embrace a gestational model of the divine. However, they must be willing to part with the cherished metaphors of kingship, patriarchy, and dominance that often run implicitly through the traditional approach and allow for the (re-)drawing of a more "fertile" analogy between God's creative and sustaining activity and the *actual biological parallels of generating life and holding it in existence* that occur in human pregnancy.[40] In so doing, we might be in a better position to see how God's creative activity, too, centrally involves a kind of loss, as the very creatures created in the divine image "fall away" from their Creator. Whether we think of this as a sort of Platonist "falling" of immaterial human souls into corporeal bodies, a Neoplatonist "flowing out" of an overabundance of divine being or love, or a more Aristotelian "conception" springing forth from an act of divine causal knowledge, the image of pregnancy and loss seems eminently compatible with the "classical" aspect of classical theism. The gestational model is also clearly well-suited to the Biblical narrative of the Fall. For all these reasons, I think that engaging in some imaginative and earnest "play"[41] with gestational models can actually help Christian philosophy, especially of the perfect-being variety, better trace the contours of its own views by providing different ways of "conceiving" the relationship between Creator and Creation.

If we follow Aquinas in assuming it is not possible for reason to determine whether the universe has a temporal beginning or exists from eternity,[42] it will be fitting to propose gestational models for both. We can thereby imagine creation as either having been "birthed" *temporally* by the pregnant God into independent existence or as being *continually* "gestated into being" from all eternity by an ever-pregnant-and-laboring God. On the former construal, the universe has already been "bodied forth" by God's pregnant self.[43] This work of love, however, is still what Scuro would call an *expellation*—a kenotic "divine-self-emptying" that gains the (wholly "good") created world through a loss of both unity and, more importantly, *unification*. On this view, God's kenotic emptying of Godself in birthing creation involves both the potential risk that humanity will go astray (which it does) and the actual loss involved in the umbilical untethering of unity into multiplicity, a common theme in medieval Neoplatonist cosmologies. The latter gestational view, according to which the universe exists from eternity, lends itself well to a kind of panentheism. Here, creation is more like the fetus than the birthed child. And we, as part of that creation, find ourselves always unborn, always dying *in utero* in Adam, always re-generated in the womb of that other unborn begotten Son, our Divine Mother Jesus (1 Cor. 15:22).[44] On this view, we are not merely *contained within* God's body, we constitute *part* of it or are otherwise always already united with it, as on Kingma's account of pregnancy. What both of these accounts bring out, however, is the longstanding teaching of the Christian tradition that distance or separation from God just *is* death, one which is indeed grievable. The whole universe, then, might be fittingly thought of as—to again invoke Scuro—*God's ontological griefwork*.

In fact, we might find that adopting a gestational model of God can help us come to see that there is a sense in which Creation is always "grievable," even where it is understood as something God wills to be and proclaims "good."[45] I take it that some of the resistance to gestational models from the perfect-being theist camps (especially of the classical variety) will have to do with the idea that God's *losing* and/or *grieving* something is incompatible with God's perfection. However, if loss really is *inherent* to pregnancy, then when the pregnant woman loses that good which she has generated and wholly desires to exist, her power is no more diminished than her inability to defy the laws of gravity. If anything, her grief is a *sign* of both her own love and her recognition of the goodness of what is lost. Just so with the pregnant God. We might say, to channel Hilde Lindemann,[46] that the pregnant God *calls us into relationship* with them and claims "It is good that you exist!" even if this vocation ultimately comes at a grievable price, namely, that of granting us our volitional (and perhaps even ontological) independence. This is the kind of agapic love that should be the centerpiece of a care-ful(l) and concerned Christian philosophy. Indeed, finding a model according to which God can grieve both *for* us and *with* us might help us develop a more humane response to the problem of evil than the traditional theodicies from the perfect-being camp have thus far been able to provide.

SECTION 7: THE MISCARRYING WOMAN AS TRINITARIAN IMAGE

Although less "birth-centric," the gestational models discussed above still take as their paradigm pregnancies in which the fetus survives and/or is birthed. Before closing, I want to discuss one more sense in which the analogy of the pregnant God can be employed and which the woman who has experienced miscarriage is in a special place to both imagine and to image. Not only is this a model that a miscarrying mother can cleave to in her time of grief; it is one that might actually help Christian philosophy make headway on a topic it has struggled with from the very beginning—namely, that of the Trinity.

This approach is brought out by Serene Jones when she poses her version of a longstanding question in Christian theology in terms that might be familiar to those who have undergone miscarriages: "What transpires in the Godhead when one of its members [namely, the incarnated Christ] bleeds away?" She notes that theologians like Moltmann and Luther "have urged us to affirm that on the cross, God takes this death into the depths of Godself,"[47] but it is unclear what this is supposed to mean, and few theologians have provided adequate solutions. Noting that the tradition has basically "told us that at this point in the story, our language breaks down, and we must simply ponder the cross and its mysteries," Jones wonders whether perhaps theology's "imaginative resources" have not been hampered by the "morphological imaginations of its mostly male theologians."[48] *Both* analytic philosophers of religion and feminist theologians have tended to miss "the rather ironic fact that the image that most effectively captures the nature of God's redeeming grace is [. . .] an image of maternal loss."[49] Indeed, it seems like the woman who has experienced a miscarriage or stillbirth is *specially positioned* to understand just how it is that "the living Godhead [can] hold death within it." Like the woman who has miscarried, the living Trinity simultaneously becomes a—or perhaps *the*—central theological landmark in Christianity, precisely by becoming a gravesite.

The metaphysics of pregnancy also become relevant here. For example, whatever its moral status, the organismal status of a fetus in relation to its mother is extremely difficult to determine. Evolutionary and immunological accounts of organismality yield different answers,[50] as do the containment and parthood approaches to pregnancy. Kingma's approach, as we have seen, characterizes the fetus as a part of the mother,[51] whereas Hilary Yancey suggests that the mother is a part of the fetus.[52] A particularly promising account by Anne Sophie Meincke proposes a *process* theory of organisms, which views the pregnant individual as a "bifurcating hypercomplex process"—one which is "neither two individuals nor one individual but something in between one and two."[53] Some Trinitarian theologians might prefer a "both-and" formulation to a "neither-nor," but understanding both what pregnancy actually is and what happens when a pregnant person miscarries might help us better understand what the Godhead is like, how death can occur within it, and how pregnant human bodies at their most vulnerable can nevertheless be powerful *specula* through which the divine reflects its Trinitarian image. In fact, however we answer the question concerning the mother-fetus relation, it might turn out that the Trinity is no more mysterious or contradictory than human biology.

I therefore submit that the further development of gestational models of God show promise for a care-ful(l) and consider-ate Christian philosophy of the future. First, it can provide a potential source for therapeutically valuable theologies that can inform rituals of grief surrounding pregnancy loss. Second, we have good reason to think that if we were to come to better understand the metaphysics of pregnancy that make such states of life and loss possible, we might find the resources to better comprehend difficult aspects of Trinitarian theology—perhaps even in a way that would satisfy even the curmudgeonly philosopher who resists the idea that those deeply invested in a topic or relying on autobiographical experience can provide the kind of "abstract" and "rigorous" insights for which philosophical theology strives.

The fact that, twenty years after Jones penned her essay, we still have not made much headway in addressing pregnancy loss in Christian philosophy might be cause for cynicism. Moreover, it is grossly unfair that the labor of such an endeavor should fall to those who have undergone such loss, while others content themselves with "disinterestedly" making more minute argumentative moves from the armchair. At the same time, even if it is not *redemptive* for us, this endeavor can nevertheless be a form of *our* griefwork, just as writing this chapter has been a laborious-yet-cathartic act of griefwork for me. Socratic midwifery itself is an inherently risky enterprise, but if we can thereby assist in the germination and gestation of new approaches to very old problems, perhaps our endeavors can result in more than the mere "heartsickness" of grief, mourning, and "hope deferred"—contributing instead to cultivating the philosophical tree of life in community and solidarity with each other.[5454]

NOTES

1. Notable exceptions include: Ann J. Cahill, Kathryn J. Norlock, and Byron J. Stoyles, eds., "Miscarriage, Reproductive Loss, and Fetal Death," Special Issue, *Journal of Social Philosophy* 46, no. 1 (2015): 1–157; Jennifer Scuro, *The Pregnancy ≠ Childbearing Project: A Phenomenology of Miscarriage* (London: Rowman & Littlefield, 2017); Karen O'Donnell, "Reproductive Loss: Toward a Theology of Bodies," *Theology & Sexuality* 25, no. 1–2 (2019): 146–59; Karen O'Donnell and Allison Fenton, eds., "Theology and Childlessness," Special Issue, *Modern Believing* 60, no. 2 (2019): 103–210; L. Serene Jones, "Hope Deferred: Theological Reflections on Reproductive Loss (Infertility, Stillbirth, Miscarriage)," *Modern Theology* 17, no. 2 (2001): 227–45; Karen O'Donnell, *The Dark Womb: Re-Conceiving Theology through Reproductive Loss* (London: SCM Press, 2022).

2. Gavin E. Jarvis, "Early Embryo Mortality in Natural Human Reproduction: What the Data Say," *F1000Research* 5 (2017): 2765.

3. For example, a 2013 survey of 1,084 valid respondents in the United States (Bardos et al. 2015) showed that a majority (55%) of participants falsely believed that miscarriages make up less than 6 percent of all pregnancies. This misperception was more common among men than women, and men were also 2.6 times more likely than women to falsely believe that lifestyle choice was the single most common cause of miscarriage, as opposed to genetic or medical causes. See Jonah Bardos et al., "A National Survey on Public Perceptions of Miscarriage," *Obstetrics and Gynecology* 125, no. 6. (2015): 1313–20.

4. Scuro, *Pregnancy ≠ Childbearing*.

5. This serves to add to the various *stigmata* that, via the debate on abortion, attach to women who miscarry. For example, the drug misoprostol and the surgical procedure of dilation and curettage (D&C), both common targets of the anti-abortion movement, are common treatments for miscarriage, since dead fetal tissue not expelled from the body can be life-threatening for a woman.

6. One might even see this latter task as an extension of the Christian injunctions to neighbor-love (Matt. 22) and the amelioration of suffering (Matt. 25).

7. Scuro, *Pregnancy ≠ Childbearing*, p. 212.

8. Shannon Withycombe, *Lost: Miscarriage in Nineteenth-Century America* (New Brunswick, NJ: Rutgers University Press, 2019).

9. Susan J. Brison, *Aftermath: Violence and the Remaking of a Self* (Princeton: Princeton University Press, 2003).

10. Amber L. Griffioen, "Nowhere Men and Divine I's: Feminist Epistemology, Perfect Being Theism, and the God's-Eye View," *Journal of Analytic Theology* 9 (2021): 1–25.

11. Amber L. Griffioen, "Therapeutic Theodicy? Suffering, Struggle, and the Shift from the God's-Eye View," *Religions* 9, no. 4 (2018): 99.

12. On the trauma surrounding pregnancy loss, cf. Jessica Farren et al., "Post-traumatic Stress, Anxiety and Depression Following Miscarriage and Ectopic Pregnancy: A Multicenter, Prospective, Cohort Study," *American Journal of Obstetrics and Gynecology* 222, no. 4 (2020): 367.e1–367.e22.

13. Jones, "Hope Deferred."

14. Ibid.

15. Cf. Christy Angelle Bauman, *Theology of the Womb: Knowing God through the Body of a Woman* (Eugene, OR: Cascade Books, 2019).

16. Elselijn Kingma, "Were You a Part of Your Mother?" *Mind* 128, no. 511 (2019): 609–46.

17. Meg Warner, "'Sing, O Barren One Who Did Not Bear': Childlessness, Blessing and Vocation in the Old Testament," *Modern Believing* 60, no. 2 (2019): 111–21.

18. Alison Reiheld, "'The Event That Was Nothing': Miscarriage as a Liminal Event," *Journal of Social Philosophy* 46, no. 1 (2015): 9–26.

19. This estimate proceeds from a 2022 world population estimate of ca. 8 billion and a global birth rate of 17.668 births per 1000 people (macrotrends.net/countries/WLD/world/population).

20. Scuro, *Pregnancy ≠ Childbearing*, p. 194.

21. Scuro, *Pregnancy ≠ Childbearing*, p. 207.
22. Scuro, *Pregnancy ≠ Childbearing*, p. x.
23. Scuro, *Pregnancy ≠ Childbearing*, p. xii.
24. O'Donnell, "Reproductive Loss," p. 153.
25. O'Donnell, "Reproductive Loss," p. 154.
26. O'Donnell, "Reproductive Loss," pp. 153–54.
27. Anastasia Philippa Scrutton, "Grief, Ritual and Experiential Knowledge: A Philosophical Perspective," in *Continuing Bonds in Bereavement: New Directions for Research and Practice*, edited by Dennis Klass and Edith M. Steffen, 214–26 (London: Routledge, 2017).
28. Scrutton, "Grief, Ritual and Experiential Knowledge," p. 215.
29. Millicent C. Feske, "Rachel's Lament: The Impact of Infertility and Pregnancy Loss Upon the Religious Faith of Ordinary Christians," *Journal of Pastoral Theology* 22, no. 1 (2012): 3.1–3.17 (p. 3.10).
30. Jones, "Hope Deferred."
31. Catherine Z. Elgin, *True Enough* (Cambridge, MA: MIT Press, 2017).
32. Cf. Grace Jantzen's claim that "it is urgently necessary for women to do some deliberate projecting of our own [. . .]"; Grace Jantzen, *Becoming Divine: Toward a Feminist Philosophy of Religion* (Bloomington, IN: Indiana University Press, 1999), p. 89.
33. Amber L. Griffioen, "Rethinking Religious Epistemology," *European Journal for Philosophy of Religion* 14, no. 1 (2022): 21–47.
34. Richard Kearney, *The God Who May Be: A Hermeneutics of Religion* (Bloomington, IN: Indiana University Press, 2001).
35. José Medina, *The Epistemology of Resistance: Gender and Racial Oppression, Epistemic Injustice, and Resistant Imaginations* (Oxford: Oxford University Press, 2013).
36. Helen De Cruz, "Seeking Out Epistemic Friction in the Philosophy of Religion," in *Voices from the Edge: Centring Marginalized Perspectives in Analytic Theology*, ed. Michelle Panchuk and Michael Rea (Oxford: Oxford University Press, 2020), pp. 23–46; Griffioen, "Therapeutic Theodicy?"
37. Michael Rea, "Is God a Man?," in *Contemporary Debates in Philosophy of Religion*, ed. Michael L. Peterson and Raymond J. VanArragon, Second Edition (Hoboken: Wiley, 2019), pp. 293–301.
38. Kathryn Pogin, "God Is Not Male," in *Contemporary Debates in Philosophy of Religion*, ed. Peterson and VanArragon, pp. 302–10.
39. Griffioen, "Nowhere Men and Divine I's."
40. In this sense, the gestational model might actually be less figurative than the patriarchal approach and perhaps better thought of as *analogical* in something like the medieval sense.
41. Cf. Rachel Wagner, "The Importance of Playing in Earnest," in *Playing with Religion in Digital Games*, ed. Heidi A. Campbell and Gregory P. Grieve (Bloomington, IN: Indiana University Press, 2014), pp. 192–213.
42. Thomas Aquinas, *Summa Contra Gentiles. Book Two: Creation*, trans. James F. Anderson (Notre Dame, IN: University of Notre Dame Press, 1976), p. 38.
43. Cf. Sallie McFague, *Models of God: Theology for an Ecological, Nuclear Age* (Philadelphia: Fortress Press, 1987).

44. For Jesus as Divine Mother, see (among others) Julian of Norwich, *Revelations of Divine Love: The Short Text (Translated from British Library Additional MS 37790), The Motherhood of God: An Excerpt (Translated from British Library MS Sloane 2477)*, trans. and ed. Frances Beer (Cambridge: D.S. Brewer, 1998), and Anselm of Canterbury, *The Prayers and Meditations of St. Anselm* (Harmondsworth: Penguin, 1973), "Prayer to Saint Paul."

45. A more cynical, deistic alternative might be to think of creation as God's "abortion"—a world expelled and left behind, except, perhaps, in the memory of a departed Deity who may or may not grieve it. Although this is a view many Christian theists will be inclined to reject, it is not without some Biblical precedent. For example, the flood narrative in Genesis 7 might speak for the idea that God might intentionally abort their own creation, while Paul's reference to himself as an abortion (ἐκτρώμα) in 1 Corinthians 15:8 points more to the imagery of miscarriage (spontaneous abortion).

46. Hilde Lindemann, *Holding and Letting Go: The Social Practice of Personal Identities* (New York: Oxford University Press, 2014).

47. Jones, "Hope Deferred," p. 242.

48. Jones, "Hope Deferred," p. 242.

49. Jones, "Hope Deferred," p. 243.

50. Jonathan Grose, "How Many Organisms during a Pregnancy?" *Philosophy of Science* 87, no. 5 (2020): 1049–60.

51. Kingma, "Were You a Part of Your Mother?"

52. Hilary Yancey, "Was Your Mother Part of You? A Hylomorphist's Challenge for Elselijn Kingma," *Quaestiones Disputatae* 10, no. 2 (2020): 69–85.

53. Anne Sophie Meincke, "One or Two? A Process View of Pregnancy," *Philosophical Studies* 179 (2022): 1495–1521. https://doi.org/10.1007/s11098-021-01716-y

54. I am so grateful to Christina Van Dyke and Lacey Hudspeth for organizing the online APA session in which I was able to present an earlier version of this paper, as well as for their continued personal support during times of grief and joy, debilitating anxiety and equally (though differently) debilitating birth. Thanks are also due to Mike Rea, Laura Callahan, and the 2021-22 cohort of fellows at the Center for Philosophy of Religion, who gave me the space to write this version and provided invaluable feedback along the way. This chapter is dedicated to my spouse, Daniel, and to our rainbow baby girl, Charlie Rae.

BIBLIOGRAPHY

Aquinas, Thomas. *Summa Contra Gentiles. Book Two: Creation*. Translated by James F. Anderson. Notre Dame, IN: University of Notre Dame Press, 1976.

Anselm of Canterbury. *The Prayers and Meditations of St. Anselm*. Harmondsworth: Penguin, 1973.

Bardos, Jonah, Daniel Hercz, Jenna Friedenthal, Stacey A. Missmer, and Zev Williams. "A National Survey on Public Perceptions of Miscarriage." *Obstetrics and Gynecology* 125, no. 6 (2015): 1313–20. https://doi.org/10.1097/AOG.0000000000000859.

Bauman, Christy Angelle. *Theology of the Womb: Knowing God through the Body of a Woman*. Eugene, OR: Cascade Books, 2019.

Brison, Susan J. *Aftermath: Violence and the Remaking of a Self*. Princeton: Princeton University Press, 2003.

Cahill, Ann J., Kathryn J. Norlock, and Byron J. Stoyles, eds. "Miscarriage, Reproductive Loss, and Fetal Death." Special Issue, *Journal of Social Philosophy* 46, no. 1 (2015): 1–157.

De Cruz, Helen. "Seeking Out Epistemic Friction in the Philosophy of Religion." In *Voices from the Edge: Centring Marginalized Perspectives in Analytic Theology*. Edited by Michelle Panchuk and Michael Rea, 23–46. Oxford: Oxford University Press, 2020.

Elgin, Catherine Z. *True Enough*. Cambridge, MA: MIT Press, 2017.

Farren, Jessica, Maria Jalmbrant, Nora Falconieri, Nicola Mitchell-Jones, Shabnam Bobdiwala, Maya Al-Memar, Sophie Tapp, et al. "Posttraumatic Stress, Anxiety and Depression Following Miscarriage and Ectopic Pregnancy: A Multicenter, Prospective, Cohort Study." *American Journal of Obstetrics and Gynecology* 222, no. 4 (2020): 367.e1-367.e22. https://doi.org/10.1016/j.ajog.2019.10.102.

Feske, Millicent C. "Rachel's Lament: The Impact of Infertility and Pregnancy Loss Upon the Religious Faith of Ordinary Christians." *Journal of Pastoral Theology* 22, no. 1 (2012): 3.1–3.17. https://doi.org/10.1179/jpt.2012.22.1.003.

Griffioen, Amber L. "Therapeutic Theodicy? Suffering, Struggle, and the Shift from the God's-Eye View." *Religions* 9, no. 4 (2018): 99. https://doi.org/10.3390/rel9040099.

Griffioen, Amber L. "Nowhere Men and Divine I's: Feminist Epistemology, Perfect Being Theism, and the God's-Eye View." *Journal of Analytic Theology* 9 (2021): 1–25. https://jat-ojs-baylor.tdl.org/jat/index.php/jat/article/view/437.

Griffioen, Amber L. "Rethinking Religious Epistemology." *European Journal for Philosophy of Religion* 14, no. 1 (2022): 21–47. https://doi.org/10.24204/ejpr.2022.3290

Grose, Jonathan. "How Many Organisms during a Pregnancy?" *Philosophy of Science* 87, no. 5 (2020): 1049–60. https://doi.org/10.1086/710542.

Jantzen, Grace. *Becoming Divine: Toward a Feminist Philosophy of Religion*. Bloomington, IN: Indiana University Press, 1999.

Jarvis, Gavin E. "Early Embryo Mortality in Natural Human Reproduction: What the Data Say." *F1000Research* 5 (2017):2765. https://doi.org/10.12688/f1000research.8937.2.

Jones, L. Serene. "Hope Deferred: Theological Reflections on Reproductive Loss (Infertility, Stillbirth, Miscarriage)." *Modern Theology* 17, no. 2 (2001): 227–45. https://doi.org/10.1111/1468-0025.00158.

Julian of Norwich. *Revelations of Divine Love: The Short Text (Translated from British Library Additional MS 37790). The Motherhood of God: An Excerpt (Translated from British Library MS Sloane 2477)*. Translated and edited by Frances Beer. Cambridge: D.S. Brewer, 1998.

Kearney, Richard. *The God Who May Be: A Hermeneutics of Religion*. Bloomington, IN: Indiana University Press, 2001.

Kingma, Elselijn. "Were You a Part of Your Mother?" *Mind* 128, no. 511 (2019): 609–46. https://doi.org/10.1093/mind/fzy087.

Lindemann, Hilde. *Holding and Letting Go: The Social Practice of Personal Identities*. New York: Oxford University Press, 2014.

McFague, Sallie. *Models of God: Theology for an Ecological, Nuclear Age*. Philadelphia: Fortress Press, 1987.

Medina, José. *The Epistemology of Resistance: Gender and Racial Oppression, Epistemic Injustice, and Resistant Imaginations*. Oxford: Oxford University Press, 2013.

Meincke, Anne Sophie. "One or Two? A Process View of Pregnancy." *Philosophical Studies* (2021). https://doi.org/10.1007/s11098-021-01716-y.

O'Donnell, Karen. "Reproductive Loss: Toward a Theology of Bodies." *Theology & Sexuality* 25, no. 1–2 (2019): 146–59. https://doi.org/10.1080/13558358.2018.1548161.

O'Donnell, Karen. *The Dark Womb: Re-Conceiving Theology through Reproductive Loss*. London: SCM Press, 2022.

O'Donnell, Karen, and Allison Fenton, eds. "Theology and Childlessness." Special Issue, *Modern Believing* 60, no. 2 (2019).

Panchuk, Michelle, and Michael Rea, eds. *Voices from the Edge: Centring Marginalized Perspectives in Analytic Theology*. Oxford: Oxford University Press, 2020.

Peterson, Michael L., and Raymond J. VanArragon, eds. *Contemporary Debates in Philosophy of Religion*. Second Edition. Hoboken: Wiley, 2019.

Pogin, Kathryn. "God Is Not Male." In *Contemporary Debates in Philosophy of Religion*. Second Edition. Edited by Michael L. Peterson and Raymond J. VanArragon, 302–10. Hoboken: Wiley, 2019.

Rea, Michael. "Is God a Man?" In *Contemporary Debates in Philosophy of Religion*. Second Edition. Edited by Michael L. Peterson and Raymond J. VanArragon, 293–301. Hoboken: Wiley, 2019.

Reiheld, Alison. "'The Event That Was Nothing': Miscarriage as a Liminal Event." *Journal of Social Philosophy* 46, no. 1 (2015): 9–26. https://doi.org/10.1111/josp.12084

Scrutton, Anastasia Philippa. "Grief, Ritual and Experiential Knowledge: A Philosophical Perspective." In *Continuing Bonds in Bereavement: New Directions for Research and Practice*. Edited by Dennis Klass and Edith M. Steffen, 214–26. London: Routledge, 2017.

Scuro, Jennifer. *The Pregnancy ≠ Childbearing Project: A Phenomenology of Miscarriage*. London: Rowman & Littlefield, 2017.

Wagner, Rachel. "The Importance of Playing in Earnest." In *Playing with Religion in Digital Games*. Edited by Heidi A. Campbell and Gregory P. Grieve, 192–213. Bloomington, IN: Indiana University Press, 2014.

Warner, Meg. "'Sing, O Barren One Who Did Not Bear': Childlessness, Blessing and Vocation in the Old Testament." *Modern Believing* 60, no. 2 (2019): 111–21. https://doi.org/10.3828/mb.2019.10

Withycombe, Shannon. *Lost: Miscarriage in Nineteenth-Century America*. New Brunswick, NJ: Rutgers University Press, 2019.

Yancey, Hilary. "Was Your Mother Part of You? A Hylomorphist's Challenge for Elselijn Kingma." *Quaestiones Disputatae* 10, no. 2 (2020): 69–85. https://doi.org/10.5840/qd20201024.

5

Mourning

A Phenomenology

Balázs M. Mezei

Mourning has a complex meaning stretching from silent sadness to loud lamentation; or on the psychiatric level from melancholy to "melancholia," that is, clinical depression. As one of the central human phenomena, mourning has been in the focus of culture and history; even more it stands at the center of so many religious forms. From Sumerian and Egyptian mythologies to Judaism and Christianity, from Hellenistic mystery cults to post-secular burial ceremonies, we face time and again the centrality of the tradition, experience, and practice of mourning. Mourning, in short, is with us in a variety of forms in our everyday life, historical existence, and cultural reflections.[1]

While one of the earliest philosophical pieces was produced on the subject matter of mourning—namely Plato's *Menexenus*—subsequent authors neglected the topic for a long time. Emile Durkheim is rarely seen as a philosopher, yet his interpretation of mourning, based on carefully collected ethnographic material, has clear philosophical implications. In his view, the phenomena of mourning can be explained by the instinctive need of a community to reorganize itself and strengthen its unity.[2] This functional approach has become characteristic of other experts such as Sigmund Freud, Walter Benjamin, or even Jacques Derrida. Their work led to claims that "mourning is the mother of all allegories"[3] or "mourning is the origin of culture,"[4] or mourning, centered around subliminal incest and patricide, is the origin of the superego.[5] "The politics of mourning"—to use Derrida's expression—appears in these approaches as an important means of various kinds of sublimation.[6]

The method of phenomenology helps us a little further. Phenomenology offers two distinct paths.[7] The first path leads to the grasping of the essence of a thing, which may be a physical object, an event, a ritual, an experience, or a scientific theory. The essence in such cases is conceived of as the ideal condition of possibility of the concrete thing in the world. In the phenomenological method, "mourning" as a phenomenon is not just a certain occurrence in the world, but rather the core by which all actual mourning may take place. This core, called essence or phenomenon, is the fundamental element of material phenomenology. However, the other path, that is, transcendental phenomenology, offers us the overall context of the phenomenological essences. This context is the sphere of intentionality in which the essences are contained and the real or actual instances of essences materialize. The sphere of intentionality is the realm of the mind; it is *per se* mental, that is, that kind of being that is capable of containing real objects in a peculiar, intentional fashion. Transcendental phenomenology scrutinizes the realm of intentionality with a special respect to its organizing center, the transcendental ego. This center is egological, because all mental events possess, by definition, a certain level of ego-centeredness in the form of the "universal a priori of correlation."[8]

The analyses of mourning in Levinas, Derrida, Dastur, and others follow the path of material phenomenology.[9] They point out the importance of mourning as the central occurrence in the real world of culture and history, an event based on the existential fact of death. Like the latter, mourning too is seen as a real-world fact and not as an intentional moment. However, these approaches do not realize that material phenomenology is logically dependent on transcendental phenomenology. Just as a real occurrence is determined by the central phenomenon of intentionality as the fundamental feature of the mental, so mourning as the central phenomenon in human history presupposes the transcendental meaning of mourning. On the basis of the intentional phenomenon, we can identify various real instances of the acts of mourning in different contexts, cultures, languages, and customs. We cannot dispose of the transcendental realm only by using a kind of phenomenological naturalism that misconceives phenomenology in terms of external or naïve experience. Some sort of what is termed transcendental phenomenology is, by definition, presupposed by any factual analysis of real things, events, or occurrences in the world.[10] In order to flesh out the meaning of mourning, we need to reach the intentional level of phenomenology; or even beyond that, we need a higher-level phenomenology on which I will say a few words below.

THE WHIRLPOOL

Sigmund Freud was the first scholar to distinguish between mourning and melancholy.[11] Mourning is the normal way to react to an important loss, mainly the loss of a human person or persons, affecting one's life. Melancholy is also a reaction, but in this case the loss of the other one turns out to be the loss of the ego itself. In "melancholia," the pathological form of melancholy, self-emptying, self-devaluation, and a comprehensive sense of losing oneself take the place of the clear and well-defined subject–object relationship characteristic of the act of mourning. We have borderline cases, so some forms of mourning may take the form of melancholy.[12] However, the time factor becomes especially important: in mourning, there is always a timeframe in which it is supposed to be carried out. In some cultures, well-defined periods are prescribed for different kinds of mourning. In melancholy, however, these well-defined forms collapse into a formless and undetermined kind of excessive mourning leading to an overall self-loss, to what Benjamin termed "the whirlpool of melancholy."[13]

Based on this fundamental analysis, one can suggest that mourning is an intentional phenomenon. Its intentional structure is such that the loss as a concrete core is perceived, understood, and interpreted in the noetic structures of mourning. These structures tend to be expressed in various acts of mourning, including procedures, cults, liturgies, customs, ceremonies, and so on. All such expressions have a well-defined timeframe beyond which certain forms of mourning must cease; especially intellectual forms may be kept or even be considered central, which never happens in the formless state of the collapse into melancholy. Melancholy can be therefore described as the collapse of the intentional structure of mourning, a collapse affecting not only psychological forms, such as the experience of the loss of the self, but also the dissolution of the external forms, such as physical appearance, nutrition, dressing, and communication. Mourning, to put it simply, is the intentional structure of the extreme loss, especially death, while death is the material core of this intentional structure.

Here we face a paradox. In normal intentional structures, the material core is something positive: a thing, an event, a perception, an idea, and so forth. In the case of mourning, the material core is *the lack* of such a positive thing. There is an emptiness in the intentional structure of mourning, an emptiness making this structure characteristically unique. This special structure makes mourning quite often the borderline case of melancholy, because the paradox is difficult to process. Melancholy can be conceived as the pathological reaction to the paradoxical structure of the intentionality of mourning. As Derrida suggests, even if death is irreducibly unique, there is an "originary mourning," in which the intentional structure of mourning is born.[14] *Pace* Derrida and others, precisely this originary act of mourning shows us the way to the transcendental understanding of death by which we are in the position of conceiving of such a loss as the core of intentionality. In this way we are led to realize that the entire transcendental realm of intentionality is based on the paradoxical structure discovered in mourning. In its ultimate form, intentionality refers to an important loss, an absolute lack into which intentionality is drawn and, at the same time, from which intentionality is born. Yet the abysmal depth of depression may devour the intentionality of mourning. Inasmuch as we *realize* this danger, we have already succeeded in getting out of the whirlpool of melancholy; the very realization of this situation entails its overcoming.

PREFIGURATIONS

Before we develop the above point into a higher-level phenomenological analysis, let me recall some of the most influential instances of mourning defining our present understanding. While we can find a number of such instances in the history of culture, I will focus only on four here: the myth of Persephone, Sophocles' *Antigone*, Plato's *Menexenus*, and an important saying of Jesus in the Gospel.

Persephone

Claudius Claudianus, one of the last Roman poets, produced his finest poems under the title *The Rape of Proserpina*. This small epic work describes the well-known story of Persephone (in Latin: Proserpina), her rape, death, and rise from the underworld. The poet himself, of Egyptian origin, used the traditional mythological material (mentioned already in the Homeric poems) to develop a sophisticated narrative on a literary level surpassed only by the greatest writers of the Golden Age of Roman poetry. The poem remained either unfinished or was perhaps truncated at some point during the history of the manuscript tradition. The text as it stands today leads the reader through the events of the life of young Proserpina including her unexpected death. When Ceres (in Greek: Demeter), the mother goddess of Proserpina, discovers the death of her daughter, she is devastated. In her mourning, she shows all the three characteristic stages: first, in the form of prophetic dreams she senses the coming tragedy; second, she discovers the abandoned palace where her daughter used to live; and third, she carries out what could be called, to use an expression of Freud, the "work of mourning" (*Trauerarbeit*), that is, the search for Proserpina around the world. The full text of the fourth stage is missing from the poem; this part must have contained the descriptions of the journeys of Ceres throughout the Greek *oikumene* while teaching humanity the art of cereal production. By having accomplished the work of mourning, Ceres creates a greater good; the goddess guides humanity to become more civilized and humane. As a result, Jupiter (Zeus) permits the return of Proserpina from Hades, that is, her rise in the form of the yearly springtime renewal. So, mourning and the renewal of nature, together with the consolation of the mother, lead to an overall renovation of nature and culture, humanity and divinity. Proserpina becomes the connecting link between the heavens and the underworld, good and evil, light and shadow, life and death. In the original myth, obviously also in the lost final part of the poem, the universal renewal is seen as the direct result of the work of mourning.

The poem may have served as an introduction to a mystery cult, which can also explain the omitting or cutting of the final part. If intentional, the omission may have been caused by Christian scribes who found that the return of Proserpina from Hades too closely resembled the resurrection of Jesus in the Gospels. In any case, we have a clear even if poetic interpretation of the work of mourning and its difference from melancholy. According to the story, some of the naiads destroy themselves because of their depression over the loss of Proserpina. They show the extreme effects of melancholy. Ceres, however, overcomes depression and begins her salvific journey by the end of which she reaches the universal integration of life and death.[15]

Antigone

Sophocles' *Antigone* is a drama on mourning. Or rather, it is *the tragedy of unmourning*. As Creon orders that the corpses of the dead brothers lie unburied, he also forbids mourning them. The prohibition of mourning is the trigger of the entire tragedy that evolves in the drama and leads to the full destruction of the House of Thebes. Teiresias' prophetic words summarize the crime of Creon who imprisoned Antigone and left the dead body of Polyneices unburied:

> For you have thrust below one who belongs above,
> blasphemously entombed a living person,
> and at the same time have kept above ground
>   a corpse belonging to the chthonic gods—
> unburied, unmourned, unholy.
> Neither you nor the heavenly powers should have a part in this,
> but your violence has forced it. Now, sent by those gods,
> the foul avenging Furies, hunters of Hell,
> lie in wait to inflict the same evils on you.[16]

Creon polluted the state and upset the order of the universe by burying a living person and leaving a dead person unmourned, "unholy." Mourning, in this context, is an integral part of the process of burial. Or, as it appears from the drama, mourning is the key element in the natural order, because it opens the way of the dead to their new home in the underworld and connects them to the gods above in heaven. For Sophocles, as for the entire age of the Greek polis, mourning is the connection between the gods and the dead, a link realized by the living in their mourning ceremonies. The fate of Creon is the fate dictated by what Freud terms melancholy, that is, the way to self-destruction. As opposed to this, the way of mourning is the way to the renewal of the order of the cosmos exemplified in the mystery cult of Eleusis.[17] In this way, the tragedy of *Antigone* is embedded in the framework of the same understanding of death and resurrection expressed by the myth of Persephone.

Menexenus

Plato offers a similar picture in *Menexenus*.[18] The short dialogue, presumably from the early period of the author, describes the art of the composition of an official funeral oration to be held at the graves of fallen soldiers. Socrates alleges that some time earlier Aspasia, Pericles' partner, taught him such an oration. He recalls and recites the entire address verbatim. While the oration is about the heroic Athenian soldiers, it actually describes the classical history of Athens, its ascendance, flourishing, and collapse in the Peloponnesian War. The symbolical, even ironical nature of the dialogue is clearly shown by the fact that the oration recited by Socrates contains references to events *after* the known death of Socrates himself, that is, to the Corinthian War of 395–387 BCE, long after Socrates' death in 399. Thus, in the dialogue a *dead* Socrates recalls the funeral oration, received from the *dead* Aspasia, on the *dead* Athenian heroes ... Yet even as a caricature the dialogue is not only about the historical Athens, but even more importantly about a symbolical Athens, an esoteric community whose members enjoy "freedom, equality and fraternity,"[19] possess virtue and insight and especially heroism in view of the brutal power of the "barbarians" (hence the meaning of Menexenus: the one standing fast against the alien). The history of Athens is tragic; to be more precise, it is dramatic, since it leads not only to the death of heroic citizens but also to a resurrection both in the philosophical sense and in the historical developments after the Peloponnesian Wars leading to the defeat of Sparta.

It would not be an exaggeration to see in this short dialogue a more philosophical and more historical story of another Proserpina. Just as the mythical Persephone, the historical Athens also goes through the drama of death and resurrection, a drama summarized in a funeral sermon offered by the dead yet living Socrates. However, the dialogue speaks about the nature of philosophy rather than the nature of history. Philosophy is not only the preparation for death, but also the understanding of *the meaning of death*. Philosophy is presented here as a kind of funeral address about heroic acts and persons; it is also about the philosophical dialogue of the living that recalls, recites, and interprets the heroism of the past. Just like Proserpina, philosophy becomes the link between the dead and the living, gods and humans. The funeral oration is one of the fundamental expressions of mourning; philosophy is shown here as the central form of mourning. Philosophy, to use again this term, is depicted here as an "originary mourning" in which the transcendental structures of intentionality are displayed, even though in a sarcastic manner often characteristic of Plato's early dialogues.

Blessed are . . .

The Gospels display in many ways an equally transcendental structure of intentionality. Let me focus merely on one saying of Jesus in Matthew 5:4: "Blessed are they that mourn: for they shall be comforted." "Blessed" is the translation of μακάριος, that is, happy, fortunate, or problem-free. The root of this expression is μάκαρ, blessed, which is used for the gods, human beings, and also for the dead. The dead are μάκαρ, because they have received the judgment after their earthly life and so they rest now in peace. Behind Jesus' saying we find the terminology of the Psalms where the expression "blessed is the one . . ." recurs several times, such as in Psalms 1:1. The Hebrew word behind μακάριος is אֶשֶׁר where the root has the meaning "plain," "smooth." Jesus must have alluded to the Psalms in his blessed-sayings, yet he further developed what we find in the Hebrew Scriptures. Especially in Matthew 5:4 we find a point paralleling the Greek mystery stories. Mourning is *at the same time* the cause and the effect of blessedness. Those who mourn are blessed, because they mourn; and they mourn, because they are blessed. Blessedness and mourning mysteriously *overlap*.

This blessed-mourning status leads to comfort, παράκλησις, a sense of παρακαλέω characteristic especially of the LXX and the New Testament—also a name of the Holy Spirit (John 14:26). To be comforted is not an effect of blessedness and/or mourning: Mourning *entails* blessedness and comfort, where the future tense of παρακαλέω is a reference to the overall structure of the situation. So, when Jesus says in the Gospel that "Blessed are they that mourn . . . ," he must have been understood not only as a prophet proclaiming his understanding of the Psalms, but also as a wisdom teacher disclosing the relationship between mourning and blessedness, sorrow and comfort, death and life. Thus, even if in a half-mythical way, Jesus revealed the transcendental structure of the intentionality of mourning, that is, the structure of the new life he opened in his own personal story of death and resurrection.

RADICAL UNMOURNING

In some cases, mourning is radically isolated from its natural contents. It is the new meaning of "radical evil," introduced by Hannah Arendt, that serves as the most important example of such a decisive separation. As she writes,

> It is inherent in our entire philosophical tradition that we cannot conceive of a "radical evil," and this is true both for Christian theology, which conceded even to the Devil himself a celestial origin, as well as for Kant, the only philosopher who, in the word he coined for it, at least must have suspected the existence of this evil even though he immediately rationalized it in the concept of a "perverted ill will" that could be explained by comprehensible motives. Therefore, we actually have nothing to fall back on in order to understand a phenomenon that nevertheless confronts us with its overpowering reality and breaks down all standards we know. There is only one thing that seems to be discernible: we may say that radical evil has emerged in connection with a system in which all men have become equally superfluous.[20]

For Arendt, "radical evil" means a new kind of evil without explanation. This evil "cannot be punished and forgiven."[21] It is beyond all our earlier conception and experience, for which every human being becomes "superfluous." This evil, being unforgiveable, *cannot be mourned*; it cannot be put into any intentional structure in which a meaningful overcoming becomes possible. This evil is simply beyond our grasp and cannot even figure as evil in a meaningful sense. There is no human or divine mourning as a response to this evil; this evil triggers radical unmourning.

Arendt was not the only one arguing for the lack of comprehensibility of radical evil, history, human beings, or even ourselves. She was not the only one underpinning the overall situation of radical unmourning in our time. For it is logically entailed in the incomprehensibility of evil that human beings are also incomprehensible; their acts, their intentions, their philosophy are such in similar ways. And it is entailed in the same proposal that we are incomprehensible to ourselves. In this total incomprehensibility, mourning becomes fundamentally impossible, as does understanding, sorrow, and forgiveness. We find a similar position in Karl Löwith's *Meaning in History*,[22] or even in Sir Karl Popper's *Open Society and Its Enemies*,[23] among a number of other works. It seems that Derrida or even Levinas suggest a similar position.[24]

The underlying experience of the Holocaust is palpable. The debates concerning the incomprehensibility of the Holocaust as the ultimate evil are well known.[25] There are some authors, such as Elie Wiesel, who stress the point of the full lack of explanation and the impossibility of interpretation of the Holocaust. Following this path, we leave behind the realm of mourning and enter the different realm of melancholy; or again, we leave behind the possibility of the work of mourning and collapse into the abyss of self-destruction. We face here the question of the possibility of mourning: if an event is comprehensible to some extent, we are granted that possibility; if it is beyond comprehension, we are deprived of the same possibility.

Going back to Kant for a second, it is obvious that he did not "rationalize" "radical evil," as Arendt mistakenly suggested. Kant too declared *the root of evil* incomprehensible. This root is the natural propensity of our freedom to evil. While this propensity is incomprehensible, its products are comprehensible, even if always in a paradoxical fashion. Yet they can be *outweighed*, because this possibility "is found in the human being as a freely acting being."[26] Freedom is able to overcome even the most radical propensity of our nature; and freedom is able to put evil in the context of understanding to some extent and in a certain sense; especially in the sense of outweighing evil by good deeds.

Among the authors discussing the problem of the Holocaust as an act of "radical evil," we find such different thinkers as Emil Fackenheim, Hans Jonas, or Viktor Frankl. Fackenheim used the Kabbalistic notion of תיקון עולם, *tikkun olam*, "mending the world" as a partial interpretation of the Holocaust.[27] His main point is that there is a certain, if paradoxical, meaning in the Holocaust and this meaning has to be explored. Hans Jonas argued in his *Gottesbegriff nach Auschwitz* that the meaning of Auschwitz can be developed theologically by using the Kabbalistic notion of *tzimtzum* (צמצום).[28] The self-contracting of God made possible the radical evil of the Holocaust; yet the point lies in the mysterious responsibility of human beings to contribute to the reality of the divine and create the meaning of that tragedy by their own efforts. In other words, for Jonas, it is possible to mourn the Holocaust and thereby to develop an interpretation, even a positive understanding. For Frankl, the same path is open: it is our task to make "the unconscious God" conscious in our acts of responsibility so that a new understanding of the human person will be possible and born in our own lives.[29] Mourning is the gateway in this development; if we are deprived of it, we are deprived of meaning. If we are granted the possibility of mourning, the way is open to a higher comprehension.

In the Oscar-winning film *Son of Saul*,[30] the protagonist is motivated by an unquenchable quest for mourning. Saul is obsessed with finding a rabbi in the concentration camp who can recite the *kaddish* (קדיש), the mourning prayer for his dead son. He is desperately trying to overcome radical unmourning. Breaking out of the concentration camp together with a few other prisoners, he hides in a barn. While hiding, a young peasant boy appears in the door and stares at the refugees; and the longer he looks, the more he smiles. Saul, even in his wretched state, smiles back; and in this exchange of smiles the possibility of mourning is born. Together with it, the vista of sorrow, comprehension, and forgiveness is also born. *Intentionality* emerges out of the abyss of radical evil . . . While we learn from the last minutes of the film that the fugitives are caught and perhaps killed, the boy's smile lingers above the tragedy and helps the audience realize that there is an inborn power of transcendence in all dramas. The search for mourning, the main preoccupation of Saul throughout the film, opens up this dimension.

APOCALYPSE

These examples serve to illustrate the difficult path from the abyss of a tragic loss to the higher realm of intentionality. The path leads through genuine mourning. Mourning is the gateway between the depths of death and the rebirth of life. It unfolds the dimension of intentionality, that is, the transcendental structures of understanding. This way has been more precisely explained in what I call "apocalyptic phenomenology."[31]

In this expression the term "phenomenology" refers both to the material and the transcendental dimensions. The word "apocalyptic" points to the fact that the overall noetic structures of understanding are disclosed under the horizon of ultimate self-disclosure, also termed revelation (ἀποκάλυψις, apocalypse). Phenomenology, properly interpreted, cannot remain merely material with a limited focus on essences in the world. It cannot even remain a transcendental phenomenology in the sense of the disclosure of the structures of understanding intentionally centered around the transcendental ego. It must go beyond this ego to the source of all egos, transcendental or real, and show the act of infinite disclosure, revelation or ἀποκάλυψις, that makes possible the noetic structures of intentionality on an absolute level as well as in every single perception, conception, insight, and interpretation in our real lives. It is in the framework of apocalyptic phenomenology that phenomenology as a method to create a new kind of thinking receives its decisive meaning. It is this phenomenology that is able to explain the meaning of mourning.[32]

Apocalyptic phenomenology is a complex structure which describes the process and the stages of self-disclosure. What I term "the principle of *refusivum sui*" stands at its center.[33] This principle is derived from the old saying, Neo-Platonic in origin: *bonum est diffusivum sui*, "goodness is self-spreading."[34] This adage expresses the nature of goodness, imagined along the lines of natural light, as spreading in the universe and being the source of life. It is interpreted as expressing the diffusion of the creative energies of divine goodness. However, this understanding cannot account for the existence of evil, not to mention "radical evil." If goodness is diffused universally in an unhindered way, what is the explanation of evil? What is the explanation for the incomprehensibility of radical evil in the sense of Kant or Arendt? How can the uninterrupted radiation of goodness, its infinite self-spreading, explain the dramatic disruptions by badness? If everything is clothed in infinite light, what is the origin of the shadow?

The principle of *refusivum sui* offers a certain answer. Instead of *bonum est diffusivum sui* we need to use the form *bonum est refusivum sui*: "Goodness (or being or reality) is such that it withdraws yet also restitutes itself." *Refundo*, the verb behind *refusivum*, has a double meaning: on the one hand, it means to refuse, withdraw; on the other hand, it means to restitute, restore, renew. Thus, *refusive* (the ablative of *refusivus*) has both a negative and a positive sense, that is, "in a rejecting and restoring, withdrawing and repairing way." The connection between the two aspects is close as both are derived from flowing, *fundere*, while the prefix "re" can mean something negative and positive at the same time. *Refusivum sui* means both "self-withdrawal" and "self-reparation," "self-negation," and "self-restoration." Hence, I apply what I term "refusive analysis" in order to highlight the fact that the positive and negative aspects of *refundo* are intimately connected; the positive and the negative are linked to one another, so that the meaning of the abyss may be conceived. To illustrate this configuration let me refer to the pattern of the "ambiguous images" (*Vexierbild*, e.g., the duck-rabbit drawing). In an ambiguous image, the two aspects of one and the same picture exist together, while it is difficult, if not impossible, to conceive them in one optical act. Yet it is always the invisible aspect of the image that not only hides behind the visible one but also supports its optical emergence.[35]

The content of the refusive analysis is different from what we usually understand by *tzimtzum* or the related idea of *kenosis*. *Tzimtzum*, in Hebrew *contraction* or *condensation*, is a term used in the Kabbalah to explain Isaac Luria's doctrine that God began the process of creation by "contracting" his infinite light in order to allow for a space in which finite realms could exist. *Kenosis* (κένωσις), on the other hand, refers to God's self-emptying in Jesus, His becoming a human being, so that the work of salvation could be carried out (cf. Philippians 2:6). The principle of *refusivum sui* in its original form refers to *bonum*, yet the importance is to be understood in both the metaphysical and the theological senses. *Ens et bonum convertuntur. . . Bonum* and being, *bonum* and the absolute are intrinsically united. Therefore, what the principle expresses about goodness, it also expresses about the overall context of reality. Accordingly, what is realized as self-withdrawal is at the same time self-reparation, self-enrichment, or self-renewal. The two moments coincide and highlight each other in the refusive circle.

Obviously, the paradox characteristic of *tzimtzum* and *kenosis* does not fully disappear in a refusive analysis. *Tzimtzum* offers an openly paradoxical view of the self-limiting of the limitless. *Kenosis* is more rational, as it offers a partial self-emptying of divine perfection. The refusive principle, nevertheless, states that it is through the self-withdrawal that self-renewal is realized; or it is through the self-renewal that the self-negation takes place. This principle, in other words, describes a close link between the negative and positive moments and as a result makes the principle meaningful. The meaning is precisely the infinite self-renewal of *bonum* or, for that matter, reality as such. This paradox is not less disturbing than what we experience in instances of natural degeneration and generation, decay and growth. This point was emphasized by St. Paul when he compared physical resurrection to the sprout of a seed after its decay in the soil (cf. 1 Cor. 15:36); or when he states that "the truth of God hath more abounded through my lie" (Romans 3:7). Renewal and decay are inherently integrated as separate yet intrinsically connected aspects of the same reality.

The refusive analysis of mourning describes this act as the paradoxical unity of death and life, a process in which both are present, linked to one another, and create a peculiar unity of fundamental differences. In the act of mourning, we mourn something or somebody lost, yet we connect this loss to the renewal already heralded in the act of mourning. Mourning is the gateway between decay and renewal, degeneration and generation. As opposed to melancholy, mourning uncovers the way to self-renovation, either at the individual or the communal level, and so it stops the "whirlpool," the self-destructive power of depression.

The traditional, religious, or secular acts of mourning signal this peculiar function in symbolic ways. "Originary mourning," that is, the mourning expressed in higher reflection, embodies, however, the gateway function in a more direct way and at a metaphysical level. In the phenomenological approach, which connects conceptual metaphysics with actual experience, it is the principle of *refusivum sui* that helps us rise to the overall meaning of mourning. This meaning has two aspects not only in the sense of connecting degeneration and generation, but also in the sense that it is through mourning that the abyss of chaos is closed. Mourning, accordingly, presents a form of healing, both emotional and intellectual, leading to a meaningful life and a complex discernment of reality. Mourning is therapeutic above all in the sense of disclosing the ultimate form of reality, that is, renewal or newness.[36]

While optically we are unable to see the unity of the individual aspects of ambiguous images, these aspects support each other. Similarly, in the act of mourning we may not be able to synthesize the instances of life and death, yet they support each other so that we can conceive them in a paradoxical unity of meaning. On the basis of the principle of *refusivum sui*, we discern that these dimensions coexist and let the higher intentionality surface above the abyss. Such a discernment is eloquently expressed in Mihály Babits's *The Book of Jonah* of 1939 where he mourns the coming destruction as well as his own terminal sickness; yet he also perceives an ultimate unity of meaningfulness arising on the horizon of all sorrow. As he writes, "The fouler depths I'm falling into though/The brighter will Thy face be in my view."[37] With these words the poet indicates the refusive meaning of mourning, a meaning leading to further possibilities in the exploration of apocalyptic phenomenology.

NOTES

1. See Xuan Huong Thi Pham, *Mourning in the Ancient Near East and the Hebrew Bible* (Sheffield: Sheffield Academic Press, 1999); Antonius C. G. M. Robben, ed., *Death, Mourning, and Burial: A Cross-Cultural Reader* (Oxford: Blackwell, 2004).
2. Emile Durkheim, *The Elementary Forms of the Religious Life*, trans. by Joseph Ward Swain (London: George Allen & Unwin, 1964), pp. 390–96.
3. Walter Benjamin, *Origin of the German Trauerspiel*, trans. by Howard Eiland (Cambridge, MA: Harvard University Press, 2019), p. 180.
4. Françoise Dastur, "Mourning as the Origin of Humanity," *Mosaic: An Interdisciplinary Critical Journal* 48.3 (2015): 11.
5. Jacques Lacan, *The Seminar of Jacques Lacan*, Book VII: The Ethics of Psychoanalysis, 1959–1960, trans. by Denis Porter (New York: Norton & Company, 1997), p. 146.
6. Pascale-Anne Brault and Michael Naas, "Introduction," in Jacques Derrida, *The Work of Mourning* (Chicago: University of Chicago Press, 2001), pp. 1–30.
7. Edmund Husserl, *The Idea of Phenomenology*, trans. by Lee Hardy (Dordrecht: Kluwer Academic Publishing, 1999), p. 33.
8. Edmund Husserl, *The Crisis of European Sciences and Transcendental Phenomenology*, trans. by David Carr (Evanston: Northwestern University Press, 1970), p. 159.
9. Emmanuel Levinas, *Ethics and Infinity*, trans. by Richard A. Cohen (Pittsburgh: Duquesne University Press, 1992); Jacques Derrida, *The Work of Mourning* (Chicago: University of Chicago Press, 2001).
10. Husserl, *The Crisis of European Sciences*, pp. 67–70, 197.
11. Sigmund Freud, "Trauer und Melancholie," *Internationale Zeitschrift für Ärztliche Psychoanalyse* 4.6 (1917): 288–301.
12. See Ilit Ferber, *Philosophy and Melancholy: Benjamin's Early Reflections on Theater and Language* (Stanford: Stanford University Press, 2013), Chapter 1.

13. Jacques Derrida, *The Gift of Death*, trans. by David Wills (Chicago: University of Chicago Press, 1995), pp. 4, 10; Ferber, *Philosophy and Melancholy*, p. 11.

14. Jacques Derrida, *Aporias*, trans. by Thomas Dutoit (Stanford: Stanford University Press, 1993), p. 61.

15. Claudius Claudianus, *Works*, Volume II, trans. by Maurice Platnauer (London: W. Heinemann, 1998 [1922]), p. 362.

16. Sophocles, *The Theban Plays: Oedipus the King; Oedipus at Colonus; Antigone*, trans. by Ruth Fainlight and Robert J. Littman (Baltimore: Johns Hopkins University Press, 2009), p. 178.

17. See Sophocles, *The Theban Plays*, p. 180.

18. Plato, "Menexenus," in *Plato: The Complete Works*, ed. and trans. by John M. Cooper (Indianapolis: Hackett, 1997), pp. 950–64.

19. Plato, "Menexenus," 238e–239b.

20. Hannah Arendt, *The Origins of Totalitarianism* (New York: Schocken Books, 1951), p. 459.

21. Hannah Arendt, *The Human Condition* (Chicago: University of Chicago Press, 1958), p. 241.

22. Karl Löwith, *Meaning in History* (Chicago: University of Chicago Press, 1949).

23. Karl Popper, *Open Society and Its Enemies* (London: Routledge, 1945).

24. Derrida, *Aporias*; Levinas, *Ethics and Infinity*.

25. See Balázs M. Mezei, *Religion and Revelation after Auschwitz* (New York: Bloomsbury, 2013), pp. 3–29.

26. Immanuel Kant, *Religion within the Bounds of Bare Reason*, trans. by Werner S. Pluhar (Indianapolis: Hackett, 2009), p. 41.

27. Emil Fackenheim, *To Mend the World* (New York: Schocken Books, 1982).

28. Hans Jonas, *Der Gottesbegriff nach Auschwitz* (Stuttgart: Suhrkamp, 1987).

29. Viktor E. Frankl, *The Unconscious God* (New York: Simon & Schuster, 1975).

30. László Nemes, director, *Son of Saul*, Laokoon Filmgroup, 2015.

31. See Balázs M. Mezei, *Radical Revelation: A Philosophical Approach* (London: T&T Clark, 2017), Chapter 6.

32. See Balázs M. Mezei, "Revelation in Phenomenology," in *The Oxford Handbook of Divine Revelation*, ed. by Balázs M. Mezei, Francesca A. Murphy, and Kenneth Oakes (Oxford: Oxford University Press, 2021).

33. Mezei, *Radical Revelation*, pp. 255–58.

34. For an early form, see Gregory of Nazianzus, "Oratio XXXVIII," in *Patrologia Graeca*, Volume 36, ed. by Jacques-Paul Migne (Paris, 1859), pp. 319–20.

35. See Carlos Montemayor and Harry Haroutioun Haladjian, *Consciousness, Attention, and Conscious Attention* (Cambridge, MA: MIT Press, 2015).

36. Balázs M. Mezei, "Introduction: Revelation as Newness," in *The Oxford Handbook of Divine Revelation*, ed. by Balázs M. Mezei, Francesca A. Murphy, and Kenneth Oakes (Oxford: Oxford University Press, 2021).

37. Mihály Babits, *Poems*, trans. by István Tótfalusi (Budapest: Maecenas, 1988) p. 85.

BIBLIOGRAPHY

Arendt, Hannah. *The Origins of Totalitarianism.* New York: Schocken Books, 1951.
Arendt, Hannah. *The Human Condition.* Chicago: University of Chicago Press, 1958.
Babits, Mihály. *Poems.* Translated by István Tótfalusi. Budapest: Maecenas, 1988.
Benjamin, Walter. *Origin of the German Trauerspiel.* Translated by Howard Eiland. Cambridge, MA: Harvard University Press, 2019.
Brault, Pascale-Anne, and Michael Naas. "Introduction." In Jacques Derrida, *The Work of Mourning.* Chicago: University of Chicago Press, 2001, pp. 1–30.
Claudianus, Claudius. *Works.* Volumes I–II. Translated by Maurice Platnauer. London: W. Heinemann, 1998 [1922].
Dastur, Françoise. "Mourning as the Origin of Humanity." *Mosaic: An Interdisciplinary Critical Journal* 48.3 (2015): 1–13.
Derrida, Jacques. *Aporias.* Translated by Thomas Dutoit. Stanford: Stanford University Press, 1993.
Derrida, Jacques. *The Gift of Death.* Translated by David Wills. Chicago: University of Chicago Press, 1995.
Derrida, Jacques. *The Work of Mourning.* Translated by Pascale-Anne Brault and Michael Naas. Chicago: University of Chicago Press, 2001.
Durkheim, Emile. *The Elementary Forms of the Religious Life.* Translated by Joseph Ward Swain. London: George Allen & Unwin, 1964.
Fackenheim, Emil. *To Mend the World.* New York: Schocken Books, 1982.
Ferber, Ilit. *Philosophy and Melancholy: Benjamin's Early Reflections on Theater and Language.* Stanford: Stanford University Press, 2013.
Frankl, Viktor E. *The Unconscious God.* New York: Simon & Schuster, 1975.
Freud, Sigmund. "Trauer und Melancholie." *Internationale Zeitschrift für Ärztliche Psychoanalyse* 4.6 (1917): 288–301.
Gregory of Nazianzus. "Oratio XXXVIII." In *Patrologia Graeca*, Volume 36. Edited by Jacques-Paul Migne. Paris, 1859.
Husserl, Edmund. *The Crisis of European Sciences and Transcendental Phenomenology.* Translated by David Carr. Evanston: Northwestern University Press, 1970.
Husserl, Edmund. *The Idea of Phenomenology.* Translated by Lee Hardy. Dordrecht: Kluwer Academic Publishing, 1999.
Jonas, Hans. *Der Gottesbegriff nach Auschwitz.* Stuttgart: Suhrkamp, 1987.
Kant, Immanuel. *Religion within the Bounds of Bare Reason.* Translated by Werner S. Pluhar. Indianapolis: Hackett, 2009.
Lacan, Jacques. *The Seminar of Jacques Lacan.* Book VII: The Ethics of Psychoanalysis, 1959–1960. Translated by Denis Porter. New York: Norton & Company, 1997.
Levinas, Emmanuel. *Ethics and Infinity.* Translated by Richard A. Cohen. Pittsburgh: Duquesne University Press, 1992.
Levinas, Emmanuel. *God, Death, and Time.* Translated by Bettina Bergo. Stanford: Stanford University Press, 2000.
Löwith, Karl. *Meaning in History.* Chicago: University of Chicago Press, 1949.
Mezei, Balázs M. "Introduction: Revelation as Newness." In *The Oxford Handbook of Divine Revelation.* Edited by Balás M. Mezei, Francesca A. Murphy, and Kenneth Oakes. Oxford: Oxford University Press, 2021.

Mezei, Balázs M. *Religion and Revelation after Auschwitz*. New York: Bloomsbury, 2013.
Mezei, Balázs M. *Radical Revelation: A Philosophical Approach*. London: T&T Clark, 2017.
Mezei, Balázs M. "Revelation in Phenomenology." In *The Oxford Handbook of Divine Revelation*. Edited by Balázs M. Mezei, Francesca A. Murphy, and Kenneth Oakes. Oxford: Oxford University Press, 2021.
Mezei, Balázs M. "Introduction: Revelation as Newness." In *The Oxford Handbook of Divine Revelation*. Edited by Balázs M. Mezei, Francesca A. Murphy, and Kenneth Oakes. Oxford: Oxford University Press, 2021.
Montemayor, Carlos, and Harry Haroutioun Haladjian. *Consciousness, Attention, and Conscious Attention*. Cambridge, MA: MIT Press, 2015.
Nemes, László, director. *Son of Saul*. Laokoon Filmgroup, 2015. 107 mins.
Pham, Xuan Huong Thi. *Mourning in the Ancient Near East and the Hebrew Bible*. Sheffield: Sheffield Academic Press, 1999.
Plato. "Menexenus." In *Plato: The Complete Works*. Edited and translated by John M. Cooper. Indianapolis: Hackett, 1997.
Popper, Karl. *Open Society and Its Enemies*. London: Routledge, 1945.
Robben, Antonius C. G. M., ed. *Death, Mourning, and Burial: A Cross-Cultural Reader*. Oxford: Blackwell, 2004.
Sophocles. *The Theban Plays: Oedipus the King; Oedipus at Colonus; Antigone*. Translated by Ruth Fainlight and Robert J. Littman. Baltimore: Johns Hopkins University Press, 2009.

6

✣

Mourning and the Recognition of Value

Cathy Mason and Matt Dougherty

INTRODUCTION

Each year, ancient Athens would celebrate its fallen soldiers by choosing a citizen to deliver a funeral oration. In Plato's *Menexenus*, Socrates recounts advice he has received from Aspasia of Miletus as to what such a speech should involve. Among other things, she recommends instructing the audience on how to mourn the dead, recounting the following instructions given to her by Athenian soldiers concerning how their fathers ought to behave in case they should die in battle:

> If they bear their sorrows courageously, they will seem to be really fathers of courageous sons—and just as courageous themselves; but if they succumb to grief, they will provide grounds for suspicion that either they are not our fathers or the people who praise us are mistaken. Neither of these must happen. On the contrary, they above all must be our encomiasts in action, by showing themselves to be true men, with the look of truly being the fathers of true men. *Nothing too much* has long been thought an excellent adage—because it is, in truth, excellent. For that man's life is best arranged for whom all, or nearly all, the things that promote happiness depend on himself. Such a man does not hang from other men and necessarily rise or fall in fortune as they fare well or badly; he is the temperate, he is the brave and wise man. He above all, when wealth and children come and when they go, will pay heed to the adage: because he relies on himself, he will be seen neither to rejoice nor to grieve *too much*.[1]

To the modern ear, the tenor of this advice seems somewhat merciless: the bereaved are advised to avoid mourning if they can and are warned that deep mourning will be so damning of their courage that either their parenthood will be doubted or the courage of their sons will be called into question. But why should such grief impugn one's courage? The answer, it seems, relies on the particular conception of the good life expressed later in the passage: that the best kind of life is one in which one's happiness depends solely upon oneself. The truly virtuous man, it suggests, would not be moved to deep grief or mourning upon the death of his son, because he would not "hang from other men" in the first place. On this view, deep grief and mourning suggest a lack of virtue because they indicate a life that fails to be fully self-sufficient and invulnerable.

This conception of the good life sounds utterly alien to the modern ear. Living a satisfying life, we tend to think, depends not on being wholly self-sufficient but, rather, on finding and being committed to purposeful, meaningful things and activities. And we envisage the paradigmatic form of this meaning and fulfillment as coming from close relationships with other people. Such relationships essentially involve the possibility of painful loss. Far from thinking that profound grief and mourning are to be avoided and self-sufficiency prized, we tend to think that deep grief and mourning, or at least vulnerability to them, are an essential part of living well, and ought to be embraced as such.

This more modern conception of mourning finds voice, for example, in Julian Barnes's discussion of mourning his wife's death in *Levels of Life*. At one point in the book, Barnes shares a portion of a letter from a bereaved friend who describes their own experience of mourning: "The thing is—nature is so exact, it hurts exactly as much as it is worth, so in a way one relishes the pain."[2] Barnes later comes to reflect on this:

> The second part of that sentence was what I stubbed my foot against: it struck me as unnecessarily masochistic. Now I know that it contains truth. And if the pain is not exactly relished, it no longer seems futile. Pain shows that you have not forgotten; pain enhances the flavour of the memory; pain is a proof of love. "If it didn't matter, it wouldn't matter."[3]

Far from the shameful exhibition of vulnerability that Aspasia presents it as, Barnes sees deep grief as purposeful. While not going so far as to say that he relishes the pain, he notes that it is "not futile," that it reveals how much he had valued and loved his wife: "pain is a proof of love." And though the final line of the passage is ambiguous, it seems to reveal that he recognizes a closer connection between love and pain as well, that love itself involves the possibility of pain: "If it didn't matter, it wouldn't matter."

While the advice recounted in *Menexenus* seems too austere and dispassionate, the line of thinking implicit in Barnes's reflections seems to lead us to a different problem: If mourning is truly a proof of love and a reflection of the value that others have for us, how could it be appropriate to move on when one has truly loved and valued someone? Assuming that it is appropriate to value others extremely highly—perhaps even infinitely—how could it ever make sense for one's grief to abate? Do loss and proper mourning present us with a choice between living well and loving well?

In this chapter, we want to vindicate the pressing nature of these questions but nonetheless argue that we do not usually need to choose between living well and loving well. In the section "Tensions between Living Well, Loving Well, and Moving on from Loss," we explain in more detail how these questions become pressing and why loving well seems to necessitate unending mourning in the case of some losses. In the section "Psychological Literature on Moving on from Loss," we turn to some empirical research about how people in fact mourn the loss of partners and close family members—research that can seem to imply that we do not tend to love well at all. And finally, in the section "Ceasing to Mourn While Recognizing the Value of Those Lost," we offer an explanation of why ceasing to mourn need not be a failure of love. In particular, we offer an account of how ceasing to mourn can be a fitting response to the object of love itself, as well as compatible with living well. In doing so, we will be understanding grief as a kind of strong negative emotional response to loss, and mourning as a somewhat wider concept encompassing grief as well as patterns of behavior that manifest or are influenced by such grief. Grief and mourning have sometimes been understood otherwise, but hopefully these conceptions of them are intuitive ones.

TENSIONS BETWEEN LIVING WELL, LOVING WELL, AND MOVING ON FROM LOSS

In addressing the above questions, we will be assuming that living well is partially within our human means and partially outside of them. The part of the ability to live well which is within our means we call virtue—excellence at living. Loss, on the other hand, is to a great extent outside of our means, in the sense that it cannot be avoided, at least not completely. As we have seen in *Menexenus*, however, *profound grief* in response to such loss can be avoided, at least in principle. We can resist fully or wholeheartedly loving anything, and thus resist making ourselves vulnerable to grief. On the assumption that doing so is no way to live, however, vulnerability to loss and grief, if not loss and grief themselves, is necessary for living well.[4] If such vulnerability is not a virtue, virtue at least entails it.[5]

To say that virtue requires vulnerability to loss, then, is just another way of saying that the good life requires love, since making oneself invulnerable is plausibly only achieved by failing to love or value, or at least to love or value fully and adequately.[6] We are thus taking for granted that our lives should involve fully and wholeheartedly loving and valuing, at least some things and at least sometimes. Our question is "What is the appropriate response to losing a thing which one has loved wholeheartedly?" Or, more specifically, "Is *any* response appropriate, apart from unending grief and mourning?" The question arises in part because of the nature of virtue and in part because of the nature of love.

Virtue, on a common conception, involves both acting well and having appropriate affective responses. For our purposes, the latter is the relevant aspect of virtue. For example, the virtuous person will admire those things that are genuinely admirable and feel angry at injustices, because these are fitting emotional responses to have. Since anger is understood as being directed at actual or perceived injustice, it is objectively fitting when the object of anger is in fact unjust, and it is subjectively fitting when the object of anger is perceived to be unjust.[7] Anger disproportionate to the injustice it is about is unfitting, as is anger disproportionate to one's perception of injustice; so, both are prima facie unvirtuous. And this is the case whether the anger is wholly misplaced or not, and whether the agent feels too much or too little anger: anger directed at a just action is inappropriate, but a lack of anger at an egregious injustice can also suggest a lack of virtue, such as insufficient care for the victim.

Similar to anger, though more attitude than affect, love is directed at what is valuable, and it is appropriate in proportion to the actual and perceived value of the thing loved. Grief and mourning, in turn, are love's converse: they are directed at (or "about") the loss of something valued or loved. They are objectively fitting when something truly valuable has been lost, and subjectively fitting when something truly *valued* is lost. So, while one might love one's guinea pig and also love one's mother, and therefore mourn the loss of each, mourning the loss of one's guinea pig more than the loss of one's mother would usually be unfitting, both objectively and subjectively.[8]

Being virtuous, then, seems to entail mourning for things that we love and have lost. The possibility of unending grief and mourning thus seems to arise because it seems both possible and desirable that we should value certain things (paradigmatically other people) extremely highly, and perhaps infinitely. If mourning for a week can be fitting after the loss of a guinea pig, say, then given that we value other people not merely a few times more than this, but with an altogether different order of care, how could infinite mourning not be called for—or, at least, mourning until the end of our lives? The idea that mourning is an appropriate response in proportion to loss seems to have the implication that in some cases virtue requires unending mourning.[9]

PSYCHOLOGICAL LITERATURE ON MOVING ON FROM LOSS

The point that another's value could only be adequately recognized by unending mourning seems especially worrying when we consider recent psychological research regarding mourning the death of partners and close family. That literature seems to suggest that the bereaved rapidly return to "baseline functioning," slewing off their grief and mourning after only a few months on average.[10] Specifically, such literature suggests that after a few months the intense emotional turmoil and sadness of initial mourning is usually overcome and the bereaved once again live a fairly normal life, both functioning in similar ways to before the bereavement and experiencing similar psychological well-being. Far from experiencing unending mourning, this evidence suggests that people tend not to mourn for a very long period at all.

A plausible response to these findings would be to take them as evidence that people do not in fact love, value, or care about their partners or close family members very deeply. And this response would plausibly be based on an idea we have expressed above: that the difficulty of enduring a loss is proportional to one's love. We value most those whose loss would be most difficult for us to endure. Relative indifference to a loss, or at least managing to "move on" from it, thus seems to reveal that we were wrong to think that we valued the thing very deeply in the first place. Dan Moller considers and rejects this conclusion. He argues that there is good reason to think that people do love and value their partners while they are alive, as evidenced by people's deep empathy with their partners and their willingness to make sacrifices for them.[11] He argues that it seems both intuitively implausible and in tension with our other behavioral evidence to conclude that people do not usually love and value their partners and close family members.

Instead, Moller comes to the following conclusion: not that we do not really love our loved ones but that we often fail to *recognize* their importance to us. He argues, that is, that people's ability to move on after the death of a loved one indicates a deficiency, not of love, but of recognizing how much they loved and cared for those they have lost:

> Our "emotional immune system," while promoting our interests by allowing us to continue functioning in the face of trauma, also renders us unable to take in and register fully the significance of our losses. Part of what being the vulnerable creatures of flesh and blood that we are means is that we are subject to staggering losses in the form of the deaths of those we love, and yet our reaction to those losses is utterly incommensurate with their value, especially after the first month or two have passed. The good of a happy relationship with a lover is one that we value more highly than almost any other, and yet when we lose that good, our response over time does not seem to reflect its preciousness to us. Resilience thus seems to deprive us of our ability to care about those we love to their full measure after they are gone, and so deprives us of insight into our own condition.[12]

Moller concludes that though the ability to move on from deep grief and mourning may have important benefits for the bereaved, it is nonetheless a "profound reason . . . for regret."[13]

Whichever of the above explanations one prefers, however, our worries about mourning only multiply. In the section "Tensions between Living Well, Loving Well, and Moving on from Loss," we offered an argument from plausible considerations about virtue and valuing that seem to suggest that we should mourn unendingly for those we care about. Namely, we argued that the virtuous person's affective responses are fitting generally, that mourning is fitting in proportion to loss, that some losses are vast or infinite, and, therefore, that some mourning should be vast or lifelong. In the present section, we have noted some evidence to think that people rarely mourn in this way and, in fact, that most bereaved people recover relatively rapidly from their losses. Whether one explains this as a lack of love or a lack of recognition of value, the implication would seem to be that we are lacking in virtue.

CEASING TO MOURN WHILE RECOGNIZING THE VALUE OF THOSE LOST

We think, however, both that this conclusion is too fast and, thankfully, that recognizing the value of someone or something need not entail unending grief at their loss. Indeed, we think that one's grief at the death of a loved one abating after a short period is fully compatible with virtue. Fully recognizing the value of loved ones, we think, does plausibly entail a period of mourning, and it does plausibly entail *some* form of ongoing and active recognition of the value of the loved one, but this need not take the form of grief. In particular, mourning can, and properly does, transform into other states (such as honoring the dead) which are also apt responses to the value that people have for us. The virtuous person, then, need not be condemned to endless grief and suffering, since they can engage in other forms of ongoing activity that recognize the value of what they have lost.

To see why this should be, let us look more closely at the argument that was offered in favor of the idea that only unending grief and mourning adequately recognize the value that loved ones have for us. That argument began with the thought that the virtuous person's affective responses to the world must be fitting. Grief, we suggested, is directed at the loss of something that is conceived of as valuable and is thus fitting when the thing lost is indeed valuable. We further suggested that grief is fitting in proportion to the value of the thing lost: the more valuable the thing, the greater the grief should be. Together with the idea that people should be (and often are) extremely highly valued, these thoughts seemed to lead to the conclusion that our grief at their loss should be prolonged, even lifelong.

However, at this point the analogy with anger with which we introduced the idea of fittingness should give us pause. Anger, we noted, is aimed at injustice, and is fitting when the object at which it is directed is indeed unjust. However, while too little anger often indicates a lack of virtue in the form of complacency about injustice or a failure to even acknowledge it, it need not do so. This is because there are other ways of responding to injustice that *also* acknowledge it as injustice. For instance, particularly after an initial period of indignant anger, one might instead begin to feel sadness at the injustice. This sadness could be an apt way of recognizing the injustice of the object. Alternatively, one may focus not on the injustice itself, but on what can be done about it, and one might instead primarily feel determination not to allow such injustices in the future. Again, this would be an appropriate response to injustice. While anger is one fitting response, then, it is not the only one. Lack of anger *can* indicate a lack of virtuous motivation and a failure to acknowledge the gravity of injustice, but it can also be a sign only that the agent is acknowledging the injustice in some other way.

The same holds for grief. Grief is a fitting response to the loss of something valuable, but it is not the only fitting response. There are other ways of recognizing the value of what is lost that are also apt. For example, a recognition of the value of someone who has died, and of how much one valued them, can take the form of celebrating their life. Such celebration seems to make sense only if the thing being celebrated is of value. Similarly, honoring can also be a way of acknowledging value. Such honoring might, for example, involve appreciative recollection of them alongside action or activity that is taken or engaged in "for their sake": taking up a project that they cared about, acting in ways that they would have wished one to, and so on.[14]

If grief is not the only way to acknowledge others' value, then moving on from grief need not suggest that one has failed to properly love or value the person who died. There seems something right about the idea that the greater the value a thing has, the more demanding it must be to fully recognize and acknowledge that value. This suggests that a fully adequate recognition of the value a loved person has for us may well require *something* of us unendingly. But such recognition of value need not specifically take the form of grief. Unendingly honoring the life of the person who has died, for example, is another fully adequate way to recognize the value that they had. Mourning is thus one way among many of acknowledging the value that others can have for us, and moving on from mourning to a different kind of recognition of value does not necessarily indicate any failure in valuing.

We began by considering Barnes's claim that "pain is a proof of love." We agree with this statement. We simply think that there are other activities and affective states that are *also* proofs of love; that is, we think that pain is not a unique proof of love. As such, pain is not the only response to loss that is compatible with full virtue: other responses to loss can be fitting.

At this point, it is worth noting that this view is not necessarily a complacent affirmation of human limitations with regard to love; the view remains fairly demanding of the bereaved. On this view, it would not be fitting or virtuous to move on and return to life *exactly* as it was before; some kind of ongoing activity of remembrance remains appropriate. And these broader kinds of activity, we think, might well be required for the rest of one's life.

We might compare and contrast this conception of adequate mourning to that suggested by Freud in "Mourning and Melancholia." He contrasts mourning, which he conceives of as a healthy response to loss, with melancholia, which he conceives of as being pathological. One important difference between the two, he thinks, is that mourning is a transitional state, whereas melancholia is not.[15] He writes, for example, that "normal mourning . . . overcomes the loss of the object,"[16] and that "when the work of mourning is completed the ego becomes free and uninhibited again."[17] We agree that mourning is an appropriate reaction to loss, as well as that ceasing to mourn after a time is also appropriate. Nonetheless, one might read Freud as suggesting that once a period of mourning has passed, the bereaved can return to the very same state as before, free to inhabit the world no differently, simply without the thing lost. His idea that once one is no longer grieving, the ego becomes "free and uninhibited" suggests a breaking of ties with the loss, a moving on from a loss that is itself left behind. On the contrary, we think that the end of grief ought to signal a return not to one's previous state and life, but to a less grief-filled way of being that continues to be shaped by one's recognition of the value that the other had for one. One may wish to think of this continued recognition as a kind of mourning, simply transformed—but even if so, it will be a kind of mourning no longer incompatible with living well.

Returning to the psychological research mentioned earlier, we suggest that, far from being reason for regret, the position we have expounded here is compatible with this research being completely innocuous. Given that there are many ways of recognizing value, the fact that the bereaved cease to grieve after a short time may simply indicate that they are recognizing the loss of the loved one in other ways. And, indeed, though the research suggests that a large portion of bereaved individuals cease to feel *painful* grief after a period of only a few months, these individuals often understand themselves as "grieving" in other ways. Moller, for instance, notes that they "sometimes report grieving for a substantial length of time, though this reported grieving appears to have little connection with measures of happiness or subjective well-being."[18] On our account, this kind of "grieving" that is compatible with emotional well-being can be a fully adequate acknowledgment of the value that the one who died had for us.[19] While full virtue is, of course, vanishingly rare, if possible at all, we think that these particular results do not suggest that humans fail to love appropriately, nor that they are, in that respect, lacking in virtue.

We have discussed virtue as involving appropriate affective responses to the world, and we have said that grief at the loss of something loved is one such appropriate response. We have now argued that there are other appropriate responses as well. However, it is important to note a further point in favor of thinking that virtue, at least eventually, *requires* moving beyond painful grieving: in most cases, the thing grieved is not coextensive with the valuable things in the world.[20] Usually, there are other valuable things, and the virtuous person will—if not in every moment, at least generally—recognize them as such in their activities as well. Deep grief usually obstructs one's ability to recognize the value of other things, and this provides further reason to think that unending grief is a barrier to living well.[21] If we can love well in other ways, however, as it seems we can, loving well need not itself be such a barrier. If we recognize that loving well requires being able to grieve well, loving wholeheartedly can remain the essential aspect of the good life which we moderns more often take it to be.[22]

CONCLUSION

To finish, we return once more to Plato. We began by noting that the exhortation which he reports seems unduly austere and valorizing of an unappealing self-sufficiency. It is worth noting that this is not the only advice that Aspasia offers. A few breaths earlier, she passes on the following advice from the same Athenian soldiers:

> And as for those of our fathers and mothers who still live, one ought ceaselessly to encourage them to bear the sorrow, should it fall to their lot, as easily as they can, instead of joining them in lamentations. For they will stand in no need of a stimulus for grief; the misfortune that has befallen them will be enough to provide that. A better course is to try to heal and soothe them, by reminding them that the gods have answered their most earnest prayers. For they prayed for their sons to live not forever, but bravely and gloriously. And that—the greatest of boons—is what they received. It is not easy for a mortal to have everything in his life turn out as he would have it.[23]

This passage suggests that the parents of the dead ought to celebrate, for they have received the great good of their sons being valiant soldiers. Their sons have lived honorable lives, and this should be a cause for celebration, or at least satisfaction. When read alongside the earlier valorization of self-sufficiency, the present advice may also seem unduly austere, but we think that it nonetheless contains truth. While sorrow is one appropriate way to recognize the value of something lost, appreciative honoring or celebrating is another. And as engaging in the latter activities, unlike engaging in unending grief, is compatible with living a life that recognizes the value of the rest of life as well, that is something to be grateful for.

NOTES

1. Plato, *Menexenus*, in *Plato: Complete Works*, ed. by John M. Cooper, trans. by Paul Ryan (Indianapolis: Hackett, 1997), pp. 950–64 (247d–248a).
2. Julian Barnes, *Levels of Life* (London: Jonathan Cape, 2013), p. 71.
3. Barnes, *Levels of Life*, p. 113.
4. Jonathan Lear ascribes a similar view to Freud: "Freud seems to be moving in the direction of treating mourning as a virtue—in Aristotle's sense—a way of living well with loss and death and destruction. We can certainly imagine an Aristotelian voice speaking of mourning as striking the mean: not caring too little about the loss of a loved one, but not going to excess of permanently exiting from life and world"; Jonathan Lear, "The Difficulty of Reality and the Revolt against Mourning," *European Journal of Philosophy* 26.4 (2018): 7. It is worth noting that Lear himself seems also to be moving in this direction, in this and other recent work—e.g., Jonathan Lear, "Mourning and Moral Psychology," in *Wisdom Won from Illness: Essays in Philosophy and Psychoanalysis* (Cambridge, MA: Harvard University Press, 2017), pp. 191–205.
5. One might conceive of the particular part of virtue that entails such vulnerability along the lines of what Alasdair MacIntyre has called "virtues of

acknowledged dependence"; Alasdair MacIntyre, *Dependent Rational Animals: Why Human Beings Need the Virtues* (London: Duckworth, 1999), p. 18. He suggests that the self-sufficiency mentioned above can never be more than the illusion of self-sufficiency, an illusion that can exclude one from certain valuable types of relationship.

6. Harry Frankfurt, for example, writes: "A person who cares about something is, as it were, invested in it. He identifies himself with what he cares about in the sense that he makes himself vulnerable to losses." Harry G. Frankfurt, *The Importance of What We Care About: Philosophical Essays* (Cambridge: Cambridge University Press, 1988), p. 83.

7. From this point onward we will be primarily discussing *subjective* fittingness. Of course, when all goes well, this subjective fittingness will align with objective fittingness.

8. There can, of course, be important differences in relationships, which influence the way we mourn their loss. For instance, we more often *expect* to experience the death of a parent than that of a child, which can make the latter experience especially painful. Even in the light of such differences, however, given that we can value parents, children, partners, etc., all extremely highly and perhaps infinitely, the problem we are concerned with (viz., of explaining how ceasing to mourn in such cases could be appropriate) still arises.

9. Marušić poses a similar question to ours: "I realize that when my mother died, I had very good reason to grieve. I also acknowledge that today, a decade after her death, I am not wrong not to grieve. But I find it puzzling why this should be so—since it does not seem that her death is any less of a loss"; Berislav Marušić, "Do Reasons Expire? An Essay on Grief," *Philosophers' Imprint* 18.25 (2018): 4. Na'aman suggests that some attitudes are "rationally self-consuming," by which he means that the longer they endure, the less fitting they become, despite the initial reasons for them persisting. He cites grief alongside attitudes such as resentment and anger as examples of these; Oded Na'aman, "The Rationality of Emotional Change: Toward a Process View," *Noûs* 55.2 (June 2021): 245–69. One potential response to the worry we have described would be to accept this view of the rationality (or appropriateness) of attitudes. However, we think that this will not resolve the problem, since we can value other people very highly, such that even if the aptness of grief diminishes over time, it remains apt throughout a lifetime.

10. For a selection of such papers, see: George Bonanno et al., "Resilience to Loss in Bereaved Spouses, Bereaved Parents, and Bereaved Gay Men," *Journal of Personality and Social Psychology* 88.5 (2005): 827–43; Andrew Futterman et al., "The Effects of Late-Life Spousal Bereavement Over a 30-Month Interval," *Psychology and Aging* 6.3 (1991): 434–41; Dale Lund, "Impact of Spousal Bereavement on the Subjective Well-Being of Older Adults," in *Older Bereaved Spouses*, ed. by Dale Lund et al. (New York: Hemisphere, 1989), pp. 3–15. Moller summarizes their findings as follows: "[T]he cumulative evidence seems to show quite clearly that most people do not experience significant long-term distress when they lose the person they have committed their lives to"; Dan Moller, "Love and Death," *Journal of Philosophy* 104.6 (2007): 304. We are, for the moment, taking this research at face value.

11. Moller, "Love and Death," pp. 307–08. He also notes that the pattern of "resilience" implied by this research is not particular to bereavement; people recover astonishingly rapidly from losses of all kinds of things that they take themselves to care about; Moller, "Love and Death," pp. 305–07.

12. Moller, "Love and Death," pp. 310–11.

13. Moller, "Love and Death," p. 301. We find it plausible that a failure to *recognize* the importance of something to oneself is a *kind* of failure to love well or adequately, but we will not take up that point here. (Relatedly, see note 2.) It is also worth noting that though we have made Moller out to use "importance" synonymously with our "value," he understands "importance" as specifically "functional importance," such that someone is important to me to the extent that they fulfill a significant and unique function in my life. We think that any functional (or, likewise, instrumental) notion of importance comes up short of the value that a loved one has for us.

14. A similar line of thinking is offered by Preston-Roedder and Preston-Roedder. They, too, argue against Moller that moving on from grief need not indicate that the deceased lacked "importance" for us; Ryan Preston-Roedder and Erica Preston-Roedder, "Grief and Recovery," in *The Moral Psychology of Sadness*, ed. by Anna Gotlib (London: Rowman & Littlefield, 2017), pp. 93–116. Their use of "importance," however, is Moller's (understood as fulfilling a unique and significant functional role within one's life), and though it is, of course, worthwhile responding in Moller's own terms, we are doubtful that such a use of "importance" captures the sense in which other people are valuable to us.

15. He does not regard this as being the only difference between the two. Another significant difference he identifies is the "direction" of one's sorrow: "In mourning it is the world that has become poor and empty; in melancholia it is the ego itself"; Sigmund Freud, "Mourning and Melancholia," in *The Standard Edition of the Complete Psychological Works of Sigmund Freud*, Volume 14, ed. by James Strachey, Anna Freud, Alix Strachey, and Alan Tyson (London: Hogarth and the Institute of Psycho-Analysis, 1953), p. 246.

16. Freud, "Mourning and Melancholia," p. 255.

17. Freud, "Mourning and Melancholia," p. 245.

18. Moller, "Love and Death," p. 304.

19. Moller also notes that the bereaved generally retained "photographs and trinkets of remembrance" and may retain "a special place in their hearts" for the person who has died; Moller, "Love and Death," pp. 301, 310. We think that his skepticism about such practices is misplaced, that they can involve an apt recognition of the value that the one who has died had for us.

20. Lear's example of the devastation of an entire way of life is a plausible exception; Jonathan Lear, *Radical Hope: Ethics in the Face of Cultural Devastation* (Cambridge, MA: Harvard University Press, 2006).

21. Marušić says: "Temporal distance does not merely make us grieve less; in many cases it seems that we are not wrong to grieve less. Indeed, there is something wrong with being stuck; there is something wrong with persistent grief"; Marušić, "Do Reasons Expire," p. 9. We agree with at least the latter sentence.

22. This is an idea—at least implicit—in much of Lear's work, including: Jonathan Lear, *Love and Its Place in Nature: A Philosophical Interpretation of Freudian*

Psychoanalysis (New Haven: Yale University Press, 1990); *Radical Hope*; "Mourning and Moral Psychology"; and "The Difficulty of Reality." We see our arguments here as contributions to that idea.

23. Plato, *Menexenus*, 247c–d.

BIBLIOGRAPHY

Barnes, Julian. *Levels of Life*. London: Jonathan Cape, 2013.

Bonanno, George A., Anthony Papa, Judith Tedlie Moskowitz, and Susan Folkman. "Resilience to Loss in Bereaved Spouses, Bereaved Parents, and Bereaved Gay Men." *Journal of Personality and Social Psychology* 88.5 (2005): 827–43.

Frankfurt, Harry G. *The Importance of What We Care About: Philosophical Essays*. Cambridge: Cambridge University Press, 1988.

Freud, Sigmund. "Mourning and Melancholia." In *The Standard Edition of the Complete Psychological Works of Sigmund Freud*, Volume 14. Edited by James Strachey, Anna Freud, Alix Strachey, and Alan Tyson. London: Hogarth and the Institute of Psycho-Analysis, 1953, pp. 243–58.

Futterman, Andrew, James Peterson, Dolores Gallagher-Thompson, Michael J. Gilewski, and Larry W. Thompson. "The Effects of Late-Life Spousal Bereavement Over a 30-Month Interval." *Psychology and Aging* 6.3 (1991): 434–41.

Lear, Jonathan. "The Difficulty of Reality and the Revolt against Mourning." *European Journal of Philosophy* 26.4 (2018): 1–12.

Lear, Jonathan. "Mourning and Moral Psychology." In *Wisdom Won from Illness: Essays in Philosophy and Psychoanalysis*. Cambridge, MA: Harvard University Press, 2017, pp. 191–205.

Lear, Jonathan. *Radical Hope: Ethics in the Face of Cultural Devastation*. Cambridge, MA: Harvard University Press, 2006.

Lear, Jonathan. *Love and Its Place in Nature: A Philosophical Interpretation of Freudian Psychoanalysis*. New Haven: Yale University Press, 1990.

Lund, Dale. "Impact of Spousal Bereavement on the Subjective Well-Being of Older Adults." In *Older Bereaved Spouses*. Edited by Dale Lund et al. New York: Hemisphere, 1989, pp. 3–15.

MacIntyre, Alasdair. *Dependent Rational Animals: Why Human Beings Need the Virtues*. London: Duckworth, 1999.

Marušić, Berislav. "Do Reasons Expire? An Essay on Grief." *Philosophers' Imprint* 18.25 (2018): 1–21.

Moller, Dan. "Love and Death." *Journal of Philosophy* 104.6 (2007): 301–16.

Na'aman, Oded. "The Rationality of Emotional Change: Toward a Process View." *Noûs* 55.2 (June 2021): 245–69.

Plato. *Menexenus*. In *Plato: Complete Works*. Edited by John M. Cooper. Translated by Paul Ryan. Indianapolis: Hackett, 1997, pp. 950–64.

Preston-Roedder, Ryan, and Erica Preston-Roedder. "Grief and Recovery." In *The Moral Psychology of Sadness*. Edited by Anna Gotlib. London: Rowman & Littlefield, 2017, pp. 93–116.

7

Grieving and Mourning
The Psychology of Bereavement
Colin Murray Parkes

As a psychiatrist, I have worked, with others, to develop a theory of the psychology of grief and mourning that is both useful and evidence-based. Within the emerging field of palliative care and bereavement support, new ways of construing grief and its vicissitudes are emerging. They have significant implications for our understanding of love, loss, and change.

I remember feeling very anxious when I first knocked on the door of a newly bereaved widow to ask her to help me with my research into the psychology of bereavement (the lasting loss of a loved person). I was afraid that either she would angrily slam the door in my face, or she would burst into tears. In either case I would have done more harm than good.

What I found was that, once I had convinced her that I was not carrying out bogus research in the hope of selling her something, a product or a religion, she was quite willing to admit me into her home and in no time she was pouring her heart out. Yes, she cried and apologized for crying as if it was a weakness rather than a natural consequence of love. By the end of the interview, she had dried her tears and, as I was leaving the house, she said "I think it's wonderful what you are doing." This response was repeated, one way or another, by most of the widows and widowers whom I interviewed and many of them were grateful for the opportunity to talk about the experience that was filling their minds. I realized that they were on the same quest as I. They too were trying to make sense of one of the most painful and shattering experiences they had ever faced. They were glad to find someone with whom they could share their confusion in the hope that they could begin to make sense of it.

Many of them said, "You're the first person I've been able to talk to like this." They had discovered that they could not speak to their family for fear of upsetting them and they did not want to become a burden on their friends for fear of losing them. "Laugh and the world laughs with you, weep and you weep alone."

I have dwelt on this dilemma because it illustrates one of the most important and challenging aspects of bereavement, the emotional turmoil. In fact, a major bereavement for which people are unprepared gives rise to many problems, the most distinctive being grief. This has two main psychological components. Stroebe and Schut, from the University of Utrecht, refer to these as *the dual process*. They point out that bereaved people tend to oscillate between pangs of grief, episodes of intense yearning or pining for the lost person, *the loss orientation*, and a longer but less passionate struggle to deal with the problem of undertaking a major revision of their assumptive world which they refer to as the *restoration orientation*. It is worth looking more closely at each of these orientations.[1]

In his book *The Expression of the Emotions in Man and Animals* published in 1873, a year after *The Descent of Man*, Charles Darwin refers to "the grief muscles" which produce the distinctive expression of the pang of grief. He suggested that the expression of grief is a muted form of the expression which we see most clearly in young children and infants when frightened or separated from their mothers for any length of time. In Figure 7.1, Dylan, my fifth grandson, was expelling air through a closed larynx (see Figure 7.1).

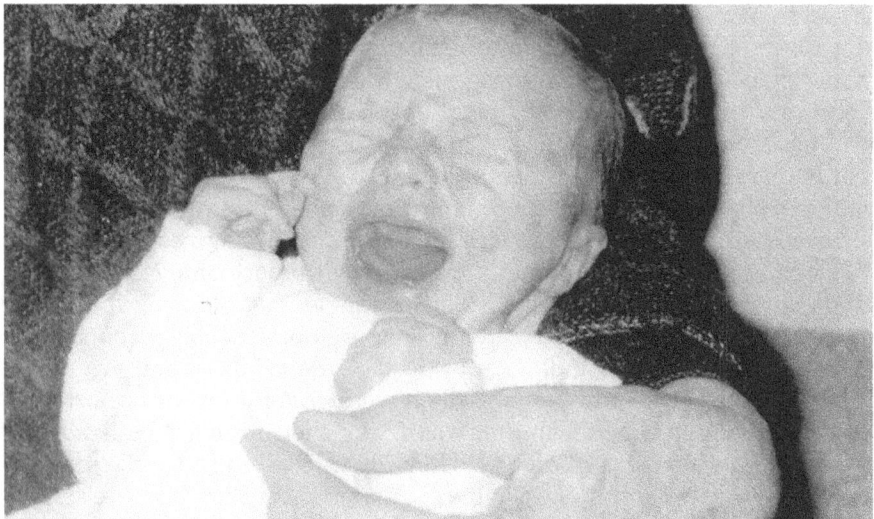

Figure 7.1. Infant expelling air through a closed larynx when frightened. *Author's own records. Consent to publish given by the subject's parents.*

This generated a loud noise through his wide open mouth. His face went red as a result of raised intravenous pressure which would have caused bleeding into his conjunctivae if he had not screwed his eyes tight shut. I had picked him up but the cry did not stop; it got louder and he hammered with his clenched fists before the noise subsided.

It is Darwin's case that this cry has survival value by signaling that the child is in need and, Bowlby suggested, it also punishes his caregivers thereby deterring them from deserting him again. Since the crying can take place immediately after birth, it cannot have been learned although, like all instinctive behaviors, it was soon modified by learning.

Crying is not the only behavior that has survival value in early childhood. Before long, babies show searching behavior, at first with its eyes and head movements, and as mobility increases, by moving towards places associated with the main caregiver, usually the mother.

By the time we reach adult life we know that death is irreversible and that crying and searching is not only irrational, but socially embarrassing. Yet newly bereaved people do just that. "Dwight, where are you?" wrote Frances Beck in her *Diary of a Widow*.[2] In one of my own studies, I found that measures of crying, preoccupation with thoughts of the dead person, and a clear visual memory of the dead person correlated significantly together; in short, the bereaved people (most of them widows) carried in their heads a clear picture of the spouse and moved restlessly around places associated with him or her.[3] They found it difficult to pay attention to other tasks and some of them admitted, "I walk around searching for him," or "I'm just searching for nothing," "It's as if I'm drawn towards him." Six widows went to spiritualist meetings in the hope of meeting the dead person and several of them received messages that seemed to confirm their hopes.

In recent years, it has become possible, for the first time, to examine the changes in the brain that accompany much human thought and behavior. fMRI (functional Magnetic Resonance Imaging) scanning traces temperature changes caused by neurons firing thereby showing the exact place in the brain that is in use. We still have a way to go to understand the complex changes that accompany bereavement, but some fascinating findings are emerging. For instance, recent studies show that when people with prolonged grief are shown pictures of the lost person, or mothers are shown pictures of children from whom they are currently separated, or drug addicts are shown pictures of their drugs and syringes, all show a similar pattern of reaction involving the reward center, the nucleus accumbens in the brain.[4]

What do these three situations have in common? The answer is a mental set to find a particular goal. Each is holding in mind a mental image which, for a moment, finds its goal in the picture. In all three cases, the instant recognition of a set goal is rapidly followed by disappointment and the overall emotion felt is usually negative. Thus, the research provides confirmation of the pang of grief as a goal-seeking emotion akin to separation anxiety.

Returning to attachment theory, the theory of love. John Bowlby included crying and searching as two of the ways by which small children regain contact with their parents when separated.[5] Although they are subsequently modified by learning, they remain at the root of the emotion of grief. Bowlby added clinging, smiling, and following as ways of maintaining proximity. Together he referred to these as *attachment behaviors*.

I come now to the *restoration orientation*. This is every bit as important as the *loss orientation* and reflects the extent to which love relationships become integrated into patterns or habits of thought and behavior which govern much of our assumptive world, the world that we assume to exist on the basis of all that we know or think we know at this moment in time.[6] Much of our assumptive world is shared. Individuals become couples and in due course, couples change into families in which each member has roles and obligations vis-à-vis each other, issues of leadership and followership, each of which leads to habits of thought and behavior which we take for granted. Differences are shelved or resolved into ways of living together, and all the small details of life become routine and more or less "comfortable." Sexuality may add spice to life but it is the security arising out of attachments that lasts and grows stronger with time.

When we lose a family member, or lose a limb or other physical functions, or are fired from a job, or have our first baby, major changes in our assumptive world are inevitable. Much of the time we are at least partially prepared for such changes, indeed our education, training, and planning enable us to enter new worlds in our imagination long before they become real. Problems arise when we are unprepared for changes because they are sudden and/or unanticipated. And we are often unprepared for the loss of those people and things to whom or which we are attached. We do not look forward to the things we do not look forward to. There are no schools for widowhood.

Bereaved people are often surprised at how disabled they feel. In one study of the response to the loss of a limb, I came across twelve people who had suffered a major bereavement at some time before the illness or accident that brought about the amputation.[7] They were all struck by the similar feelings of disorientation they had faced and many described it as a form of grief. Yet they had not lost a loved person and it seemed that their response to amputation required a different explanation.

Part of the problem is that our assumptive world is all we have. Our ways of coping with stress involve other people and without them many have lost a rudder or support just when they needed it most. The consequence is a feeling of disorientation. The familiar world suddenly feels unfamiliar, we have lost our bearings and feel weak and helpless. We have always known that disasters happen, but they happen to other people, and our safe, secure world now feels very unsafe and insecure, nothing can be taken for granted. "My world has been turned upside down." Life seems to have lost its meaning.

For a while we may even feel that we have lost everything good that came with the other person. Yet that is not strictly true, for attachments do not end when somebody dies. There is truth in the statement "He (or she) lives on in my memory." While the loss orientation is prompting us to search outside ourselves for the lost person, we are repeatedly disappointed, yet it is only when we let go of the dead outside ourselves that we find that we never lost them inside.

After the unexpected death of her husband, one woman found her eyes repeatedly drawn to his favorite chair. Even when watching television or talking to her friends, she would keep glancing towards him. "But I solved all that," she told me, "I went and sat in the chair myself, then I felt that I had him within me." Freud spoke of this as "internalizing the lost object"[8] but in fact it is more a matter of rediscovering what was never lost in the first place.

The process is described here in more detail by Raymond Tallis in his sensitive and scholarly account of how the bereaved deal with the problem of "outliving" the dead.

To understand the problems that sometimes cause bereaved people to seek psychiatric help we need to look more closely at the roots of love in early childhood. One of Bowlby's trainees was a Canadian psychologist, Mary Ainsworth, who developed a scientific way of studying child–mother and mother–child attachments during and after brief four-minute periods of separation in a strange situation.[9] They are important because they identified patterns of behavior that persisted and colored other relationships even into adult life. To sum up a very large amount of research, Ainsworth identified four *patterns of attachment* (see Table 7.1):

Table 7.1. Type of Attachment Pattern

	Secure	Insecure		
		Anxious / Ambivalent	Avoidant	Disorganized
Parenting Style	Encouraging play within safe limits.	Anxious, controlling, intrusive parenting inhibiting play.	Ignoring or punishing clinging, and intolerant of closeness.	Grieving or abusive parents, unable to care for or rejecting the child.

Patterns of attachment according to Mary Ainsworth

1. *Secure* infants tolerate brief separation well. They continue to play fitfully when mother leaves the room but stop playing and go to her for a cuddle when she returns. They have parents who encourage play but provide protection when it is needed and set reasonable limits on dangerous behavior;
2. *Anxious/ambivalent* infants (*clingers*) dislike the strange situation from the outset. When mother leaves, they start crying, and when she returns, the volume increases and they seem angry. They have mothers who are anxious, overprotective, and often intrusive, controlling the child and inhibiting play and adventure;
3. *Avoidant* infants seem unperturbed by the short separation and take little notice when mother returns. Even so, their heart rate increases greatly and they show other evidence of physiological arousal when separated. They usually have mothers who are intolerant of closeness and ignore cries or punish clinging.
4. *Disorganized* infants, as the name implies, have no clear pattern. Sometimes they rock back and forth, or freeze, at other times they run towards mother then turn away. They seem lost and helpless. Their mothers are usually preoccupied with their own problems, many have suffered major losses at the time of the child's birth and their grief or depression interferes with their ability to provide consistent mothering, a few are outrightly abusive or rejecting of the child.[10]

It seems that these patterns influence the acquisition of two important sources of security. *Secure infants* learn reasonable degrees of self-trust and trust in others; *clingers* learn to be dependent on others; while the *avoidant* learn to stand on their own feet from an early age, to keep a safe distance from others, and often to control others by assertiveness or aggression; and finally, the *disorganized* have no effective strategies for coping with others and turn in on themselves (see Table 7.2).

With regard to *gender*, although avoidant patterns of attachment are no more frequent in young boys than they are in girls, this tends to change with *adolescence*. In many social animals, it is the dawning of sexual development that causes males to become more assertive, dominant, and

Table 7.2. **Trust in Others**

		High	Low
Self-Trust	High	Secure	Anxious / Ambivalent
	Low	Avoidant	Unpredictable

The effect of patterns of attachment on child's trust

aggressive. Displays of bravery and mastery serve two evolutionary ends: to drive away competing males from receptive females and to establish a lasting place in the dominance hierarchy. In most mammals, females are less overly aggressive and achieve their status by attracting high status males. Human beings pride themselves on their ability to behave in more rational ways, but it would be idle to pretend that we have escaped entirely from the consequences of our evolution.

Although my own studies rely on retrospective data and need confirmation by longitudinal studies, they seem to show that each pattern of attachment influences the response to bereavements later in life.[11] The *clingers* tended to grieve intensely and persistently, so much so that some psychiatrists have proposed that intense, prolonged grief can impair worthwhile life to the extent that it should be regarded as a mental illness. The *avoidants* find it hard to express grief and other emotions. Their grief is delayed or inhibited and they tend to blame themselves for their inability to show feelings throughout their lives. The *disorganized* suffer "learned helplessness" and are prone to anxiety, depression, and often alcohol abuse. Even the *secure* can be thrown off course by betrayals and by unduly traumatic losses for which their secure upbringing has left them unprepared. They lack the tough carapace of the long-traumatized (see Table 7.3).

Human beings are more subtle and less driven by "blind emotion" than other species. They still need to achieve the same ends if they are to perpetuate their genes, but their larger cerebral cortex provides them with a wider range of alternative strategies along the way. Within each society many and varied beliefs and rituals attend the predictable turning points in life. These are most obvious at times of trauma, change, and death. Humans may be the only creatures who ought to know that they, and those they love, are doomed to die, but their high intelligence, social and cultural influences have enabled most of them to find ways of rationalizing this. In the past, and in many parts of the world to this day, attachment to God or Gods provide an "invisible means of support" at

Table 7.3. Type of Attachment Pattern

	Secure	Insecure		
		Anxious / Ambivalent	Avoidant	Disorganized
Response to Loss	Normal grief but vulnerable to traumatic or undue loss.	Intense and persistent grief, sometimes leading to Prolonged Grief disorder.	Difficulty in expressing emotions leading to delayed or inhibited grief.	Prone to anxiety and depression due to "learned helplessness."

Responses to loss in later life influenced by patterns of attachment in early childhood times of bereavement and loss. This said, bereavement can be a test of faith, as Father Conran will show, and those without faith face a different set of problems including the lack of a clear context of meaning for death itself.

One major difference between cultures is in the ways in which grief and other emotions are expressed.[12] It does appear that countries at war and those in which martial arts and macho behavior play a large part in determining status within and between societies are also inclined to inhibit the overt expression of grief and other powerful emotions. Peaceful and secure societies are more in touch with their feelings. It is perhaps no coincidence that both Freud's "Mourning and Melancholia" (1917) and Erich Lindemann's "The Symptomatology and Management of Acute Grief" (1944) were written near the end of World War I and II, respectively. By contrast, there are other societies in which powerful expressions of emotion are expected and even promoted by the employment of professional wailers whose role it is to lead the way. In the Maori Tangi the body of the deceased person is displayed in the meeting house. The immediate family and closest friends spend three days and two nights engaged in emotional chanting including expressions of anger, tears, and much else. As a Maori GP said to me, "After three days you've had enough." The Maoris see themselves as warriors and it may be that there is a special need for this kind of ritual in such societies.

But we would be unwise to assume that all pathological grief is attributable to the repression of grief. When I carried out my early studies in the aftermath of World War II, avoidance and repression of emotion did seem to give rise to more psychiatric problems than they do today. In recent years it is severe, prolonged, and disabling grief that is the most frequent problem; this, as we have seen, cannot be explained by repression and most therapists find dependent patients difficult to treat. Part of the problem is that we may inadvertently treat people who see themselves as sick, weak, or helpless as if this were indeed so. Out of pity we may reinforce their negative assumptions about themselves by treating them as if they were the helpless sufferers they appear to be. But pity belittles people; what they most need is respect for their intrinsic value and potential.

In recent years much controversy has arisen between the proponents of therapies aiming at encouraging the expression of grief and therapies that help people to identify and change the ways they think about their problems (Cognitive Behavior Therapy or CBT). Henk Schut et al., working at the University of Utrecht, compared the use of emotive therapy and CBT by assigning people who had sought help for problems following bereavement to three groups: problem-focused cognitive therapy; emotion-focused therapy; and a waiting list control group.[13] On follow up, both therapies were more effective than the controls but an important difference was found between men and women. The men who, given a choice, would probably have opted for problem-focused therapy, actually benefited most from emotional expression, while the women benefited most from problem-focused therapy. Now I am not suggesting that all men need one therapy and all women another. There are many women who have difficulties in emotional expression and men who have difficulty in re-organizing their assumptive worlds. Suffice it to say that there is no single therapeutic approach or counseling that will solve all bereavement problems.

In conclusion, we have seen that, while most people will come through the stress of bereavement without the need for help from outside their own family and network of friends, there is a substantial minority who need and will benefit from help.[14] Since all of the problems discussed here arise from insecurity, clients are all likely to need a person and place that makes them feel safe enough to begin to talk about the things that make them feel unsafe. Given that prerequisite, some, who tend to repress feelings, will need expressive forms of therapy, while others will benefit from more "cognitive" approaches.

It may be that, in the years to come, drug companies will find a medication for grief but none has been found to date. Anxiolyticas and antidepressants may reduce some of the pain of severe anxiety and depression, but they do not affect the course of grief. Today it is widely assumed that grief, however painful, is a normal process that must be allowed to run its course. Similar arguments were used in the nineteenth century against the introduction of drugs and anesthetics to relieve the pains of childbirth. But it was not the doctors but Queen Victoria's use of chloroform during her frequent parturitions that changed the fashion and reduced much of the suffering of women in childbirth.

For the time being, we rely on the support of friends and family along with organizations, such as *Cruse Bereavement Care* whose volunteers are carefully selected, trained, and supervised to provide a range of services to bereaved people. They, in turn, need well-trained psychologists, psychiatrists, social workers, and clergy to help with the more complex difficulties. To quote from the ending of my book of selected papers *The Price of Love*,

> Love and loss, it seems, can contribute to some of the darkest, saddest and most painful aspects of life. Indeed, the cost of commitment can be very high. Any simplistic and sentimental ideas we may have had that love solves all problems must be set aside. And yet our commitment to care, which is another aspect of love, may also hold the key to solving those problems and to discovering that the price of love can be a price worth paying.[15]

NOTES

1. M.S. Stroebe and H. Schut, "Models of Coping with Bereavement: A Review," in *Handbook of Bereavement Research: Consequences, Coping and Care*, ed. by M.S. Stroebe, R.O. Hansson, W. Stroebe, and H. Schut (Washington, D.C.: American Psychological Association, 2001), pp. 375–404.

2. Frances Beck, *Diary of a Widow* (Boston: Beacon Press, 1965).

3. Colin Murray Parkes, "'Seeking' and 'Finding' a Lost Object: Evidence from Recent Studies of the Reaction to Bereavement," *Social Science & Medicine*, 4 (1970): 187–99.

4. Harald Gündel, Mary-Frances O'Connor, Lindsey Littrell, Carolyn Fort, and Richard D. Lane, "Functional Neuroanatomy of Grief: An fMRI Study," *American Journal of Psychiatry*, 160 (2003): 1946–53.

5. John Bowlby, *Attachment and Loss. Volume 1: Attachment* (London: Hogarth, 1969).

6. Colin Murray Parkes, "Psycho-Social Transitions: A Field for Study," *Social Science & Medicine*, 5 (1971): 101–15.

7. Colin Murray Parkes, "Psycho-Social Transitions: Comparison between Reactions to Loss of a Limb and Loss of a Spouse," *British Journal of Psychiatry*, 127 (1975): 204–10.

8. Sigmund Freud, "Mourning and Melancholia," in *The Standard Edition of the Complete Psychological Works of Sigmund Freud. Volume 14*, ed. by James Strachey, Anna Freud, Alix Strachey, and Alan Tyson (London: Hogarth Press and the Institute of Psycho-Analysis, 1957).

9. Mary D. Salter Ainsworth, Mary C. Blehar, Everett Waters, and Sally Wall, *Patterns of Attachment: A Psychological Study of the Strange Situation* (Hillsdale, NJ: Erlbaum, 1978).

10. Ainsworth et al., *Patterns of Attachment*.

11. Colin Murray Parkes, *Love and Loss: The Roots of Grief and Its Complications* (London: Routledge, 2006).

12. Colin Murray Parkes, Pittu Laungani, and Bill Young, eds., *Death and Bereavement Across Cultures*, 2nd Edition (London: Routledge, 2015).

13. H. A. W. Schut, M.S. Stroebe, J. van den Bout, and J. de Keijser, "Intervention for the Bereaved: Gender Differences in the Efficacy of Two Counseling Programs," *British Journal of Clinical Psychology*, 36 (1997): 63–72.

14. H. Schut, M. S. Stroebe, J. van den Bout, and M. Terheggen, "The Efficacy of Bereavement Interventions: Determining Who Benefits," in *Handbook of Bereavement Research: Consequences, Coping and Care*, ed. by M.S. Stroebe, R.O. Hansson, W. Stroebe, and H. Schut (Washington, D.C.: American Psychological Association, 2001), pp. 705–37.

15. Parkes, *The Price of Love*, pp. 230–31.

BIBLIOGRAPHY

Ainsworth, Mary D. Salter, Mary C. Blehar, Everett Waters, and Sally Wall. *Patterns of Attachment: A Psychological Study of the Strange Situation*. Hillsdale, NJ: Erlbaum, 1978.

Beck, Frances. *Diary of a Widow*. Boston: Beacon Press, 1965.

Bowlby, John. *Attachment and Loss. Volume 1: Attachment*. London: Hogarth, 1969.

Darwin, Charles. *The Expression of the Emotions in Man and Animals*. London: John Murray, 1873.

Freud, Sigmund. "Mourning and Melancholia." In *The Standard Edition of the Complete Psychological Works of Sigmund Freud. Volume 14*. Edited by James Strachey, Anna Freud, Alix Strachey, and Alan Tyson. London: Hogarth Press and the Institute of Psycho-Analysis, 1957.

Gündel, Harald, Mary-Frances O'Connor, Lindsey Littrell, Carolyn Fort, and Richard D. Lane. "Functional Neuroanatomy of Grief: An fMRI Study." *American Journal of Psychiatry*, 160 (2003): 1946–53.

Lindemann, Erich. "The Symptomatology and Management of Acute Grief." *American Journal of Psychiatry*, 101 (1944): 141–48.

Parkes, Colin Murray. "'Seeking' and 'Finding' a Lost Object: Evidence from Recent Studies of the Reaction to Bereavement." *Social Science & Medicine*, 4 (1970): 187–99.

Parkes, Colin Murray. "Psycho-Social Transitions: A Field for Study." *Social Science & Medicine*, 5 (1971): 101–15.

Parkes, Colin Murray. "Psycho-Social Transitions: Comparison between Reactions to Loss of a Limb and Loss of a Spouse." *British Journal of Psychiatry*, 127 (1975): 204–10.

Parkes, Colin Murray. *Love and Loss: The Roots of Grief and Its Complications*. London: Routledge, 2006.

Parkes, Colin Murray. *The Price of Love: Selected Works of Colin Murray Parkes*. London: Routledge, 2016.

Parkes, Colin Murray, Pittu Laungani, and Bill Young, eds. *Death and Bereavement Across Cultures*. 2nd Edition. London: Routledge, 2015.

Schut, H.A.W., M. S. Stroebe, J. van den Bout, and J. de Keijser. "Intervention for the Bereaved: Gender Differences in the Efficacy of Two Counseling Programs." *British Journal of Clinical Psychology*, 36 (1997): 63–72.

Schut, H., M. S. Stroebe, J. van den Bout, and M. Terheggen. "The Efficacy of Bereavement Interventions: Determining Who Benefits." In *Handbook of Bereavement Research: Consequences, Coping and Care*. Edited by M. S. Stroebe, R. O. Hansson, W. Stroebe, and H. Schut. Washington, D.C.: American Psychological Association, 2001, pp. 705–37.

Stroebe, M. S., and H. Schut. "Models of Coping with Bereavement: A Review." In *Handbook of Bereavement Research: Consequences, Coping and Care*. Edited by M.S. Stroebe, R.O. Hansson, W. Stroebe, and H. Schut. Washington, D.C.: American Psychological Association, 2001, pp. 375–404.

8

Bereavement, Grief, and Mourning

John Cottingham

DIMENSIONS OF BEREAVEMENT

At the time of writing, it is too early to say just how devastating will be the damage done by the global pandemic that began at the end of 2019. Clearly nothing will be able to erase the loss of life, and the suffering of the relatives and friends of those lost. And there will be much human misery accruing from the economic catastrophe that the virus brings in its wake. But I want to start by referring to an aspect of the crisis that may at first seem minor by comparison with the horrors just mentioned, but whose implications turn out, I believe, to be of strong relevance to the idea of mourning. I refer to something experienced by very many people during the "lockdown" period when the virus first got a grip on the planet, namely the sense of disorientation and loss caused by the sudden enforced isolation from the company of other human beings.

Humans are by nature social animals. So being deprived of the company of friends and relatives, colleagues and neighbors, is a loss that cuts deeper than can be expressed in a simple utilitarian calculus. Not for nothing is isolation, solitary confinement, regarded as the most severe and most feared of the punishments that prison authorities have at their disposal. Not being allowed to mix with our fellow human beings for a prolonged period is not just unpleasant; it cuts at the roots of our nature, undercutting our sense of meaning, leaving us not living but merely existing.

Being deprived of association with others is a source of grief in itself, but it also carries with it the further grief at being deprived of all the enriching human activities that are predicated upon association with others. What is lost in isolation is not just ordinary social intercourse such as eating together or sharing a walk in the country, but more structured and organized social activities such as participating in choral singing, playing in an orchestra, taking part in a dramatic performance, playing a sport, engaging in philosophical discussion—the list is endless, though for any given individual there will probably be two or three such activities that are prized as especially enriching, and which serve to lift the spirits and give life meaning and point.

To be told that one will not be able to participate in any of these precious human activities for a protracted period is a kind of bereavement. This applies to everyone affected, but it may be worth adding that for those in the last decade or so of their lives, there is a special extra dimension of distress—there is grief at something taken away, and there is the additional sadness that the time remaining for such activities would in any case have been short, so that the opportunity for renewing them in the future is correspondingly diminished.

Is it pretentious to talk of the pain of loss in such cases as a bereavement, or as a cause for mourning? It is certainly the case that many people did indeed describe the enforced isolation during the pandemic as a kind of bereavement, and this accords with a long-standing use of the term to denote that state or condition which, in the words of one nineteenth-century writer, "in its essence is always the loss of some object accustomed to draw forth the soothing or cheering reactions of the soul."[1] Added to this, one effect of the isolation was to produce a kind of foretaste of the bereavements that await us all sooner or later, if we survive long enough. The human condition is such that the grim facts of aging and advancing bodily and mental decline are destined to deprive us, perhaps slowly and progressively, perhaps through sudden onset of disease, of the chance to engage fully in the social activities that are the bedrock of our happiness. And to these bereavements will, for many people, be added the ever-increasing risk of personal bereavement, the loss of a partner with whom one's life is shared, and through whose presence life's joys are enhanced and sorrows mitigated.

Being deprived of future happiness one might otherwise have hoped to enjoy is of course a grievous blow not just for the old but for all; and since the young, for whom the expected future is longer, have potentially more to lose in this respect, such deprivation can be reckoned to be all the worse. One might also suppose that a special kind of compensation for the loss of happiness is available to the old, namely they are likely, other things being equal, to have had a larger existing store of happy experiences they can look back on; so when disaster strikes and truncates happy activities, the mourning of old age will be alleviated by the memory of all the past happiness that is "in the bank," as it were. But fathoming the way human grief and loss are actually felt by human beings often defies such calculations. Yes, the old person facing loss should no doubt rationally be consoled by the past happiness they have been fortunate to enjoy, but this does not accord with the way grief for such loss is actually experienced. For in the real world, as Dante so vividly pointed out, the memory of past happiness only seems to exacerbate present misery:

> Nessun maggior dolore
> che ricordarsi del tempo felice
> nella miseria . . .
>
> No greater grief
> Than to remember happiness gone by
> In time of sorrow.[2]

Something fundamental is expressed here about the phenomenon of mourning. The grief of bereavement is not just a pang in response to something bad that has happened; it is a longing for something good that cannot be recovered. The Latin noun for longing, *desiderium*, often (like its ancient Greek counterpart πόθος [*pothos*]) used in connection with mourning, conveys this idea of a painful reaching out towards something that is out of reach, as in Horace's fierce lament for Quintilius, where the poet asks what restraint or limit there can be to this *desiderium*, this longing, this regret, this grief, for so dear a friend:

> Quis desiderio sit pudor aut modus
> Tam cari capitis?[3]

In existential terms, grief and mourning are emotions that are pregnant with our human finitude. *Alle Lust will Ewigkeit*, says Nietzsche[4]—we yearn for joy to continue; but when, brutally and against our will, it is brought to an end, we are confronted with the clash between our infinite longings and our inherently finite nature. This does not just hurt, but it produces a profound sense of disorientation. The ground on which we were standing crumbles from under us, and we seem to be sliding into an abyss of meaninglessness.

THE PERVASIVENESS OF GRIEF

Understanding the deeper existential nature of bereavement, grief, and mourning is complicated by the tendency, particularly prevalent among philosophers, to overintellectualize. We schematize grief as related to the loss of one or more goods that enrich our lives, and thus construe it in terms of a kind of calculus, where its degree is proportionate to what has been subtracted from the list of goods. But what such an account leaves out is the peculiar phenomenological character of grief. Clearly, it is an unpleasant feeling, something painful as opposed to pleasurable, a sorrowful as opposed to joyful sensation. And suitably qualified and elaborated, these ideas no doubt capture something of what is going on. But perhaps the most important aspect of the way grief is experienced, and the most damaging to our equilibrium, is its *pervasiveness*. Grief is like a held pedal note on the organ that continues to sound, pervasively affecting the way in which we hear whatever else is being played above on the keyboards. So, what might otherwise have been a brilliant and uplifting melody is now suffused with a sinister or melancholic undertone that radically alters the character of what is heard. The poet John Keats used another analogy, that of a sounding bell that "tolls me back to my sole self," bringing his imagination back down to the earth, even as it strives to lose itself in visions of far off lands where the nightingale's song is heard.[5] And even in the more mundane and prosaic settings of our everyday lives, something similar can occur: the pedal note of grief is the first sound heard in the morning as the sleeper, after a blessed forgetful instant of "normal" waking consciousness, swiftly recalls their situation: all is as bad as it was the night before; the loss remains. The droning pedal note resumes, and continues sounding throughout the day, infusing the felt quality of every activity and experience. One may strive to divert the mind, but the grief for what is lost constantly intrudes, sapping the concentration, dulling the motivation, souring even those pursuits that might otherwise have been a cause for joy. In that great poem of mourning, *In Memoriam*, Alfred Tennyson depicts this peculiar intrusiveness of grief when he describes the first Christmas after a bereavement, when the family has to go through normally joyful and bustling activities of putting up the Christmas decorations under a dark rain cloud that seems to "possess the earth," the gloomy sky outside mirroring the black cloud of grief that hangs permanently over them.[6]

The inner world of feeling and the outer world of nature do not always coincide in this way, but where they do not, the very dissonance can itself serve to exacerbate the grief. In the magnificent spring that England enjoyed in 2020, when the death toll from the virus was mounting daily, many reported that there seemed to be something uncanny or even sinister about the unusually rich profusion of blossom to be seen on every tree and hedgerow. A signal proof here of the power of grief to infuse our perceptions, almost as if the color and richness of the spring scene no longer lifted the spirits but lowered them. Instead of the exuberance of nature finding an echo in the joy of the human heart, nature now seemed to threaten, like the alien, proliferating presence of the virus, calling to mind Housman's anxious line "I, a stranger, and afraid, in a world I never made."[7] The benign, calm sense of being at home in the world, what Heidegger called *Zuhause-sein,* is an undramatic but vital ingredient of human happiness. The "uncanny" spring of 2020—the German word for uncanny, *unheimlich,* is particularly apt here—managed to be so disorienting partly because those very wonders of nature that normally, in the spring season, make us feel peculiarly at home in the world, now seemed to emphasize the sinister threat concealed beneath nature's exuberance and bounty.[8]

MOURNING THE HUMAN CONDITION

Grief and pain for what is lost often relates to something very specific, as in the case of the deprivations of isolation discussed above. But there may also be a case for thinking it is in some form or other an intrinsic part of the human condition. The human finitude and vulnerability of which we are always implicitly or explicitly aware may give rise to a generalized sense of loss that lies in waiting, ready to be mourned, an inchoate sadness beneath the surface that may bubble up at any moment. Gerard Manley Hopkins beautifully describes this in "Spring and Fall," a poem about what might at first seem a sentimentalized and fanciful case, that of a young girl seen weeping at the sight of the dead leaves falling in autumn:

> Margaret, are you grieving
> Over Goldengrove unleaving?
> Leaves like the things of man, you
> With your fresh thoughts care for, can you?

The initial feeling of the onlooker is almost one of surprise or bemusement that tears could be shed over trees losing their leaves. Perhaps indeed these are (to quote the opening of another poem, by Tennyson) "tears, idle tears"; or perhaps (as that poem goes on to imply) no tears are really "idle," but are rather signs whose meaning is not yet fully understood.[9] At all events, in the Hopkins poem, the pregnant phrase "leaves *like the things of man"* already proleptically hints that this young life will before long have more to grieve at than the annual falling of leaves. Soon enough, all too soon, the girl will not spare a sigh for any number of such sights, and yet the tears will come, for reasons that will be only too clear:

> Ah! as the heart grows older
> It will come to such sights colder
> By and by, nor spare a sigh
> Though worlds of wanwood leafmeal lie;
> And yet you will weep and know why.

The lines that now follow, in the final three couplets of the poem, gently address the child, taking away any earlier faint suggestion of bemusement that mere falling leaves could trigger tears, and acknowledging that her tears betoken something universal. The "springs of sorrow" in the human soul are shared by all, and so her grieving is recognized as having been called forth by something that could not be articulated in words, or intellectually expressed, but echoes of which were faintly heard by the heart, or guessed at deep within the soul:

> Now no matter, child, the name:
> Sorrow's springs are the same.
> Nor mouth had, no nor mind, expressed
> What heart heard of, ghost guessed:
> It is the blight man was born for,
> It is Margaret you mourn for.[10]

Notwithstanding the final line, it would trivialize the message of the poem to infer that Margaret's grief is selfish or autocentric. Yes, she mourns for herself, but as surrogate or representative of all humankind. Her seemingly idle tears at the decay of the woods are intimations of the "blight man was born for," the pain and loss that is inseparable from human existence. Hopkins's universalism here enables us to put into perspective the tendency we all have to say "poor me!"—to place special emphasis on the woes that beset us personally, or those of our immediate circle. So, without retracting the point made earlier, about the special force and poignancy that attaches to the griefs of the old, one may also acknowledge the vivid sharpness and intensity of grief felt in youth, and the peculiar anguish characteristic of the pains and disappointments of middle age. For clearly the truncating of worthwhile activities and the sudden elimination of sources of joy can happen at any age, and there is perhaps something distasteful about quantitative judgments as to which types of loss are more grievous. The "blight man was born for" does not discriminate, and the specter of grief and mourning (though some may be fortunate enough to escape it longer than others) hovers in the background for all of us.

MOURNING AND MEANING

Although there are many contexts in which the terms "grief" and "mourning" are virtually interchangeable, the concept of mourning has a more formal flavor than that of grief. Grief, as already suggested, is the pain that pervades our consciousness when we suffer serious loss, while mourning often denotes an enactment, a formalized ritual, or a liturgy owed to the one for whom we grieve. As with many spiritual practices, mourning has a potentially healing function: it is an attempt to find closure to grief, or at least to find a ritualized way of expressing it, so that it can contribute to some kind of understanding of what has happened, and perhaps, in due course, enable us to come to terms with it.

But can one mourn for oneself, as the last line of Hopkins's poem implies? Not clearly in the formalized sense in which one engages in the rituals of mourning in order to pay one's respects to the dead. But there may be an analogous kind of mourning for oneself, an act in which one explicitly acknowledges and confronts the pain of loss. Margaret, in Hopkins's poem does not do this, though the implied onlooker, the speaker of the poem, does it for her, acknowledging on her behalf the grief and loss that awaits her simply as a member of the human race. And in another beautiful poem of mourning, "At Castle Boterel" by Thomas Hardy, we find a remarkable fusion of mourning for another and mourning for oneself. With a keen sense of loss, the poet glimpses through the rain the vision of a "girlish form benighted," the lover with whom, many years ago, in "dry March weather" he once climbed the hill that is "now glistening wet":

> Primaeval hills front the road's steep border
> And much have they seen there, first and last,
> Of the transitory in Earth's long order;
> But what they recall in colour and cast
> Is—that we two passed.

The pervasiveness of grief hangs over the scene, and the narrator is all too aware that the one he loved, whom he walked and talked with on that distant March day, is now no more. The bitter truth is that she is gone—as a later line of the poem has it, "Time's unflinching rigour with mindless rote has ruled from sight the substance now"—and all that remains is the phantom figure of his imagination:

> I look back and see it now, shrinking, shrinking,
> I look back at it amid the rain
> For the very last time; for my sand is sinking,
> And I shall traverse old love's domain
> Never again.[11]

So, what is mourned is, yes, the grievous and irreparable loss of the loved one; but there is also an awareness of all else that inevitably passes, the endless roll call of the "transitory in Earth's long order"; and then finally, as the poem reaches its resonant and elegiac cadence, the rueful acknowledgment that this life too, the life of the poet who contemplates all this, is drawing towards its close. What is conveyed here with consummate skill is not just the fact of mortality, but the gap between longing and reality that is the essence of mourning. We see stretched out before us what might have been, what will perhaps be for others; but for this one protagonist, who knows that his sand is sinking, that old domain of love will be traversed "never again."

Hardy is mourning here: mourning his first love, but also mourning himself. Yet in the poem we perhaps see not just the expression of grief, but also a kind of closure, the kind of recognition and acknowledgment that has something in common with what the formalized rituals of mourning are designed to bring. What is expressed by the end of the poem is not just pain, and certainly not mere self-pity, but a kind of acceptance of finitude. The poet takes his own place amid the "transitory of Earth's long order," and will soon himself go the way of the loved one whom he is mourning.

None of this takes away the genuine sadness of the poem, but it does indicate that a kind of meaning has been achieved. Not a full meaning, not a full reconciliation: for there is still anger at the loss caused by "Time's unflinching rigour" with its "mindless rote." But at least the materials of suffering have been caught up and woven into a pattern, a pattern of loss and memory, of past revisited, and of a wider temporal flow of which the protagonist is now willing to acknowledge that he himself is a part.

It is one of the tasks of great art, whether in music or painting or poetry, to enact the kind of meaning that cannot always be found in life itself. So, for example, in the set of beautiful choral motets entitled *Songs of Farewell* by the composer Hubert Parry, we find music of mourning and consolation that has uplifted many listeners. Grief is there, but also a kind of serenity. And perhaps in our ritualized acts of mourning, which themselves so often draw on music and poetry not as mere embellishment but as an intrinsic and essential part of what is enacted, we seek after just such a sense of meaning, so that we can hold on to something of enduring value and significance in the midst of desolation.

Yet grief remains particularly hard to bear, and mourning finds it hard to achieve its goal of closure, in cases where the circumstances of our loss are such that their meaning stubbornly eludes us. So, to come back to the pandemic example with which we began, that sense of painful disorientation which so many felt was surely bound up with a sense of the *meaninglessness* of the disaster. Millions were cowering in their homes, deprived of the social intercourse that is the very signature of our humanity, yet for no grand reason or noble cause, but from mere fear—fear of something that had suddenly come upon them without warning, without meaning—not even an adversary like a tyrant whose malign purposes they could take pride in resisting, but a minute random strip of genetic coding, something not even alive in its own right, unraveling its devastation indiscriminately, blindly, and without plan or purpose.

Such kinds of bereavement are hard to mourn properly, hard to knit up into any sort of narrative that might offer the hope of reconciliation or closure. Of course, there were many such attempts among the commentators and pundits who hurried to point out the possible lessons to be learned, the connection between the spread of the infection and the global scale of our human exploitation of the planet. And to be sure, these analyses did and do highlight the risks and terrible costs of our greed and selfishness in treating the world as a set of commodities to be plundered for our short-term gratification. But one does not have to deny the importance of any of this in order to feel that such attempts to read off meaning from the disaster nevertheless left out something crucial. It seemed, if one may put it like this, as if they tried too hard to force the occurrence into a meaningful framework without acknowledging the extent of its brute contingency. The pandemic may have been an accident waiting to happen, but it was, for all that, an accident, something dependent, as with so many natural disasters, and so many of the tragedies of everyday life, on a long and complex chain of contingent circumstances, a small change in any one of which might have averted the ensuing horrors.

Though we like to imagine ourselves as in charge of our destinies, the human condition is such that a minute variation in any one of a thousand circumstances can at any time reveal our vulnerability. The ancient Greeks, as often, had a phrase for this: σμικρὰ ῥοπή [*smikra ropē*]—the tiny nudge of the balance that can tip the scales to tragedy.[12] How is it possible to come to terms with this? The sheer irrationality and contingency of it all threatens to swamp our natural human impulse to seek meaning and closure. Music and poetry, as just suggested, are among the most potent resources we have at our disposal for transmuting our grief into something of enduring value. But where the loss seems the result of blind irrational processes, the grief risks mutating into helpless sorrow and impotent pain.

MOURNING AND TRANSFORMATION

There are no simple answers here, since how far the arts may offer a healing role in assuaging human grief will depend on complexities of context that may vary from generation to generation. The sonorous consolations offered by Parry's *Songs of Farewell* (1916–18), or the resonant cadences of Laurence Binyon's famous poem "For the Fallen" (September 1914) have found echoes in many hearts, but to many others they now seem somehow overblown, too bound up with imperial justifications for warfare, and too tainted with dubious concepts of the "glory" of dying in battle. The search for meaning requires a certain keenness of gaze, and where that gaze is distorted by sentimentality, the attempt at closure may founder. Rather than trying to unravel these puzzles here, let me end by moving from the domain of art to that of religion, and looking at one scriptural example of the search for meaning in the midst of grief and loss.

I have in mind the famous story in Luke's gospel of the journey of two disciples who encounter a stranger on the road to Emmaus, following the disastrous events leading up to the Crucifixion.[13] Luke vividly depicts the emotional reaction of the disciples as the stranger asks them what they are discussing—first the sullen confusion, next the "burning" of the hearts as the scriptures are expounded so as to explain how the messiah was destined to suffer, then the warm impulse of offering hospitality to the stranger ("Stay with us, for the evening is come and the day is far spent"), and the final opening of their eyes at the breaking of the bread. As narrated by Luke, the transformation is partly an intellectual one, caused by the stranger's exposition of the scriptures, but the outcome also involves a profound emotional shift, or rather it hinges on that intricate interplay of the affective and the cognitive that is crucial to the possibility of moral and spiritual transformation.

For those who accept the message put forward by Luke, the remarkable change from despair to hope is to be understood in theological terms—terms which many in our present culture may reject. But the message is also partly to be understood in human terms. For there is a remarkable capacity in the human heart to bring joy out of sorrow, to find consolation in the midst of grief. And what is required for this purpose is not a clinical analysis of the facts, which may often provide little to console, but rather a determination to hold fast to the good in the midst of distress, and to open oneself, as the two disciples did in the story, to the possibility of change and renewal. The story opens with the deepest grief, grief at having lost what had been longed for. But it ends with the discovery of a wholly different perspective on what had happened, and a new resilience and empowerment.

However, one understands the narrative of tragedy and triumph at the climax of the Gospels, the grief and the deep mourning it engenders are an irreplaceable part of the story. And it cannot be otherwise, since our finite and vulnerable human lives cannot escape the ever-present risk of loss. What is more, the hope that emerges does not amount to an easy solution, or glib assurance that all will suddenly be well. But it is an affirmation of the power of the human mind to draw on resources that will find a way through grief to renewal. Sometimes in human life, to be sure, the loss or pain will be too heavy for such a way to be found.[14] Yet that is no reason not to cultivate, in so far as our weak natures allow, the virtues of resilience and hope. This, of course, is the goal of many traditional spiritual practices, though whether the power they seek can come from our own resources alone is a metaphysical question that cannot be adjudicated here. What is clear is that if mourning is not to collapse into depression and despair, we will need to be fortified with faith that it will have an end, or at least that its sharpest and most anguished aspects will in time somehow be assuaged. We will need to hold on to something like the thought expressed by the Psalmist, a thought not based on clinical assessment of the evidence, but on a deep conviction of the enduring power of goodness: "Heaviness may endure for a night, but joy cometh in the morning."[15]

NOTES

1. W. R. Alger, *The Solitudes of Nature and of Man* [1866], quoted in the *Oxford English Dictionary*, 2nd ed. (Oxford: Oxford University Press, 2004), s. v. "Bereavement."

2. Dante Alighieri, *La Divina Commedia* [c. 1310–14], *Inferno*, Canto V, 121–23; trans. J. C.

3. Quintus Horatius Flaccus, *Odes* [*Carmina*, 23 BC] I, 24.

4. Friedrich Nietzsche, *Thus Spake Zarathustra* [1883-5], Third Part, Second Dance Song, trans. by Alexander Tille (London: Dent, 1958), §59.

5. John Keats, "Ode to an Nightingale" [1819]: "Forlorn! the very word is like a bell /To toll me back from thee to my sole self!"

6. Alfred Tennyson, *In Memoriam A.H.H.* [1849], section 30.

7. A. E. Housman, "The Laws of God, the Laws of Man," in *Last Poems* (London: Richards Press, 1922), p. xii.

8. See Martin Heidegger's discussion of "uncanniness" or "unhomelikeness" (*Unheimlichkeit/ das Nicht-zuhause-sein*) in *Being and Time* [*Sein und Zeit*, 1927], trans. by Edward Robinson and John Macquarrie (Oxford: Blackwell, 1967), §40, pp. 188–90. It should be added that while for Heidegger the state of not being at home is the root of human anxiety, he is also wary of the "tranquillized familiarity" and "self assurance" of those who are too much at home, uncritically absorbed in ordinary life.

9. Tennyson, "Tears, idle tears," from *The Princess* [1847].

10. Gerard Manley Hopkins, "Spring and Fall" [1880].

11. Thomas Hardy, "At Castle Boterel" [1913].

12. Sophocles, *Oedipus Tyrannus* [c. 429 BC], line 961; cf. *Trachiniae* [c. 421 BC], line 82.

13. Luke 24:13–35.

14. See Eleonore Stump, *Wandering in Darkness* (Oxford: Oxford University Press, 2010), p. 480.

15. Psalm 30 (*Book of Common Prayer* translation).

BIBLIOGRAPHY

Heidegger, Martin. *Being and Time*. Translated by Edward Robinson and John Macquarrie. Oxford: Blackwell, 1967.

Housman, A. E. "The Laws of God, the Laws of Man." In *Last Poems*. London: Richards Press, 1922.

Nietzsche, Friedrich. *Thus Spake Zarathustra*. Translated by Alexander Tille. London: Dent, 1958.

Stump, Eleonore. *Wandering in Darkness*. Oxford: Oxford University Press, 2010.

9

✝

Mourning and the Second-Person Perspective

Mikołaj Sławkowski-Rode

The time of mourning is a time of coping with the effects of loss.[1] The "work of mourning," as it is sometimes called after Freud, is a process which is often hard, implying intense emotional and psychological strain, and one that can remain "unresolved."[2] But despite a clear sense that "a resolution" that will put an end to grief is what is desired, there is no consensus as to what exactly this resolution consists in. This is partly because the way loss affects us is idiosyncratic. This is how we may understand the great insight about the human condition, expressed by Tolstoy in the first line of *Anna Karenina*: that happiness brings people together and makes others intelligible to us, while unhappiness and pain make others opaque, and inaccessible, that joy is more easily shared than pain. Hence the interest of the book, which attempts to bring the unhappiness particular to Anna Karenina into focus. In line with Tolstoy's view, Freud believed that loss effects our withdrawal from the world, making the forming of new bonds and engaging in new projects difficult. However, unlike Tolstoy, Freud sought to offer an explanation of the experience of loss, which would show its effects to be treatable, in the same way as other psychological conditions he identified might be.

Freud psychologized the process of mourning, and, invoking the technical vocabulary he invented to describe the human psyche, argued that it is a condition in which the subject is inhibited by desires it can no longer fulfill. In his famous essay "Mourning and Melancholia," he claims that in this way the object of loss becomes a burden to the ego, and needs to be buried in the unconscious in order that the world can again become familiar and manageable.[3] Consequently, Freud considers the inability to overcome loss and finally lay its object to rest pathological.[4] Freud's speculative theory was given support by Erich Lindemann, who, inspired by Freud, conducted empirical studies of the physical symptoms of grief. Based on his research Lindemann created a taxonomy of the stages of grief, which coincided with Freud's descriptions, and was widely believed to confirm Freud's core claim: that "emancipation from emotional bondage to the deceased" was the goal of the work of mourning.[5]

This approach became dominant in the twentieth century and indeed continues to be the most influential. For example, the latest 2013 update to the Diagnostic and Statistical Manual of Mental Disorders (DSM-5) differs from its predecessors in that it no longer includes a provision which allowed symptoms that are typical of depressive disorders not to be diagnosed as pathological when they are linked to bereavement. This, in effect, makes lasting grief a condition that requires treatment, and medicalizes the "inability to move on."[6] To be sure, it is a legitimate concern that cases of depression requiring treatment might be overlooked due to their connection with the experience of significant loss and the ensuing grief. However, the fact that depression has many features in common with those experiences does not entail that they cannot be distinguished, even if they happen to be concurrent. In fact, conflating depression with the process of coping with loss may muddy the waters, making both the diagnosis and treatment of depression, as well as finding a resolution to mourning, more difficult.

One reason to take this view is that we may be skeptical as to whether an individual's psychological wellbeing, which is what the psychologist aims to achieve, is synonymous with what we expect from a resolution of the struggle with loss. In this chapter, I will suggest how we might understand one important aspect of experiencing and coping with loss which should be distinguished from any psychological condition which might require therapy. I will further argue that this aspect of the experience of loss can be a guide to reinterpreting the process of mourning, and its desired ends. The most fundamental difference between therapy and mourning in this sense is that the former is concerned with the individual who has suffered the loss, while the proper object of the latter is the person who has been lost. I will propose that the aspect of loss in question and the ends of mourning appendant on addressing it may be usefully analyzed by appeal to second-personal relatedness. I believe that this aspect of the experience of loss, and the way that it can be addressed, cannot be adequately represented simply in terms of the grieving individual's mental health. If this is right, then it follows that limiting the way we approach this experience to the grieving person's own psychology risks undermining at least some of the ends of mourning.

The idea that mourning is not about the person who suffers loss but rather the person lost is of course by no means new. Indeed, this might be considered the most widespread pre-theoretical assumption, which is endorsed in most religions and cultures where mourning is practiced. The dead, although lost to us in some respects, in these traditions often continue to play a relevant part in our lives as objects of piety, or sources of hope, and sometimes even as supernatural agents who are able to act in aid of the living. Against this background the approach introduced by Freud is a relatively new development. Freud's ambition was to demystify the inner world of human psychology in the way Darwin had done for human biology. This played no small part in why he saw the continued attachment and appeal to the dead expressed in the process of mourning as a potentially harmful delusion, which can prevent the mourner from accepting and engaging with the real world. One way in which we can understand the subsequent domination of Freud's approach is that it precipitated an association between the focus on individual psychology, and a rational treatment of the way we cope with loss, condemning everything else as necessarily falling short of that standard.[7]

Now, it is a platitude that it is easier to cope with difficulties if we see them as a common predicament that we share with others, and it is by shifting focus to the individual affected by loss that Freud provided a framework for a standardized approach to dealing with grief. The complex interpersonal dynamics underlying even the most meaningful relationships are, on this view, reduced to a psychological burden every individual must equally take on when in mourning. However, a resolution to grief that we hope mourning might bring must intuitively rely on acknowledging the aspects that are particular to the loss which causes it, at least as much as, if not more so than, the features it shares with the experiences of others. In what follows I will substantiate that intuition and show that the aspects peculiar to the loss are largely dependent on the person mourned and the way they shaped the relationship with the mourner, and not merely on the character of the mourner's attachment. In particular, I will claim that relationships with others change us in ways that we come to identify with, yet that are often difficult to preserve once we are deprived of the other's presence in our lives. I will suggest that these changes pertain to the way we stand to others and experience the world, and that the "work of mourning," if it is to bring resolution to grief, should involve an effort to reclaim, or at the very least come to terms with, the ways in which our own individuality has been formed by the lost person's presence.

This aspect of mourning is arguably emphasized by Kierkegaard. In an important section of *The Works of Love*, entitled "The Work of Love in Recollecting One Who Is Dead," he suggests that, contrary to Freud, the impossibility of fulfilling desires that are appendant on the other person's presence does not mandate letting go of our attachment, but on the contrary, calls on us to reaffirm it.[8] Indeed, it is only through the work of mourning that we express our love most fully and confirm its lasting nature and sincerity. This is precisely because, as Kierkegaard explains, mourning presupposes the impossibility of reciprocation and so, paradoxically, it is only then, after its object is gone, that our love for the other can manifest itself most purely, as it is finally released from the shadow cast by the expectation of one's own satisfaction. But Kierkegaard also believes, characteristically looking to the future to understand the past, that whether we succeed in reaffirming our relationship despite the other's death determines our own individual character. If we fail to uphold our commitment to those we have lost, we are exposed as emotionally and spiritually deficient, and incapable of genuine love in the first place. Thus, our own integrity depends, according to Kierkegaard, on our ability to keep the object of our affection alive through our love towards it.

Kierkegaard was of course himself a melancholiac, who suffered from depression and anxiety.[9] Yet, this does not mean that we should dismiss his view. For it is possible that there are more important goods at stake than psychological wellbeing when we are faced with loss, and that a healthy relationship to those we have lost must involve a degree of pain which we learn to live with rather than shirk. The key question here is how ought we to understand our dependence on the other person such that the effort required to maintain our emotional attachment in the process of mourning is also an effort to maintain our individual integrity? How can we be so dependent on others that their loss could diminish our ability to meaningfully engage with the world, and not because we remain burdened by our attachment, but because we find it hard to hold on to it?

The shock of loss and the ensuing grief can expose the degree to which we are not self-sufficient. This fact is perhaps one reason why philosophers have typically considered too open an acknowledgment of these experiences to be a sign of weakness and lack of control.[10] This might also be another reason why Freud's approach was so readily endorsed—not only because of its claim to rationality, but also on account of its seeming vindication of earlier criticisms of traditional expressions of grief—and which has allowed philosophers to leave the subject to psychologists with a clear conscience. However, recent contributions to the discussion have increasingly challenged this prevailing view, emphasizing various negative consequences that may be entailed by "moving on" too quickly or distancing oneself too much from the lost object of affection. Instead, these new positions advocate different versions of living with the effects of loss or maintaining bonds with the deceased.[11] In what follows I will look at some of the more important and developed of these positions, highlighting the main arguments in their favor. I will then propose my own analysis of the experience of loss, and the role of mourning in working through grief, which builds on these views. I will argue, however, that these positions, in different ways, do not go far enough in moving beyond the individual psychology of the mourner to acknowledge the role that the person being mourned has in the process.

In his recent book Michael Cholbi persuasively defends the idea that loss, grief, and how we respond to them raise important philosophical questions, which cannot be fully addressed by other disciplines.[12] Moreover, he argues that these questions are unavoidable because loss and the need to respond to it are not merely symptoms of something having gone wrong in our lives but rather hallmarks of the human predicament as such.[13] We cannot avoid thinking about grief without failing to fully appreciate important aspects of our identity as human individuals. Cholbi proposes an interpretation of grief which emphasizes this view and suggests that we may have a duty not to turn away from grief. He appeals to Christine Korsgaard's notion of "practical identity," understood as consisting in the descriptions under which we value ourselves, and which provide us with reasons for action.[14] Cholbi argues that loss diminishes our sense of identity as we invest our practical identities in others, and when they die, the "patterns of, and possibilities for, our relating to them" are profoundly altered.[15] We face a dual challenge when we lose someone we are invested in: we must retrospectively take stock of the significance of the relationship before the person we were invested in died, but we must also look prospectively at how this relationship will fit into our future life.[16] In other words, we are forced to reexamine how we understand our practical identity historically, as well as redescribe the values constitutive of our identity when engaging in future projects.[17] This in some cases might turn out to be impossible or even incoherent.[18]

Nonetheless, Cholbi, like Kierkegaard, believes that letting go of our attachment in the face of loss is a kind of moral failure.[19] He puts forward a case for thinking that, in fact, we have a duty not to avoid the pain which is caused by the absence of the deceased.[20] Indeed, he argues that the duty implies being "invested in grief." The investment should be understood as bearing the pain entailed by grief, as a necessary cost of being committed to a good that is the purpose of grief.[21] That purpose, Cholbi maintains, is self-knowledge.[22] Since our practical identity is invested in the deceased, and their loss causes a disruption to that identity, grief is a "species of sustained emotional attention to one's relationship" with them.[23] The goal of grief, and the good that investing oneself in it can yield, is the reconstitution of, or even the increase in, self-knowledge, which is a prerequisite for moral development, or more general self-improvement.[24]

Now, Cholbi certainly offers a compelling picture of how the work of mourning might involve the continuation of bonds with the deceased, without becoming a form of stagnant brooding, but rather developing towards a resolution of grief. He also succeeds in illuminating the depth of the disruption of the familiar self and world occasioned by loss, and the importance of allowing oneself to grieve in response. However, ultimately, Cholbi's proposal does not fully exclude the undesirable aspects of the Freudian framework identified above. It is true that his suggestion is that there might be value in holding on to our attachment to the deceased, which is what Freud denies. However, this seems to be a difference in means only, since in both cases the goal of facing grief remains the same: the improvement of the mourner's individual predicament. Cholbi acknowledges this when he describes grief as essentially "egocentric" and "self-focused."[25] In fact, for Cholbi, it is when the self-focus is not being actualized that grief may become a sickness which jeopardizes the mourner's wellbeing, which echoes Freud's understanding of mourning as, in effect, self-rescue from the uncanny pull of death.[26] In both cases a putative psychological benefit is the goal of mourning, which, when achieved, brings resolution to the struggle with grief.

My view here is that whatever the previously unacknowledged benefits of mourning may be to the bereaved, these do not exhaust its meaning. To limit our understanding of mourning to these benefits is to overlook the value of continuing the relationship with those whom we have lost in a way that mourning can make possible. Even if Cholbi is right about the way our identities are invested in others, and the need to reconstitute them after we suffer loss (and I believe that this is largely on the right tracks), this still leaves the need to address the dead themselves unsatisfied. Answering to that need, conversely, might still be possible if a successful reconstruction of our practical identity proves impossible. In some cases, it might even be necessary, temporarily or indefinitely, to choose between adequately addressing the dead, and a satisfactory reconstruction of our practical identity. It seems, additionally, that there is no reason to suppose that the self-knowledge Cholbi claims is the goal of mourning could not be acquired without the particular loss that happens to occasion it. As Cholbi represents it, there is nothing that is specifically relevant to the person we have lost in the way we grieve, as it is essentially our own investment in the deceased, or our own capacity to value ourselves and assent to reasons for action, which we aspire to reclaim, or reinterpret, when working through loss. On the contrary, it seems to me that if we are to address the dead in how we approach the work of mourning, it is also by acknowledging and understanding how they were invested in us, and not merely how we were invested in them.

Such mutual investment, which Kierkegaard sees in love, can also be understood in terms of what Thomas Fuchs calls the "expansion and mutual overlap of selves."[27] In an important paper on the phenomenology of grief, Fuchs argues that the most essential presupposition of grief is the mutual interdependence of selfhood and otherness: the fact that human beings are "fundamentally related to and in need of others, that indeed our self is permeable and open to them."[28] Fuchs describes this openness after Arthur and Elaine Aron's account of the psychology of close relationships wherein we observe an "inclusion of other in the self."[29] On this view, the inclusion of other in the self consists in an identification with the other on the one hand, and a "self-expansion" on the other. The former involves assuming the other's characteristics or ways of relating to the world as one's own, while the latter is comprised of an opening up of potentialities that one would otherwise not have.[30] Thus, Fuchs argues, a loss which ends a relationship that has these features is experienced both as an absence we feel in how we relate to the world and as a contraction of the self. Simultaneously, however, we remain aware of the foreign elements in our experience of both the world and our subjective selves and associate these with the other's presence. Hence the "ambiguous" nature of grief which involves a dynamic between the experience of the absence of the person we have lost, but also their continued presence in the way we apprehend the world and ourselves. Fuchs calls these two aspects of grief the "de-presentifying" and "presentifying" intentions, and he suggests that they constantly compete for dominance in the experiential field.[31]

Fuchs proposes that the work of mourning proceeds by an effort to end this oscillation, which is a source of confusion and pain, and readjust oneself to the new situation. This resolution of grief requires a fundamental reorganization of both one's identity and the ways in which one relates to the world. However, as Fuchs suggests, it also offers an opportunity to gain a new relation to the deceased, which overcomes the ambiguity of grief in two complementary ways: by identification and representation.[32] The first transformation implies seeing the lost person, or certain elements of their personality and behavior, as part of ourselves. This might mean noticing, for example, certain mannerisms of a deceased parent in how we comport ourselves. Assuming certain traits of the lost person maintains their presence in how we perceive ourselves, but in a way that is reintegrated with our identity, rather than forcing a split in it. The second transformation pertains to the way we relate to the world and implies recollection and symbolization as ways of acknowledging the loss, which are at the same time commemorative, for example by associating places or events with the deceased person in a way that both emphasizes our connection with them and their absence from the world. Like Cholbi,

Fuchs believes the first aspect of grief's resolution may lead to personal development and growth. The second has a wider cultural significance as a way in which human communities develop a deeper self-understanding and maintain continuity across generations.[33]

One advantage of Fuchs's account is that it is sensitive to the need to address the dead themselves in the process of working through grief. It seems clear that the kind of resolution the mourner seeks, on this view, depends as much on an effort to understand ourselves as it does on an effort to understand the dead, and consequently, if successful, leads to both greater knowledge of ourselves and of those we have lost. While in Cholbi, as in Freud, grief is a matter of individual psychology, Fuchs makes a case for understanding grief as a form of maintaining a relationship with the deceased insofar as they continue to play an important role in how we develop our identity and relationship with the world. This approach has the non-negligible benefit of supplying a rationale for traditional, pre-theoretical approaches to loss. Indeed, Fuchs's suggestion that the way the relationship we have with the dead is maintained, both individually and by the community, is significant for the development of the whole culture has a considerable degree of intuitive plausibility. It seems that if continuity of interpersonal dependence is relevant for individual relationships, then it will also have importance for establishing and maintaining group identity where symbolic representation connects past generations to the meanings and values constitutive of the present, and promises the endurance of these values into the future. This is what Robert Hertz had in mind when he claimed that by "establishing a society for the dead, the society of the living regularly recreates itself."[34]

The account of the overlap between the self and other, which Fuchs takes to be a precondition for understanding the effects of loss in the way he proposes, is less convincing, however. The social psychology research on which Fuchs relies to establish the key aspects of the mutual interdependence of the mourner and the person they have lost seems unable to support such far-reaching conclusions. The experiments conducted by Arthur and Elaine Aron do suggest that we have a tendency to share resources with those we know rather than strangers (even when self-interest and anticipation of reciprocity are controlled for), that we are more responsive to images of those we are in a close relationship with than to those of strangers (even when they are well-known celebrities), and that we are more attentive to traits of character that we are familiar with in those close to us than if we attribute such traits to strangers (even when they are well-known celebrities).[35] Now, the conclusion that the Arons draw from these results, and which Fuchs accepts, is that, on some fundamental level, we *confuse* or *identify* those we are close to with ourselves (in terms of interest in acquiring resources, self-recognition, and familiarity with character). As appealing as Fuchs's theory might be, and regardless of what interpretative power it may have in relation to the experience of loss and grief, it is not sustained by the evidence upon which it purports to rely. On the contrary it seems that the results of the relevant experiments can be easily explained in terms of motivations which do not derive from 'confusion' or 'identification' with others in the deep sense being suggested, but simply reflect the individual's own psychological traits.

Additionally, the account of the self–other overlap proposed by Fuchs and the Arons seems to entirely bypass the question of why, if our sense of self were so fundamentally dependent on the other, it does not just feel that way. If our identity and sense of self were so deeply connected to the other person, how could the problem of solipsism ever arise? Would the other's presence not amount to an indubitable datum available to us simply by introspection? It seems, rather, that part of the severity of loss is due to a sense that the other always remains out of reach, and that death shrouds the hope that we harbor towards the living of ever reaching across the gap that divides us from them. This struggle to encounter the other person as subject is something that Sartre captures particularly well when he discusses the dynamic between the self and other. The fundamental obstacle for encountering others, and the source of the problem of other minds, according to Sartre, is the fact that the other as a subject is a negation of me.[36] This makes the distance between the self and other absolute as there is no possible internal relation that can exist between a subjective sense of self and its negation.[37] What Sartre means here is that subjectivity, or the sense of self, is perspectival and so it is not an object we can encounter in the world but a view onto it. As such, one perspective we take cancels out other possible perspectives as we cannot simultaneously occupy more than one vantage point. If this is right, and I believe that it is, then the claim that one confuses or identifies the other with oneself is best understood figuratively and not literally: it is a suggestive metaphorical expression for a set of habitual responses to our environment which are conditioned by, or predicated on, a familiarity, and proclivity to associate, with those close to us.

Nonetheless, this is arguably already quite a lot to go on when considering the effects of loss. If the death of another is experienced as a disruption in the way we habitually respond to our environment, then any meaningful form of addressing this disruption has to take into account the nature of the relationship, which shaped these responses rather than merely focus on individual psychology as Freud advises. This does not, however, furnish a justification or explanation for why holding on to that relationship might be desirable. After all, if our habits cease to be a reliable guide for navigating reality, we are well advised to change them. Fuchs's conclusion concerning the resolution of grief, or, in his terms, the overcoming of its ambiguous structure, however, is not inconsistent with letting go of our attachments, and involves continuing the relationship with the deceased in nothing more than a symbolic sense. In fact, Fuchs himself describes the process of "re-establishing" the relationship with the deceased as "losing them a second time," and containing our sense of absence through recollection, and commemoration.[38] It seems that despite appearances, Fuchs's theory does not give us a satisfactory account of what maintaining a relationship with the dead might consist in. Again, as with Cholbi's account, this approach points to important aspects of the experience of grief and gives a compelling picture of what a resolution of grief may involve. Yet, the picture seems incomplete.

The death of someone in whom we are invested, in the way Cholbi describes, or to whose influence we are permeable as Fuchs has it, raises the question of the nature of loss in a special way. This is because, on a fundamental level, we do not really know what it is we have lost. Of course, we lose many tangible things like future plans we shared with the deceased, their companionship, intimacy, support, advice, or even criticism which in turn is enhanced by the knowledge they might have had of us. None of these things may be retained when we lose the other person. But at the same time, we resist the conclusion that their presence is fully reducible to these things. After all, we might grieve the loss of someone whose presence does not benefit us in those ways, for example someone who lives far away and with whom we seldom have contact. There is a, perhaps, less tangible sense in which we discern the other's presence as something that we are vulnerable to lose in a way that is different from how we might lose the things we value in our relationship with them. This sense of the other's presence is connected to their being a self, or a subjective center of consciousness, just as we are, and so it is connected to the problem of solipsism signaled above. In order to answer the question about what we lose when we lose the other person as a subjective center of consciousness, we have to address the question of what it means for another person to be present to us as a subjective center of consciousness. For this reason, I believe that loss and the way we relate to the dead may give us a new angle on the problem of other minds. In the final part of this chapter, I will look at what I take to be the most promising recent proposal in conceptualizing loss, grief, and the ends of mourning which bears on this issue.

Matthew Ratcliffe has produced some of the most interesting recent work on loss and grief relating these experiences to the growing literature on second-person relatedness.[39] Ratcliffe considers the way our identity and practically meaningful ways of engaging with the world are affected by loss to be a very important aspect of grief, which suggests that it is not a self-centered process. He believes, however, that this aspect of the experience does not exhaust the "interpersonal phenomenology of grief."[40] The other person, Ratcliffe argues, is not just experienced as present within the world where we encounter them; they also constitute an intelligibility condition for that world.[41] Ratcliffe models the sense in which the other may be an intelligibility condition of the world we experience after Merleau-Ponty's notion of personal "style," and how one may be affected by it.[42] This consists, according to Ratcliffe, in having the possibilities of engaging with the world open to me being somehow altered by the encounter with another.[43] The "style" of another person is the temporally unfolding pattern of possibilities of engaging with and experiencing the world, which the other person instantiates. In "genuine" encounters with others, we are confronted with the style of the other person in such a way that it influences and shapes the ways in which it is possible for us to experience and engage with the world, in effect expanding it. With close relationships, Ratcliffe suggests, the integrity and intelligibility of one's world may come to depend on the relationship with another.[44]

Thus, the death of a person we are related to in this way entails not only the loss of an object in the world (even an object around which much of our world has been organized), but the ability to relate to the world as such. This may include the ability to relate to ourselves too, as part of the experience of the world to which we become open when we become open to the other's experience is the experience of ourselves as experienced by the other. C. S. Lewis records and evocatively expresses both of these aspects of the experience of loss in his famous account of grieving after the death of Joy Davidman, his wife. He describes grief as having a non-local and a local aspect: the first of these is more pervasive and all embracing; Lewis compares it to an "invisible blanket" separating him from the world.[45] Then in a famous passage he expands on this with the statement, "The act of living is different all through. Her absence is like the sky, spread over everything."[46] Of the other aspect he says: "there is one place where her absence comes locally home to me, and it is a place I can't avoid. I mean my own body. It had such a different importance while it was the body of H.'s lover. Now it's like an empty house."[47] Most revealingly Lewis adds to this: "but don't let me deceive myself. This body would become important to me again, and pretty quickly, if I thought there was anything wrong with it."[48] It is as though Lewis is unable to see himself as a subject in the way he was seen by Joy. It is as though he is only able to apprehend himself as a mere "darkness crammed with organs," which Merleau-Ponty claims is what the other would be reduced to were it not for the fact that we see the other person as a locus of experience.[49]

The loss of the intelligibility and integrity of the experienced world, on Ratcliffe's view, is crucially not merely due to one's own inability to relate to it in the usual ways, but also to the inability of the other to do so. This aspect of the experience of loss is a form of continued second-person relatedness to the deceased. It is, as Ratcliffe puts it, a "kind of participation" in the death of another that encompasses their inability to continue to participate in and shape the shared world, including the bereaved person's place in it.[50] Ratcliffe suggests that it is this breakdown of the phenomenological structure which loss implies that makes our response to loss, and what it means for grief to reach a resolution, philosophically interesting.[51] On this view, grief is not merely something that follows the recognition of loss; it is partly constitutive of that recognition.[52] In other words, the experience of loss and the ensuing grief can tell us something about the nature of our relationships with others—something that is perhaps uniquely discernible in those circumstances. This is certainly in line with Kierkegaard's claim that our response to the death of another is the ultimate test of the nature of our relationship with them. If our response to loss is self-centered, this would suggest that our relationship to the other while they were alive was also self-centered—even if our world was organized around their presence. It was self-centered because even if the meanings and values around which we organized our lives were dependent on our relationship with the other person, both these meanings and values, and the relationship with the other person, were apprehended solely from our own perspective to the exclusion of the other's perspective.

The question that arises here is whether our world is not in fact irredeemably self-centered in this way. A natural response is to point out that just as we cannot partake in the other person's sense of subjective self, so too we cannot see the world as it appears to them. In both cases, we might say, this is because a perspective, a view onto the world, is itself self-centered in the sense that whatever the objects of subjective experience may be, they necessarily are "out there" as objects of my experience, or no matter how they appear, they necessarily appear to me. In a way, this is obviously true. This is just what it means to be a subject of experience—to apprehend the world from a self-centered vantage point. However, there is, I believe, a way to put pressure on this point. Many philosophers have argued that interactions with others can have a transformative effect on the set of possibilities of experience we have.[53] In a manner relevant to the present discussion, Sartre construes this in terms of losing one's world to the other. We may cease to experience the world in terms of the possibilities open to us, and instead assume the role of an object in the other person's world.[54] Ratcliffe appeals to the idea of empathy as a way of "expanding the range of intelligible experiences" open to the subject.[55] He develops the approach proposed by Edith Stein in her doctoral thesis *On the Problem of Empathy*.[56] Stein believes that "the subject of the empathized experience . . . is not the subject empathizing, but another. And this is what is fundamentally new in contrast with the memory, expectation, or the fancy of our own experiences."[57] Ratcliffe takes this to imply that empathy includes the recognition of the other person as a locus of experience and agency.[58] If this is right, then not only does this give a new meaning to what we lose when we lose another person, but it also suggests, as I have indicated above, that the experience of loss can give us a new way to approach and challenge solipsism.

I believe that Ratcliffe's approach has a great deal of intuitive plausibility. At least some instances of grief do seem to reveal how our own experience of the world depends on the person lost, as for example in the case of Lewis. If so, then it seems that understanding the nature of the loss will require employing a richer account of interpersonal relatedness than the one implied by Freudian psychology. This does not mean that individual psychological wellbeing should be dismissed as irrelevant when we are thinking of the desired ends of grief. It is simply that aiming for psychological wellbeing addresses only one aspect of what the experience of loss might consist in. The same goes for the personal moral growth stressed by Cholbi, and the symbolic commemoration described by Fuchs. Both ways of conceptualizing the nature of loss, and coping with its effects, seem to pick out salient features of the experience. These accounts also offer something that is largely missing from Ratcliffe's: an idea of what the resolution to grief, and so the purpose of mourning, might be.

I will end by briefly sketching a suggestion that I have developed and argued for elsewhere.[59] If we accept the idea that our experience of the world is in a meaningful sense expanded for us by apprehending it as the object of the other's experience, and that we might be vulnerable to the loss of the ways of relating to the world that have been opened up to us in this manner when the other person dies, then the goal of mourning may be construed as the effort of holding on to or reconstituting this experience. If a relationship with another person may have the consequence of our coming to share some of the ways in which they experience the world, we could see ourselves as custodians of that form of experience, and the meanings and values it makes pellucid in the world. It might be difficult to hold on to the way we saw the other experience and relate to the world (including ourselves), but surely if anything of the other's presence can be retained in our own experience, it is precisely this. I believe this investment in keeping the other alive, as Kierkegaard would say, is closer in spirit to Stein's account of empathy than Fuchs's account of identification discussed above. This is because, for Fuchs, the identification with the deceased relies ultimately on seeing given traits and behaviors we associate with them as ours, whereas Stein understands empathy as, conversely, having experiences which we identify as those of the other person. On the other hand, the connection which Fuchs makes between grief and the development of culture is even more pertinent on the present view. If the community preserves the ways of experiencing the world in the same manner as individuals who mourn their dead do, then culture consists in a cumulative expansion of possibilities of experiencing and relating to the world. In that case, the melancholic attitude of Kierkegaard was not just sentimental naval-gazing, or a sign of an unbalanced psyche, but an expression of a deep investment in the human spirit. Conversely, Freud would seem here to have thrown the baby out with the bathwater, for what would we be left with were it not for all the attachments that can no longer be fulfilled?

NOTES

1. This research was supported by the University of Oxford project 'New Horizons for Science and Religion in Central and Eastern Europe funded by the John Templeton Foundation. The opinions expressed in the publication are those of the author and do not necessarily reflect the view of the John Templeton Foundation.

2. The problem of the badness of loss can be seen as paralleling the more widely discussed problem of the badness of death. Classic treatments of this problem range from Epicurus's denial that death is bad to Samuel Johnson's view discussed by Jerry Valberg in Chapter 1 of the present volume. For a recent discussion of this problem in the context of indefinite extension of life, see Ralph Weir, "Transhumanist Immortality Is Neither Probable or Desirable," in Daniel Came and Stephen Burwood, eds., *Transhumanism and Immortality*, Trivent Publishing 2023.

3. Sigmund Freud, "Mourning and Melancholia," in *The Standard Edition of the Complete Psychological Works of Sigmund Freud*, Vol. 14, ed. James Strachey (London: Hogarth Press, 1963), pp. 237–60.

4. Freud is himself careful to distinguish the condition he identifies as "melancholia" from "regular mourning," which he accepts does not require medical treatment, but rather its effects are expected to be overcome within a certain period of time. However, being structurally the same, the only real difference he sees between both conditions is that by "reality checking," the mourning person comes to accept the absence and inaccessibility of what has been lost on their own accord, and "willingly abandons" their attachment, which can no longer be fulfilled. See Freud, "Mourning and Melancholia."

5. Erich Lindemann, "Symptomatology and Management of Grief," *American Journal of Psychiatry* 151, suppl. 6 (1994): 141–49.

6. In DSM-4 (1994) a period of two months was considered the period where a severe reaction to loss should be considered part of healthy grief, and a diagnosis of depression deemed not possible due to the potential overlap. DSM-5 considers the severity of the symptoms to be sufficient for diagnosis with no provision for the time since the loss occurred.

7. This is true even of the attempts to rehabilitate mourning practices which rely on maintaining some sort of relationship with the dead, where many authors propose that a more nuanced and holistic approach to working through loss may need to involve going beyond the rational, and including séances, dreams, premonitions, and various "signs." For a recent study and defense of such approaches, see Vinciane Despret, *Au bonheur des morts: Récits de ceux qui restent* (Paris: La découverte, 2015).

8. Søren Kierkegaard, "The Work of Love in Recollecting One Who Is Dead," in *The Works of Love*, ed. and trans. Howard V. Hong and Edna H. Hong (Princeton: Princeton University Press, 1988), pp. 345–59.

9. See for example *Kierkegaard's Journals and Notebooks, Volume 5: Journals*, ed. and trans. Niels Jørgen Cappelørn, Alastair Hannay, David Kangas, Bruce H. Kirmmse, George Pattison, Joel D. S. Rasmussen, Vanessa Rumble, and K. Brian Söderquist (Princeton: Princeton University Press, 2013), p. 47: NB6, 65 (July to August 1848); p. 184: NB8, 76 (December 1848); p. 321: NB10, 105 (February to April 1849).

10. In the introduction to his recent *Grief: A Philosophical Guide*, Michael Cholbi offers a good survey of the most influential positions expressing this sentiment and shows how it remains influential even today. See Michael Cholbi, *Grief: A Philosophical Guide* (Princeton: Princeton University Press, 2021), pp. 1–20.

11. See for example: Dennis Klass, Phyllis R. Silverman, and Steven L. Nickman, eds., *Continuing Bonds: New Understandings of Grief* (London: Routledge, 1996); Dennis Klass and Edith Maria Steffen, eds., *Continuing Bonds in Bereavement: New Directions for Research and Practice* (London: Routledge, 2018); Edith Maria Steffen and Adrian Coyle, "Sense of Presence Experiences and Meaning-Making in Bereavement: A Qualitative Analysis," *Death Studies* 35 (2011): 579–609.

12. Cholbi, *Grief*, pp. 11–13.
13. See especially ibid., pp. 10–12.
14. Ibid., pp. 30–31.
15. Ibid., pp. 79–80.
16. Ibid., p. 80.
17. Ibid., p. 158.
18. Ibid., p. 30.
19. Ibid., pp. 155–58.
20. Ibid., Chap. 6.
21. Ibid., p. 114.
22. Ibid., p. 83, p. 157.
23. Ibid., pp. 83–85, also Chap. 2.
24. Ibid., pp. 99–100.
25. Ibid., pp. 92–93.
26. Ibid., pp. 28–33, pp. 109–13, pp. 172–73.
27. Thomas Fuchs, "Presence in Absence: The Ambiguous Phenomenology of Grief," *Phenomenology and the Cognitive Sciences* 17 (2018): 43–63 (p. 49).
28. Ibid., p. 48.
29. Arthur Aron, Elaine N. Aron, et al., "Close Relationships as Including Other in the Self," *Journal of Personality and Social Psychology* 20 (1991): 241–53.
30. Fuchs, "Presence in Absence," p. 49.

31. Ibid., pp. 51–54.
32. Ibid., pp. 57–59.
33. Ibid., pp. 59–60.
34. Robert Hertz, *Death and the Right Hand*, trans. Rodney Needham and Claudia Needham (London: Cohen and West, 1960), p. 72.
35. Aron, Aron, et al., "Close Relationships."
36. Jean-Paul Sartre, *Being and Nothingness*, trans. Sarah Richmond (New York: Washington Square Press, 2021), Part III, Chap. 1.2.
37. Ibid.
38. Fuchs, "Presence in Absence," p. 60.
39. See especially, Matthew Ratcliffe, "The Phenomenological Clarification of Grief and Its Relevance for Psychiatry," in *Oxford Handbook of Phenomenological Psychopathology*, ed. Giovanni Stanghellini et al. (Oxford: Oxford University Press, 2019), pp. 538–51; Matthew Ratcliffe, "Grief and Phantom Limbs: A Phenomenological Comparison," *New Yearbook for Phenomenology and Phenomenological Philosophy* 17 (2019): 77–96; Matthew Ratcliffe, "Relating to the Dead: Social Cognition and the Phenomenology of Grief," in *Phenomenology of Sociality*, ed. Thomas Szanto and Dermot Moran (London: Routledge, 2015), pp. 202–16; Matthew Ratcliffe, "Towards a Phenomenology of Grief: Insights from Merleau–Ponty," *European Journal of Philosophy* 28 (2020): 657–69.
40. Ratcliffe, "Towards a Phenomenology of Grief," p. 663.
41. Ibid., p. 660, see also Ratcliffe, "Relating to the Dead," p. 206.
42. Ratcliffe, "Towards a Phenomenology of Grief," pp. 663–65.
43. Ibid.
44. Ibid.
45. C. S. Lewis, *A Grief Observed* (New York: Harper One, 1994), p. 3.
46. Ibid., p. 11.
47. Ibid., pp. 11–12.
48. Ibid., p. 12.
49. Maurice Merleau-Ponty, *The Prose of the World*, trans. John O'Neill (Evanston, IL: Northwestern University Press, 1973), pp. 133–34.
50. Ratcliffe, "Relating to the Dead," pp. 209–12.
51. Ratcliffe, "Towards a Phenomenology of Grief," p. 661.
52. Ratcliffe, "Relating to the Dead," p. 205.
53. See, for example, Maurice Merleau-Ponty, *Phenomenology of Perception*, trans. Colin Smith (London: Routledge, 1962); Emmanuel Levinas, *Totality and Infinity: An Essay on Exteriority*, trans. Alphonso Lingis (Pittsburgh: Duquesne University Press, 1969).
54. Sartre, *Being and Nothingness*.
55. Matthew Ratcliffe, "Phenomenology as a Form of Empathy," *Inquiry* 55 (2012): 473–95 (p. 474).
56. Edith Stein, *On the Problem of Empathy*, trans. Waltraut Stein (The Hague: Martinus Nijhoff, 1964).
57. Ibid., p. 11.
58. Ratcliffe, "Phenomenology as a Form of Empathy," p. 476.
59. Mikołaj Sławkowski-Rode, "The World Shared," forthcoming.

BIBLIOGRAPHY

Aron, Arthur, Elaine N. Aron, Michael Tudor, and Greg Nelson. "Close Relationships as Including Other in the Self." *Journal of Personality and Social Psychology* 20 (1991): 241–53.

Cholbi, Michael. *Grief: A Philosophical Guide*. Princeton: Princeton University Press, 2021.

Despret, Vinciane. *Au bonheur des morts: Récits de ceux qui restent*. Paris: La découverte, 2015.

Freud, Sigmund. "Mourning and Melancholia." In *The Standard Edition of the Complete Psychological Works of Sigmund Freud*, Volume 14. Edited by James Strachey, 237–60. London: Hogarth Press, 1963.

Fuchs, Thomas. "Presence in Absence: The Ambiguous Phenomenology of Grief." *Phenomenology and the Cognitive Sciences* 17 (2018): 43–63.

Hertz, Robert. *Death and the Right Hand*. Translated by Rodney Needham and Claudia Needham. London: Cohen and West, 1960.

Kierkegaard, Søren. "The Work of Love in Recollecting One Who Is Dead." In *The Works of Love*. Edited and translated by Howard V. Hong and Edna H. Hong, 345–59. Princeton: Princeton University Press, 1988.

Kierkegaard, Søren. *Kierkegaard's Journals and Notebooks, Volume 5: Journals*. Edited and translated by Niels Jørgen Cappelørn, Alastair Hannay, David Kangas, Bruce H. Kirmmse, George Pattison, Joel D. S. Rasmussen, Vanessa Rumble, and K. Brian Söderquist. Princeton: Princeton University Press, 2013.

Klass, Dennis, Phyllis R. Silverman, and Steven L. Nickman, eds. *Continuing Bonds: New Understandings of Grief*. London: Routledge, 1996.

Klass, Dennis, and Edith Maria Steffen, eds. *Continuing Bonds in Bereavement: New Directions for Research and Practice*. London: Routledge, 2018.

Levinas, Emmanuel. *Totality and Infinity: An Essay on Exteriority*. Translated by Alphonso Lingis. Pittsburgh: Duquesne University Press, 1969.

Lewis, C. S. *A Grief Observed*. New York: Harper One, 1994.

Lindemann, Erich. "Symptomatology and Management of Grief." *American Journal of Psychiatry* 151, suppl. 6 (1994): 155–60.

Merleau-Ponty, Maurice. *Phenomenology of Perception*. Translated by Colin Smith. London: Routledge, 1962.

Merleau-Ponty, Maurice. *The Prose of the World*. Translated by John O'Neill. Evanston, IL: Northwestern University Press, 1973.

Ratcliffe, Matthew. "Phenomenology as a Form of Empathy." *Inquiry* 55 (2012): 473–95.

Ratcliffe, Matthew. "Relating to the Dead: Social Cognition and the Phenomenology of Grief." In *Phenomenology of Sociality*. Edited by Thomas Szanto and Dermot Moran, 202–16. London: Routledge, 2015.

Ratcliffe, Matthew. "The Phenomenological Clarification of Grief and its Relevance for Psychiatry." In *Oxford Handbook of Phenomenological Psychopathology*, edited by Giovanni Stanghellini, Matthew Broome, Andrea Raballo, Anthony Vincent Fernandez, Paolo Fusar-Poli, and René Rosfort, 538–51. Oxford: Oxford University Press, 2019.

Ratcliffe, Matthew. "Grief and Phantom Limbs: A Phenomenological Comparison." *New Yearbook for Phenomenology and Phenomenological Philosophy* 17 (2019): 77–96.

Ratcliffe, Matthew. "Towards a Phenomenology of Grief: Insights from Merleau–Ponty." *European Journal of Philosophy* 28 (2020): 657–69.

Sartre, Jean-Paul. *Being and Nothingness*. Translated by Sarah Richmond. New York: Washington Square Press, 2021.

Sławkowski-Rode, Mikołaj. "Title." *Publication* (forthcoming).

Steffen, Edith Maria, and Adrian Coyle. "Sense of Presence Experiences and Meaning-Making in Bereavement: A Qualitative Analysis." *Death Studies* 35 (2011): 579–609.

Stein, Edith. *On the Problem of Empathy*. Translated by Waltraut Stein. The Hague: Martinus Nijhoff, 1964.

Weir, Ralph. "Transhumanist Immortality Is Neither Probable or Desirable." In *Transhumanism and Immortality*, edited by Daniel Came and Stephen Burwood, Budapest: Trivent Publishing, 2023.

10

Mourning Academic Mentors and Mentees

Douglas J. Davies

Shaped by the world's diverse cultural economies of death, mourning's two-sided coin ever aligns the private and public faces of bereavement. While public mourning almost always accords primacy of place to those mourning a parent, a spouse, or a child, the death of more distant kin, friends, or associates frequently occupies a secondary position. Yet other deaths lie beyond all kinship charts and family politics, finding their home in distinctive relationships that are simply ignored by core family groups. This chapter is dedicated to one such instance, namely the relationship between living academics and their deceased mentors and mentees. Forged through a mutual participation in knowledge, this link is often crucial not only for successful doctoral research but also for helping to sustain academic life more broadly. While some might question whether this relational context merits consideration as a distinctive form of "mourning," it certainly intrigues me and, for the moment, I simply invite academic colleagues at large to see what they make of it.

APPROACH, REFLECTION, AND METHOD

My approach is both autobiographically reflective and collegial, seeking to share experiences that others may also have felt over the years, but which seldom find either public expression or disciplinary recognition. As for the "method" informing this exploration, I adopt an informal "conversation" between personal experience and longstanding anthropological and theological research on mortality in general, complemented by some limited comment from other academic colleagues.[1] As for "reflection," it is something that, for the moment, I distinguish from the more developed social-scientific fashion of "reflexivity" for reasons that will become apparent. Similarly, despite the fact that this chapter is not a formal essay on grief theory, I will introduce three theoretical topics to provide some direction for the flow of argument, namely Disenfranchised Grief, Uncommon Losses, and Continuing Bonds. Finally, since my focus concerns a type of mourning engendered by a mutual participation in "knowledge," I will invoke a brief formulaic approach to ideas, emotions, and identity as interlinked facets of the distinctive academic way of life.[2] My hope is that these interplaying considerations may allow colleagues at large, as well as some Death Studies specialists in particular, to gain their distinctive purchase on this otherwise meditative consideration of shared knowing.

A Theoretical Triad

In one early and creative twentieth-century account of "Death, Grief, and Mourning," as his title has it, anthropologist Geoffrey Gorer tended to merge these topical concepts in what was an extended theoretical consideration of his own very English experience of loss that he contrasted with his knowledge of worldwide rites of passage as cultural means of sustaining bereaved people in their loss.[3] There followed half a century of growing interest in bereavement's psychology, anthropology, and sociology, involving something of an exponential growth from the 1990s. This explosion of concern included an ever-expanding typology of grief whose lexicon now embraces "Normal, Anticipatory, Disenfranchised, Complicated, Chronic, Absent-Delayed, Inhibited-Distorted, Unanticipated, and Masked" forms of grief.[4] From this vast literature I single out but three elements for their potential in theoretically illuminating my account of, for want of a better term, pedagogical mourning.

Disenfranchised Grief

This relatively recent notion of disenfranchised grief speaks of the emotional complex surrounding relationships where the death of someone's significant "other" is not recognized by that person's dominant family or social circle.[5] This maps ordinary expectations of how deaths are to be felt, and who should legitimately mourn them. This attitude easily leaves some outside the circle of life-affecting ties, as in cases where, for example, the sexual orientation or some other dynamic of a person's life is either unknown to, or rejected by, their family. This sets the "unacceptable" partner outside the deceased figure's funeral ceremonies and, being "beyond the pale," that can leave the bereaved person without a circle of explicit support at the very time when their sense of identity is assailed by the loss. While differing somewhat from those situations, this chapter does portray interpersonal relationships that are simply not, or very seldom at least, recognized as involving "mourning."

Uncommon Losses

One recent addition to the mortality lexicon is that of "uncommon losses." This notion also includes "nonfinite loss" (*sic*) understood as a "continuing presence of the loss itself, and not simply the ongoing presence of the individual's grief."[6] While not considering academic loss and mourning as such, this does offer one umbrella category that signals and, perhaps, welcomes this particular phenomenon that, to my knowledge at least, has not hitherto been formally addressed.

Having said that, however, one earlier potential location for our concern is worth mentioning. It occurs when Gorer depicted "ordinary and extra-ordinary modes of mourning" in his chapter on "Types of Bereavement."[7] There he documents interview-based research on the most common British family losses of "father, mother, husband, wife, brother or sister," and finally "death of a child," all in that order, and with the last "the loss of a grown child" being described as seemingly "the most distressing and long lasting of all griefs."[8] While his research and deeply personal interest in death remains within those bounds, the "extraordinary" element that I wish to incorporate into this chapter can be developed from his "Appendix One" on theories of mourning. There, Gorer draws from Freud's famous 1915 essay, "Mourning and Melancholia," with its account of mourning as "the reaction to the loss of a loved person, or to the loss of some abstraction which has taken the place of one, such as one's country, liberty, an ideal, and so on."[9] I cite this because that closing mention of "some abstraction . . . an ideal, and so on" precisely furnishes an opportune lacuna for our concern with the loss of a personal relationship that embodies the ideal of knowledge and intellectual exchange. Moreover, the phrase "some abstraction" prompts a certain indefinable mystique of knowledge shared, and of the creative venture of exploratory discussion. Interestingly, theologians often allude to "reflection" rather than to "analysis," in a convention that seems to me to resonate with a "venture" rather than a "project," and with more personal than impersonal endeavors.

Continuing Bonds

It is just that mutuality underlying the academic mentor–mentee venture that finds one theoretical catalyst in the notion of the "Continuing Bonds" theory that heralded something of a paradigm shift in the mid-1990s.[10] This advocated the value of ongoing relationships between the living and the dead, especially between kin, rather than the Attachment and Loss model of grief held by psychologists and bereavement specialists for most of the twentieth century, and which still remains influential. Rooted in notions of interpersonal relationships, especially of mother and child, that dominant model emerged from Freud's psychodynamic theories and the much later and ethologically influenced work of John Bowlby for whom successful adaptation to loss involved the "grief-work" of redirecting attachment from the deceased to living agents.[11] Numerous variants of this approach emerged and, for many, remain of clinical use and, realistically, there are useful elements in each of these general perspectives and a sense of complementarity is wiser than any sharp opposition.[12]

PROPERTIES OF MUTUAL KNOWING

Working from these theoretical cameos it is time to consider the diverse forms of research that comprise the contexts for that mutual knowledge-generation lying at the heart of this chapter's concern with mourning. Whether in archive and library, in diverse forms of fieldwork, or in laboratory and clinical-based settings, different dynamics and modes of leadership, learning, and feedback run in parallel. They also encounter all the joys and sorrows of life's opportunities and constraints whether in academic mentor or mentee for it is, of course, far from unusual for doctoral researchers to experience periods of uncertainty, doubt, shifts in perspective, as well as a variety of illness and disruption in their own personal circumstances; so, too, with their supervisors. All such vicissitudes surround our rather niche topic of knowledge-sharing and loss, and whether or not "mourning" is its appropriate category, I remain with it since it touches something of the depth of our emotional lives that often lies beyond both our personal telling and social recognition. So, to pursue the positive dynamics of mourning's emotions I will now mark their capacity to foster our sense of identity through a series of theoretical assumptions, explanations, and intuitions, illustrated by complementary material drawn from some academic colleagues and acquaintances, beginning with "self-knowledge."

Self-knowledge?

Earlier, I made a distinction between this chapter's reflective nature and the more specifically theoretical notion of reflexivity popular in some contemporary disciplines. I did this because, despite every kind of earnest search for transparency—not least in the deconstructed postmodern self—a certain opacity often delivers us from an all-knowing tyranny, while helping to foster both our survival and flourishing. Indeed, this creative interplay of survival and flourishing sets the emotional force-field for the kind of mourning I have in mind, one for those who are "friends" of a most distinctive kind and who, perhaps, evade precise designation. While "soul-friend" has a certain cultural availability to it, though perhaps with too spiritual an overload,[13] "mind-friend" would also seem too misleading. Moreover, because our intuitive, grammatical, need merits a sentence more than a phrase to capture the image I have in mind, let me speak more of those with whom we have shared ideas: "shared" both in the sense of times past, and in the bonding-present. To be more specific, I am not thinking of our life-partners, family, or "ordinary" friends, nor of the various forms of bereavements following their death. We all have such experiences, especially as we age. I am, rather, thinking of that narrow band of "intellectual friends" comprised, more likely than not, of academic associates, mentors, and mentees, and more specifically doctoral supervisors and their postgraduate researchers.

The Rare Category

These deceased "friends," it seems to me, belong to a particularly special and relatively rare category, one that fosters a distinctive sentiment of "mourning." I draw attention to these persons because scarce, if any, attention has been paid to them as is understandable in societies where "the family" is accorded pride of place in its members' emotional kaleidoscope and where dedicated scholarship and research, and their mutuality of knowledge-generation, is a rare activity. To provide some rationale for this connectivity I will now propose a two-fold theoretical perspective. One offers a way of depicting the influence of emotion upon ideas and the sharing of ideas, while the other advocates a specific model of personhood that facilitates both the awareness of sharing and a very particular approach to memory. My hope is that this duality will provide a coherent sense of this kind of ideas-grounded relationship and a corresponding sense of "mourning."

Transforming Ideas—Forging Identities

What, then, of ideas, their shared power and impact both upon our sense of identity and upon those friendships that foster academically sourced forms of memory and mourning? With apologies to philosophical colleagues, let me propose a rather simple response to these complex issues by drawing from a formulaic scheme that I have, in recent years, used to analyze various social contexts and which is especially germane here.[14] Beginning with the simple fact that the world is full of "ideas," often abstract notions and names for "things," this approach proposes that if and when an idea becomes pervaded, framed, or sustained by an emotional dynamic, it is transformed into a "value": formulaically speaking, an emotion-pervaded idea generates a value.

For our purposes, this is where words like "grief," "bereavement," and "mourning" are of special interest. "Grief," for example, is an abstract term both for many young and some older people in societies where personal loss tends to occur in middle or even older age. Then, as life progresses, and the death of those we love makes its impact upon us, that abstraction becomes emotionally "meaningful" at a personal level with the "idea" of grief being transformed into the "value" of grief. Many other analogies could be cited as with "divorce," "betrayal," "conversion," or perhaps even "fame." By contrast, yet other "values" are, from the outset, acquired as emotion-filled ideas within intimate interpersonal contexts, with baby-talk's "mama" words affording foundational examples. Similarly, for those socialized from babyhood and infancy in religious ritual-symbolic behavior, this would also be true of religious words and names for the divine. It often strikes me, for example, that one test of a good actor is how authentically he says "God," "Our Lady," or "The Lord" in Christian contexts, or "The Prophet, peace be upon him," in an Islamic frame. Even the domestic appellations "Mum" or "Dad" can be a challenge, for when acquired and used "naturally" they have an embodied ring of truth to them that is more difficult to catch when acted.

What these examples easily demonstrate is that to speak of "shared values" involves complex, yet often unconsidered, assumptions over life's experiences and the shared emotive force of concepts. This is what makes a phrase such as "British Values" rather problematic when invoked by politicians, because not all UK sub-groups and social classes emotionally engage with what many might regard as fundamental "ideas," but that is an argument for another day. What is relevant here is the way this formulaic progression from idea to value can be taken a step further when we see how some values contribute quite directly to our sense of identity, to that reflection on who we are, and on how others see and engage with us.[15] This distinctive perspective involves the core clustering of values that helps configure a person's sense of identity, usually within a community that shares their emotional tone. Indeed, to allude to tonality is significant precisely because it is an often ignored aspect of social-scientific analysis which is unfortunate in contexts of memory, memorialization, and grief.

Empowering Academic Titles

And what of words, names, and modes of reference in academic worlds? Here, too, titles such as Doctor, Professor, Dean, Vice-Chancellor, and so on, are far from being neutral and abstract nouns. For our present purpose, this includes phrases such as "my supervisor," "my research student," and perhaps even "my colleague." While likely to be abstract, abstruse, and irrelevant to the population at large, these carry considerable import for doctoral students, postdoctoral fellows, and university connections at large. Parenthetically speaking, it is worth noting how during the emotion-pervaded cultural crisis around COVID-19, professorial titles and university provenance became increasingly marked in the media as the need for valid expert opinion increased.

Another rider to this academic domain of emotion-carrying status-names is evident in the business-like cards that increasing numbers of western academics now own and share at conferences and the like. In stating titles, degrees, department, and university, such cards not only inform others of formal and rather abstract information, but also communicate an emotional tone through the luster of association or accomplishment. Indeed, the greater the achievement, the more likely and protocol-recommended it is that only the most prestigious postnominals will be cited. Interestingly, as the market for academic posts becomes ever more competitive, it is now an emerging fashion for postgraduates to mark their postgraduate status, department, and university with similar cards. All such cards, titles, and shifting trends coalesce in expressing a person's contextual identity and academic relationships.

Returning to my formulaic schema of ideas-values-identities, though with slightly less significance for this chapter, it goes on to consider the notion of "belief" as a means of describing identity-enhancing values, stressing that such "beliefs" may consist of cultural, political, and ideological, as well as religious factors. Moreover, to do justice to that "religious" factor, especially with the "world religions" and their sense of some ultimate meaningfulness of things in mind, the argument goes even further and includes a terminal point of "destiny."[16] This is because these religious traditions foster emotional commitments to "ultimate" ideas as part of how they frame their devotees' sense of identity, fostering it through ritual-symbolic activity, as I have shown in the case of Mormon religious culture.[17] Still, for many in more westernized, secular domains, "destiny" is far less relevant than is the identity-level of emotionally significant clusters of values. This helps explain the position of those who define themselves more existentially, not least those often designated as "spiritual" but "not religious." Indeed, in the briefest shorthand, secularization might be said to consist in the demise of destiny.

What, however, has all that to do with mourning in an academic context? While it may be only of tangential significance, I do wonder whether a kind of "spirituality" or even of "destiny" might not carry some valence among those for whom knowledge and even "truth" are intrinsic to their life, and even to their "vocation" as Max Weber would have described it.[18] Is there, perhaps, some quality of knowledge-sharing experience that invites such descriptions? I am thinking of the capacity of the ritual-symbolic domain of research and supervision that becomes so embodied in a scholar's teaching, research, and supervision that it resonates with their mentees. Still, though I doubt if many academics regard their work as so significant as affording a sense of "destiny," I have spoken to at least one well-known "public" scientist for whom his "books" seemed to offer something of an afterlife-status, and perhaps he is not alone in that.

Transforming Relationships: Individuality, Dividuality

My prime reason for taking some time over these considerations and especially over the progressive transformational schema of ideas was as a prelude to grasping the significance of the distinctive mentor–mentee friendship identified in this chapter and of its ensuing form of memory. We have seen how some ideas become so pervaded by an emotional dynamic that it generates a value, how values may help resource our sense of identity, and in some rare cases how even the allure of destiny may be excited. This way of thinking I will now set within another theoretical perspective upon the relationship of shared knowledge. It is one that involves a theory of personhood rooted not in a stark "individualism" but in the notion of "dividuality."

"Dividuality," partitive, or complex personhood, as this perspective is known, may be unfamiliar to some, especially since the familiar notion of "the" individual holds sway in much western intellectual thought and, despite notions of deconstruction, still functions as almost a natural credo of postmodernity. For many, however, especially when it comes to memory and death, it may be that the dividual approach to the bonding of myself and some very special "others" provides a more adequate account of existence, something I have discussed elsewhere.[19] Dividuality understands personhood as constituted in and through the many people who help make us what we are. It concerns the constitution of our identity, not simply in the sense of others having influenced our formation, much as a social learning theory might envisage, but as participating in our embodiment. "They" have become part of me: hence partible personhood. This shift in discourse easily affects and effects a most significant mode of personal awareness and "self-understanding." It helps us appreciate that we are not simply an isolated entity as John Donne's "No man is an island, entire of itself" reminded us, not to mention the entire Christian tradition of both the Communion of Saints and of Christians as members of the Body of Christ.

When the American anthropologist McKim Marriott identified this notion of complex personhood as a way of depicting his work in India, he paved the way for some anthropologists working in other parts of the world, not least in Melanesia.[20] His perspective with its distinctive idioms made considerable sense when, for example, he analyzed the role of food, cooks, and commensals by means of "substance-codes" that conveyed distinctive messages concerning social-cultural contexts and behaviors, including hierarchy. Such codes can also apply to other forms of communication, including verbal modes, as with a mantra a Guru might impart to a devotee. Indeed, the History of Religions could easily furnish an extensive range of images that identify sacred speech and holy texts as their own form of sustenance of the soul. The image of the Guru is, in fact, instructive for the approach I am developing here in that such a figure is often identified as the embodiment of understanding, or of wisdom—a notion to which we will return. Simply to be in one's Guru's presence is bliss, so too with the effect of a Guru's glance towards a devotee. And this is, I think, instructive for the "shared ideas" and mutual "knowing" of mentor and mentee in a strictly academic context. For "knowledge," when viewed as its own "substance," can be "coded" in a variety of ways. "Supervision," for example, offers one such form. It, too, may help constitute a habit of thought, one that endures after a supervisor dies. Here, I acknowledge that I am condensing points that could, and perhaps should, be expanded at length. And also that I am pressing Marriott's perspective to cover some "western" situations of knowledge-generation embedded in interpersonal relationships.

Contexts of Influence

To think of such shared intellectual bases is, inevitably, to think of the process of study, whether in those library, archive, laboratory, or fieldwork contexts mentioned earlier. Each elicits its own affective mode and habit accompanying the teaching and supervision of "ideas." In the process we often become committed to some idea or idea-cluster, theory, tradition, or school of thought. If we have ourselves discovered some idea, developed a theory, or enhanced an existing approach, we easily become attached to it with such "ideas" becoming "values." Moreover, they may quite easily help develop a certain sense of identity and, whether we are alert to it or not, we become rooted in them. Such values, in our hands and teaching, can also generate a kind of charisma of their own. The attractive pull of a concept can be great, but it is often indistinguishable from its vehicle in the form of the scholar-teacher who, as the medium of the message, also becomes charismatic. However, as sociology has long argued, it is wiser to think of charisma as a quality of relationship between leader and devotee, and not simply as an attribute of the sole leader.[21] It is this very bonded relationship that highlights what has been shared and "known." Indeed, considerable significance lies in the property of insight and of the moment when the student "sees," "gets," and appropriates some idea. Such moments of discovery mirror aspects of revelation in religious experience.[22] Its contextual process lies in talking, critical analysis, and encouragement. Moreover, it is not only the student who experiences "change" through discovery: the teacher is also affected when the student "sees," let alone if he or she comes to understand an issue more deeply through the mutual discussion.

Gratitude and Responsibility

What, then, of that mentoring teacher's death? If what has already been proposed is accurate, we can anticipate some change in the student. A complex sense of gratitude for insight may combine with an appreciation of the deceased's personal characteristics of care, academic direction, humor, idiosyncrasy, punctiliousness, or the like. Having already alluded to India's Gurus, we can also, with some justification, extrapolate to advantage from one element of Judaism's Talmudic tradition. Notably, its formal recognition that

> the gratitude that one should have for the teacher who bequeaths spiritual and eternal life, and the honor due that teacher, is even greater than the gratitude one must have for the biological parents who bequeathed physical existence.[23]

What that tradition prescribes, many a surviving student from diverse traditions could spontaneously replicate. While that Talmudic tradition affords a culturally recognizable status-relationship between teacher and taught, non-Jewish societies seldom offer such an immediately explicit framework for self-orientation, though they may still carry implicit similarities as with the traditional German academic role of the *Doktorvater*. One of my German academic friends speaks of that status as one resembling "some kind of God" who might invite someone to pursue doctoral studies in a relationship "often characterized through dependency." But times have changed with increasing numbers of doctoral students and with the emergence of the somewhat rare reference to the *Doktormutter* figure influencing shifts in attitude. Just how death might have affected such relationships is for other German colleagues to discuss.

Having said that, it is often the case that many disciplines in many countries enjoy scholarly heredity. To have had a well-known or even renowned supervisor is something not to be kept hidden. Perhaps in such a student's early academic career this carries its own kind of ascribed status by association, while, in later years, it can engender other forms of reference including the fact that the death of a supervisor can be a freeing event, as is quite often the case in the death of an adult's own biological parents. To assume a responsible leadership role in the next generation almost inevitably involves a degree of going further than one's teacher did—at least in some cases, most especially when the doctoral candidate now becomes the doctoral supervisor. This transition almost inevitably involves an emotional appropriation of some habits of thought and practice, at least when that relationship had been positive. Whatever might be involved in contexts of negative relations lies beyond my present concerns.

Loss of Shared Resource

From this chapter's reflective stance, the influence of positive relationships inevitably touches our interior state following the loss of one who has, to some degree, "understood" what I understand. To have experienced a dependable reference-point in someone with whom one does not have to engage in preliminary discussions is an inestimable benefit amidst our human relationships, notably in an academic mentor. This takes time to develop, much as in mutual "understanding" developed in some marriages and partnerships. There is, in other words, an enormous potential life-benefit that may accrue from the experience of such a mentor–mentee alliance. This, perhaps, is one reason why academic teaching and research is often more of a vocation than a simple job. Together, these easily become widely consuming of time, attention, and endeavor that sometimes becomes problematic for family and wider relationships and commitments.

Leaving aside the potentially germane issues of status-enhancement and professional profiling associated with leading research groups and having excellent postgraduates, other existential dimensions also remain important for supervisors, not least that of contributing to ongoing generations and the life of one's "discipline." Here, for example, I can but allude to the kind of psychological analyses of people such as Erik Erikson concerning "generativity," a concept embracing creative lives and that desire to foster upcoming and ongoing generations.[24] This profoundly significant dynamic within academic life allows for the integration of cumulative knowledge with some basic human needs, not simply for rational "meaning," but for emotional worth gained through human interaction, and as such it can bring the fortunate mentor to the cusp of wisdom. While such "wisdom language" may not be common or even popular, it is deeply germane to academic mentors as their own form of cultural resource, one whose validity is enhanced through educational sharing and mentorship. Almost taking that as read, at least to some extent, let me move on to the relationships engendered by such generativity and, more pointedly still, to their loss.

Shared Emotional Knowing?

The world of doctoral ideas brings some to an enchanted maze, others to a fixed path, albeit one whose turnings often obscure its destination. For the mentee, this direction of flow involves that key person who has been there, passed nearby, glimpsed that place, and shares it. This domain resonates when two people discover it in one another, and it is that kind of identity-friendship that lies at the heart of this chapter. It may become even more pronounced in some, limited, contexts of religious research, where it might engender a form of destiny-friendship when involving a process of acknowledging a radical shift in previous doctrinal certainties. For some a sense of new freedom from former confining certainties offers its own kind of destiny, or at least a reshaping of identity.

Here, perhaps, the broad notion of theory of mind mirrors the shared-knowledge syndrome, when the credibility of likeness to myself extends into a mutuality of understanding and for realistic communication. To say that is, of course, to make enormous assumptions about the personal-private dynamics of others and fosters a humbling theory, reflecting the cautionary fact that we do not know how others "really" think, see, and feel. In practice, we simply have an inkling of shared worlds, "deutero-truths," that suffice for social mutuality—up to a point—but perhaps to a point of considerable significance.[25] While Freud may have led us to think of hidden depths open only to the analyst, and many currently in diverse forms of counseling find valuable new vistas of self, much remains unsaid, and unknown. St. Paul, for example, speaks of his age as one in which we both speak and see only in part and enigmatically. His hope, and the faith and love complementing it, looked for a day when face-to-face knowledge would prevail, perhaps indicating a clear knowledge of himself as one who has, in turn, been clearly known by the Divine (1 Corinthians 13). Perhaps theories of mind, emotion, and even of revelation have something in common, not least in terms of identity and destiny.

RECORDING MEMORIES

From these theoretical considerations we can now move on to materials drawn largely from personal contact with a small number of academic colleagues who found some personal resonance with my notion of a mentor's death and responded to an inquiry from myself. There is, however, nothing systematic, random, or sociologically methodological in these; they simply speak for themselves. To them I will add some accounts taken from Internet postings of "memorials" of yet other scholars whom I have known. I try to avoid categorizing these responses by simply citing and gloss quotations and indirect speech, to touch on key points made. As a reader you will make your own sense of this while, perhaps, noting some relation with the theoretical materials already discussed above. Some future researchers could develop appropriately random social surveys and online resources to develop this line of argument, but that lies beyond my current goal. For them, I simply note that these cases emerged from biblical-theological, sociological, and philosophical scholars and just how wider disciplines might compare would be a question in its own right, as would issues of gender that are frequently significant when it comes to death, grief, and mourning. With such themes in mind, and maintaining anonymity, it is time to rehearse what the following range of scholars have said about their academic mentors.

Shared Publisher: "but can't tell him."

One North American biblical scholar, now at a US university, had worked for her doctorate under the supervision of a fellow American but in the context of a well-known Scottish university. She spoke of having had an "easy transition to friend and colleague, although his role as a mentor never truly went away." She had "sought his advice on a number of occasions." Only some seven months or so after his death she recalled "receiving a book deal," and that the "first thing" she wanted to do was to call him "to tell him." They now shared the same publisher: "so there is a shared connection there even though I can't talk about it with him." She goes on to say that everything she does "as a scholar is filtered through his impact on my life and his memory." They had enjoyed "hanging out together" at conferences or when she was able to be in Scotland. She felt that "what makes his loss extra hard is because it hits on so many different types of relationships—mentor, friend, fellow-scholar." At this point in her life this colleague could say,

> Everything I do as a scholar is filtered through his impact on my life and his memory. It is a mixture of gratefulness, warm memories, sadness for his absence, and a determination to honor him and his legacy through my work.

Stealing a Technique

Another biblical scholar, a Briton supervised by a Briton at an English university, spoke not only about being "lucky enough to get on well with him in his capacity as a PhD supervisor" but also in wider social contexts, something that we neither can nor should ignore since, for him, this is "one reason why I keep returning to memories of good times drinking and chatting for several hours about whatever topic (typically academic). Maybe nostalgia clouds memory here but I've only met a handful of people like that over the years." If I were to add but one personal element to those comments, it would be to recall this younger colleague taking a telling part in the funeral of that supervisor, someone I also counted as a friend and colleague. That moment might, perhaps, add a funeral to the "socializing" times they and, indeed, a small group of us spent together. This friend's response to my request for his reflections took two notably interesting turns. In one he speaks of looking back and of even being "fairly conscious of this at the time," of thinking it "important post-PhD to find my own voice and style," away from an influential supervisor. Even so he still wonders what his supervisor would "make of something I'm working on because I respected his judgment and knew he was very effective with counterarguments. So, when I'm researching something and writing it up, I still think about where he might pick holes and weak spots and try to make sure I can answer them." Then, in another mode he describes how he now finds himself

> unintentionally stealing one particular technique of his when he was answering questions. He wasn't really an engaging public speaker, but he was the master of a patient response which, when backed up with the necessary detail, was a rhetorically and intellectually persuasive move on his part. The thing is that I immediately recognize that I've tried copying him—only after I've done it!

A Last—Lost Meeting

One colleague, a philosopher, reflected on the relatively recent death and funeral of his doctoral supervisor in such a way as to offer a kaleidoscopic pattern of awareness. He speaks of his personal surprise at not seeming to possess "thoughts and moods" on the death, or at least "much less than I would have anticipated." At the funeral, when the coffin was centrally located, he had "this sharp sense that this is in some way the last time I'm going to be in the same room with him." A reflection then rephrased to mark the sense that this was a place in which the deceased was "perceptibly not" present. Complementing that sense of absence was a sense of "comfort" as the eulogies emerged, "all warm, and full of admiration," and yet, as he put it:

> I had a peculiar feeling of everyone being somehow out of orbit, like cocked wheels spinning inertly. Crunched together in the reception hall, all in black, the gathering looked like a solar system imploding on itself after its sun had gone out.

This involved a sense of unease, partially avoided "semi-consciously" by "nervous laughter at appropriate jokes." Something of that "weird laudatory function at which he couldn't be present (after all, bad health now!)" lasted for some time. His present reflections circle around conversations once held, questions he once had in mind to ask but which did not emerge at meetings as conversations took their different turns. The sense of "missed opportunities" and even personal annoyance at them still emerge as new topics come to mind but which, inevitably, will never be discussed with him. This engenders a "mix of feelings" that, he thinks, "is now developing into a sense of loss—but still mostly feels like an unexpected new inability on my part." Somehow, his loss involves the fact that when he reads his former supervisor's work "it seems less rich" because the possibility of discussing it no longer exists.

> Now, more and more, I find myself simply with the bare fact I'm not sure how to understand this or that, or able to tell in what spirit something is said, or unsure what would the expression on his face be had I heard him saying it in person.

MOURNING'S PARADOX: TIMES RECENT, TIMES PAST

These are early days of loss for this last colleague where "mourning" is framed by conversations past, points never raised and now inevitably impossible. For each of us the interplay of memory and current desire constitutes the mourning potential of our lives. Time tells itself differently as years pass and yet it can be immediately intensified as a moment demands it. What is so evident is the significant place of personal presence, in the moment, or in anticipation of the moment, and is no more. The relationship between the distance between the time of death and subsequent recall is itself part of the paradox of mourning captured in the difference between the "time heals" phrase, and those who speak of their loss as something carried for decades and, sometimes, upsurging as real as ever. There is something about the nature of mourning that is so embedded within the imagination of our dividual personhood that some momentary thought, context, or cue can make the past immediately present. Within the nature of symbolic thought, each recall has the capacity to reframe each past remembrance in ways that allow our ongoing lives to reshape themselves in some small way. In that sense, the dead remain creative.

SAD SERENDIPITY

It so happened that while writing this chapter, two deaths occurred in late June 2020 that bear upon this work, those of the very well-known New Testament scholar James Dunn FBA, a personal colleague at both Nottingham and Durham Universities, and Ken Threlfall, a retired senior executive within the National Health Service, a friend and fellow supporter of the Order of St. John of Jerusalem, notably its eye-hospital work in Jerusalem and the surrounding region, and the St. John Ambulance UK. Let me comment on each in terms of shared knowledge.

Almost immediately following James Dunn's death, some of his previous colleagues and doctoral students rapidly posted reflections that are easily accessed online and need not be repeated here, but they highlight the current significance of online platforms for mourning and the sharing of memories.[26] These individuals emphasize his influence both through doctoral supervision and his personal interest in and concern for his students: they also recall the warmth of his wife's hospitality. The immediate responses from a number of these early career academics will doubtless evolve through their own ongoing teaching and supervision. For the moment, the character of the supervisor combines with his scholarly work, and their sketched memories highlight their community as his doctoral students—now intensified at this time of memorialization. This very shared and collective group brings its own significance to that notion of shared personhood discussed above. It is inevitable that when they meet at international conferences, reminiscences of Jimmy will prevail and, in the strange way that discussions of the departed can induce, he will "be present."[27]

Then, in a note of respect for Ken Threlfall, I pinpoint but one element, that which captures a moment in the force of shared ideas. About a month before I wrote this piece, I contacted him about a potential research venture relating to the COVID-19 crisis period for which his former professional NHS expertise and current charity involvement with the Order of St. John of Jerusalem and St. John Ambulance might prove valuable. I had a sense that he would "understand" and be "interested." He was, responding almost instantly. An extended conversation followed, intended to be the first of a series that would embrace the venture. Ideas flew this way and that as we anticipated a variety of research opportunities. We finished but, almost immediately, he rang again with additional comments on his professional career, aptitudes, and limitations as might affect the project. It was, then, a surprise when, relatively soon after, I learned that he had been admitted to hospital, now under COVID-19 constraints, and a few days later died there. Shortly afterwards I attended his funeral and, with social distancing in place and limited family members in attendance, heard the service while standing just outside the crematorium with other representatives of St. John. This cameo captures a moment in which one person's responsive positivity was encouraging as the potential project came alive as a "shared" grasping of possibilities. While the moment can be recalled, it is essentially unrepeatable.

MENTEES' DEATHS, SHARED KNOWING, AND MOURNING

To complement these sketched cases of mentors and colleagues, let me add a further cameo that reveals another aspect of the mourning of shared knowledge, this time in the persons of two of my own previous doctoral students. It was thinking about them that first set me pondering issues of mourning "lost" shared knowledge, or more humanly speaking, of those individuals with whom one had "thought" a great deal. Here some deep personal relations frame the emotional and intellectual dynamics involved in reversing mortality's chronology within the academy where, as elsewhere, the older usually dies before the younger. However, even in alluding to parental loss I am emphatically not implying anything of a parallel in terms of psychological distress.[28]

Still, as with all bereavement, the nature of loss is closely related to the nature of people's prior relationships, their enormous temperamental variability, grief history, health and wellbeing, and cultural context. From amid all such factors my stress in this chapter lies with shared knowledge, with emotion-framing ideas that foster belief-like values that help sustain identity. This is in addition to the power of shared ideas in forging a distinctive type of relationship arising from a student's experience of coming to "understand." The vernacular notions of "seeing it" or "getting it" capture the transformations involved when lone-learning is enhanced through shared insight and when intellectual activity almost inevitably generates a degree of emotional resonance between persons. In terms of dividual personhood, such times partially reconfigure both the teacher's and the student's sense of who they are: each identity is changed in the process. To speak of this is to mark the way in which knowledge becomes embodied and, while it recalls my previous allusion to Indian-derived contexts of "wisdom" in the teacher, it can also mark the wisdom that teachers derive from their learners.

What, then, *is* "lost" when such a person dies? At its most obvious and impersonal level, a mass of knowledge is lost. Partly acquired through the direction of a supervisor, and partly through extensive personal labor, this material had been uniquely processed by the distinctive capacities of the early career researcher and embodied by him or her, while always lying open to further and future development. It is knowledge with promise. For the supervisor, this "knowledge" represents far more than a quantum of library-acquired materials. Rather than being simply encyclopedic, it also carries extensive symbolic weight with a capacity for creative adaptation in the future. But that future has been curtailed.

At the risk of being paradoxical, let me say that while this whole topic has required me to be personal, I should say that I am not always persuaded by the "reflexivity" that has become a style, if not a method, of its own in many social sciences. This is partly because of the opacity mentioned at the outset, partly because of the human potential for deception, whether conscious or otherwise, and also because methodological styles easily become formulaic. Because I have something of a theoretical-ethical-aesthetic disinclination to describe the essentially personal and private aspects of lives and relationships, I have largely avoided them here. As for my students included in this reflection, it suffices to say that each had, as it happened, been seriously ill during the course of their doctoral work which, inevitably, involved an even closer relationship with them, their hopes and fears, than with many another researcher. Still, each went on to begin their academic careers. What I must note is the fact that each left publications for the scholarly public.[29] Moreover, for a supervisor, when such volumes also relate strongly to underlying doctoral research, their arguments, insights, and the cameos of fieldwork underpinning it all carry nuances of discussions, moments, events, and times when real insight occurred. Moments when the researcher "saw" what he had in hand, and when the supervisor "saw" it too. And it is just such knowledge-events that can assume a life of their own within memory with potential entailments of and for mourning.

EPILOGUE

To bring these thoughts to a close, let me reiterate my opening formulaic progression from ideas to emotion-pervaded values, and identity-framing beliefs. While I also alluded to "destiny," albeit with due caution, it recurs yet again, hinting at the possibility that wisdom can be a property of destiny. Of course, in terms of everyday life this may sound all too elaborate, fabricated, and fanciful, but, in everyday life, "knowledge" and the quest for insight can itself easily sound trite, especially when superficial media and celebrity outshine hard-won expertise. Finally, while I have not burdened this chapter with issues of nostalgia, legacy, or the like, I hope that enough has been said to illuminate aspects of the private and public faces of bereavement carried on mourning's two-sided coin.

NOTES

1. Douglas J. Davies, *Death, Ritual and Belief: The Rhetoric of Funerary Rites* (New York: Continuum, 2002), pp. 1, 3–7; Douglas J. Davies, *Mors Britannica: Lifestyle and Death-Style in Britain Today* (Oxford: Oxford University Press, 2017), pp. 1–10.

2. Douglas J. Davies, *Death, Ritual and Belief: The Rhetoric of Funerary Rites*, third edition (London: Bloomsbury, 2017), pp. 5–8.

3. Geoffrey Gorer, *Death, Grief, and Mourning* (London: The Cresset Press, 1965).

4. Sangeeta Singg, "Grief, Types of," in *Encyclopedia of Death and the Human Condition*, ed. by Clifton D. Bryant and Dennis L. Peck (Los Angeles: Sage, 2009), pp. 538–42.

5. Kenneth J. Doka, ed., *Disenfranchised Grief: New Directions, Challenges, and Strategies for Practice* (Champaign, IL: Research Press, 2002).

6. Cynthia L. Schultz and Darcy L. Harris, "Giving Voice to Nonfinite Loss and Grief in Bereavement," in *Grief and Bereavement in Contemporary Society: Bridging Research and Practice*, ed. by Robert A. Neimeyer, Darcy L. Harris, Howard R. Winokuer, and Gordon F. Thornton (London: Routledge, 2011), pp. 237–38.

7. Gorer, *Death, Grief, and Mourning*, pp. 84–109.

8. Gorer, *Death, Grief, and Mourning*, p. 107.

9. Gorer, *Death, Grief, and Mourning*, p. 119; Sigmund Freud, "Mourning and Melancholia," in *Sigmund Freud: The Collected Papers, Volume 4*, ed. by Ernest Jones (New York: Basic Books, 1917), pp. 152–70.

10. Dennis Klass, Phyllis R. Silverman, and Steven Nickman, eds., *Continuing Bonds: New Understandings of Grief* (London: Taylor and Francis, 1993); Christine Valentine, *Bereavement Narratives: Continuing Bonds in the Twenty-First Century* (London: Routledge, 2008); Dennis Klass and Edith Maria Steffen, *Continuing Bonds in Bereavement: New Directions for Research and Practice* (London: Routledge, 2018).

11. John Bowlby, *Attachment (Attachment and Loss, Vol. 1)* (New York: Basic Books, 1969).

12. Davies, *Death, Ritual and Belief*, pp. 53–78.

13. Kenneth Leech, *Soul Friend* (London: Sheldon Press, 1977).

14. Davies, *Death, Ritual and Belief*, pp. 5–10, 54, 183.

15. Douglas J. Davies, *Emotion, Identity, and Religion: Hope, Reciprocity, and Otherness* (Oxford: Oxford University Press, 2011).

16. Douglas J. Davies, "Ritual, Identity, and Emotion," in *The Oxford Handbook of Early Christian Ritual*, ed. by Risto Uro, Juliette J. Day, and Rikard Roitto (Oxford: Oxford University Press, 2019), pp. 55–73.

17. Douglas J. Davies, *The Mormon Culture of Salvation* (Aldershot: Ashgate, 2000), pp. 92–95.

18. Stephen Shapin, "Weber's Science as a Vocation: A Moment in the History of 'Is' and 'Ought,'" *Journal of Classical Sociology* 19.3 (2019): 1–18.

19. Davies, *Death, Ritual and Belief*, pp. 75–78.

20. McKim Marriott, "Hindu Transactions: Diversity without Dualism," in *Transactions and Meaning: Directions in the Anthropology of Exchange and Symbolic Behavior*, ed. by Bruce Kapferer (Philadelphia: Institute for the Study of Human Issues, 1976), pp. 109–42; Marilyn Strathern, *The Gender of the Gift* (Cambridge: Cambridge University Press, 1988); Cecilia Busby, "Permeable and Partible Persons: A Comparative Analysis of Gender and Body in South India and Melanesia," *Journal of the Royal Anthropological Institute* 3.2 (1997): 261–78; Sabine Hess, "Strathern's Melanesian 'Dividual' and the Christian 'Individual': A Perspective from Vanua Lava, Vanuatu," *Oceania* 76.3 (2006): 285–96; Benjamin R. Smith, "Sorcery and the Dividual in Australia," *Journal of the Royal Anthropological Institute* 22.3 (2016): 670–87.

21. Davies, *Emotion, Identity, and Religion*, pp. 115–17.

22. C. Daniel Batson and W. Larry Ventis, *The Religious Experience: A Social-Psychological Perspective* (Oxford: Oxford University Press, 1982).

23. Solomon Schimmel, "Gratitude in Judaism," in *The Psychology of Gratitude*, ed. by Robert A. Emmons and Michael E. McCollough (Oxford: Oxford University Press, 2004), pp. 51–52.

24. Dan P. McAdams and Jack J. Bauer, "Gratitude in Modern Life: Its Manifestations and Development," in *The Psychology of Gratitude*, ed. by Robert A. Emmons and Michael E. McCollough (Oxford: Oxford University Press, 2004), pp. 81–99.

25. Roy Rappaport, *Ritual in the Making of Humanity* (Cambridge: Cambridge University Press, 1999), pp. 304–12.

26. Michael Arnold, Martin Gibbs, Tamara Kohn, James Meese, and Bjorn Nansen, *Death and Digital Media* (London: Routledge, 2018).

27. Valentine, *Bereavement Narratives*, p. 174.

28. Marcia Levetown, "Children, Caring for When Life-Threatened or Dying," in *Macmillan Encyclopedia of Death and Dying*, ed. by Robert Kastenbaum (New York: Macmillan Reference USA, 2003), pp. 147–54.

29. Matthew Wood, *Possession, Power and the New Age: Ambiguities of Authority in Neoliberal Societies* (Aldershot: Ashgate, 2007); Chang Won Park, *Cultural Blending in Korean Death Rites* (London: Continuum, 2010).

BIBLIOGRAPHY

Arnold, Michael, Martin Gibbs, Tamara Kohn, James Meese, and Bjorn Nansen. *Death and Digital Media*. London: Routledge, 2018.

Batson, C. Daniel, and W. Larry Ventis. *The Religious Experience: A Social-Psychological Perspective*. Oxford: Oxford University Press, 1982.

Bowlby, John. *Attachment (Attachment and Loss, Vol. 1)*. New York: Basic Books, 1969.

Busby, Cecilia. "Permeable and Partible Persons: A Comparative Analysis of Gender and Body in South India and Melanesia." *Journal of the Royal Anthropological Institute* 3.2 (1997): 261–78.

Davies, Douglas J. *The Mormon Culture of Salvation*. Aldershot: Ashgate, 2000.

Davies, Douglas J. *Emotion, Identity, and Religion: Hope, Reciprocity, and Otherness*. Oxford: Oxford University Press, 2011.

Davies, Douglas J. *Mors Britannica: Lifestyle and Death-Style in Britain Today*. Oxford: Oxford University Press, 2017.

Davies, Douglas J. *Death, Ritual and Belief: The Rhetoric of Funerary Rites*. Third Edition. London: Bloomsbury, 2017.

Davies, Douglas J. "Ritual, Identity, and Emotion." In *The Oxford Handbook of Early Christian Ritual*. Edited by Risto Uro, Juliette J. Day, and Rikard Roitto. Oxford: Oxford University Press, 2019, pp. 55–73.

Doka, Kenneth J., ed. *Disenfranchised Grief: New Directions, Challenges, and Strategies for Practice*. Champaign, IL: Research Press, 2002.

Freud, Sigmund. "Mourning and Melancholia." In *Sigmund Freud: The Collected Papers, Volume 4*. Edited by Ernest Jones, New York: Basic Books, 1917, pp. 152–70.

Gorer, Geoffrey. *Death, Grief, and Mourning*. London: The Cresset Press, 1965.

Hess, Sabine. "Strathern's Melanesian 'Dividual' and the Christian 'Individual'. A Perspective from Vanua Lava, Vanuatu." *Oceania* 76.3 (2006): 285–96.

Klass, Dennis, Phyllis R. Silverman, and Steven Nickman, eds. *Continuing Bonds: New Understandings of Grief*. London: Taylor and Francis, 1993.

Klass, Dennis, and Edith Maria Steffen. *Continuing Bonds in Bereavement: New Directions for Research and Practice*. London: Routledge, 2018.

Leech, Kenneth. *Soul Friend*. London: Sheldon Press, 1977.

Levetown, Marcia. "Children, Caring for When Life-Threatened or Dying." In *Macmillan Encyclopedia of Death and Dying*. Edited by Robert Kastenbaum. New York: Macmillan Reference USA, 2003, pp. 147–54.

Marriott, McKim. "Hindu Transactions: Diversity without Dualism." In *Transactions and Meaning: Directions in the Anthropology of Exchange and Symbolic Behavior*. Edited by Bruce Kapferer. Philadelphia: Institute for the Study of Human Issues, 1976, pp. 109–42.

McAdams, Dan P., and Jack J. Bauer. "Gratitude in Modern Life: Its Manifestations and Development." In *The Psychology of Gratitude*. Edited by Robert A. Emmons and Michael E. McCollough. Oxford: Oxford University Press, 2004, pp. 81–99.

Park, Chang Won. *Cultural Blending in Korean Death Rites*. London: Continuum, 2010.

Rappaport, Roy. *Ritual in the Making of Humanity*. Cambridge: Cambridge University Press, 1999.

Schimmel, Solomon. "Gratitude in Judaism." In *The Psychology of Gratitude*. Edited by Robert A. Emmons and Michael E. McCollough. Oxford: Oxford University Press, 2004, pp. 37–57.

Schultz, Cynthia L., and Darcy L. Harris. "Giving Voice to Nonfinite Loss and Grief in Bereavement." In *Grief and Bereavement in Contemporary Society: Bridging*

Research and Practice. Edited by Robert A. Neimeyer, Darcy L. Harris, Howard R. Winokuer, and Gordon F. Thornton. London: Routledge, 2011, pp. 235–45.

Shapin, Stephen. "Weber's Science as a Vocation: A Moment in the History of 'Is' and 'Ought.'" *Journal of Classical Sociology* 19.3 (2019): 1–18. DOI 10.1.1177/1468795X19851408.

Singg, Sangeeta. "Grief, Types of." In *Encyclopedia of Death and the Human Condition*. Edited by Clifton D. Bryant and Dennis L. Peck. Los Angeles: Sage, 2009, pp. 538–42.

Smith, Benjamin R. "Sorcery and the Dividual in Australia." *Journal of the Royal Anthropological Institute* 22.3 (2016): 670–87.

Strathern, Marylin. *The Gender of the Gift*. Cambridge: Cambridge University Press, 1988.

Valentine, Christine. *Bereavement Narratives: Continuing Bonds in the Twenty-First Century*. London: Routledge, 2008.

Wood, Matthew. *Possession, Power and the New Age: Ambiguities of Authority in Neoliberal Societies*. Aldershot: Ashgate, 2007.

11

Mourning and Memory, Private and Public Dimensions

Anthony O'Hear

Tuis enim fidelibus, Domine, vita mutatur, non tollitur, et dissoluta terrestris hujus incolatus domo, aeterna in caelis habitatio comparatur. Et ideo, cum Angelis et Archangelis ... hymnum gloriae tuae canimus ...

—Preface of the Mass for the Dead

S'ancor si piange in cielo/ piangi sul mio dolore/ e porta il pianto mio/ al trono del Signor

—Elisabetta in Verdi's *Don Carlo*, Act V

Then tell me, love,/ How that should comfort us—or anyone/ Dragged half-unnerved out of this worldly place,/ Crying to the end "I have not finished."[1]

—Geoffrey Hill, *Funeral Music*

Do we join the angelic hosts in singing a hymn to God's glory at the death of a loved one, because his life is changed, not taken away, and changed into something with which this life cannot compare? Even if we do, it is surely not without fear; the desired change is preceded by judgment. Fear aside, even for a saint death can hardly come about without some regret at what is being lost in the change. Even if those around the death bed are calm in faith and consoled in hope, they will still mourn the passing of a saint, as did the followers of St. Francis. So, do we unashamedly pray that our tears may be carried to the throne of the Lord? Or do we echo the defiance Geoffrey Hill attributes to a Plantagenet noble being dragged to his execution in the fifteenth century—a passage I have heard read to great effect at a Christian burial service by Geoffrey Hill himself?

Few of us then, even if Christian, can celebrate the death of a loved one quite as straightforwardly as the Requiem Mass preface enjoins, certainly not without an accompanying sadness, nor should we. Other parts of the Mass are more somber, not least the *Dies Irae* ("quidquid latet, apparebit": whatever is hidden will appear—terrifying!). The passing of one who had played a part in our lives, even if a somewhat negative one, leaves a gap which cannot be filled, and of course this gap is the more poignant, the more affecting, the closer in affection we are to the one who has died. And even in the case of the death of an enemy, or of one from whom we have become estranged, many will mourn the impossibility of any kind of reconciliation or resolution.

Even in the most Christian of eras tears of mourning were permitted. It was the heathen Socrates who brusquely forbade them, death in his view being not just a transition to a better place, but a cure for the sickness that this life is. Christ, who had not foresworn this life, knew better than that. He was moved by the tears of Mary to summon Lazarus from the grave (John 11:33). Other Greeks too thought differently, as we see in Homer and with Sophocles' Antigone. The dead are to be mourned and accorded decent burial, something acknowledged by both sides in the *Iliad* and, of course, denied by Creon in *Antigone*.

So Elisabetta is not wrong to want her tears carried to heaven. The melodramatic posturing of Heidegger's *Sein zum Tode*—being towards death—notwithstanding, death is not a destination, so much as an interruption. No life is ever finished in a wholly balanced or satisfying way, subjectively or objectively, nor do we live life as if we were simply awaiting death. Death is not the destination we are steadily and smoothly approaching, as an intended telos, but a derailment while still on the track. It is true that some nuns slept in their coffins, but, until they died, they got up each morning and set about their tasks, spiritual and temporal. No doubt they made all sorts of this-worldly plans, even while contemplating the four last things, and so did the Orders to which they belonged as they built their convents and chapels. Some lives are ended voluntarily, but almost always because life itself has become unbearable. Real death cults are very much the exception to the religious life, and even there the parents and relations of suicide bombers and the like frequently mourn their passing, to say nothing of what they see as the tragedy of a young life cut short by a fanatical ideology. From the outside at least there seems to be plenty of mourning at the funerals of those who have sacrificed this life for a martyr's paradise. Further, far too many lives are, like that of Hill's Earl Rivers, cut unnaturally short by human actions, a point to which we will return.

Mourning the dead is clearly natural to us as human beings, if anything is. The earliest remains of Neolithic human beings from fifty of more millennia ago are usually seen as being to do with burials and other commemorative ceremonials. I remember in the 1960s a hippyish disparagement of such things, maybe in reaction to what they saw as the empty, even hypocritical services of the established churches and authorities (and maybe in the bitterness of the Vietnam War there was a degree of hypocrisy in the military funerals of the time). But simply disposing of dead bodies as if they were any other piece of refuse, to be cremated "within hours of death," and the ashes "thrown out with the trash," as was advocated by a well-known Hollywood star of the time, did not catch on. Even the star's own family, themselves gilded countercultural rebels, did not abide by their father's wishes. Today the trend among the non-religious is for ever-more embarrassingly personalized services of remembrance, whose baroque mawkishness makes some yearn for the formal, impersonal, and hallowed forms of the Latin Requiem Mass or the *Book of Common Prayer*'s Order for the Burial of the Dead.

At first sight Aristotle's view that a dead body is not a human body, and that a severed hand is not a hand, might seem to militate against treating the bodies of the dead with honor and respect.[2] This is because in his scheme a *human* body is something endowed with life, with all the capacities and potential which being human involves. A dead body, less even than an embryo, has no such potential, and so, unlike an embryo, is not actually human. A severed hand is a piece of inorganic matter, without the potential to do what a human hand does, and so, strictly, is not a hand, even though the matter of which it is composed once was. Profound truths are bound up in the Aristotelian picture, truths which should help us to guard against the temptation to treat a dead body as if it were still, in some sense, the person who has died. But I see nothing in what Aristotle says that would lead him or us to see anything but the deliberate and vainglorious dishonoring of a great man in Achilles' treatment of the corpse of the Hector he has just slain, dragging it behind his chariot three times round the walls of Troy. Our memories of and feelings towards the dead coalesce around the material remains of what was once the body of the deceased, the place the person had filled, a recognition indeed of their very embodiment. The body, or its remains, is naturally the focus of those memories, eliciting a concrete recognition of and respect for the person who is now dead. It is an acknowledgment of the unique and sacred mystery of the embodied person that once lived and moved and had its incarnate being among us, its incarnate being *there*. This is why we treat the corpse with respect and mourn in its physical presence before ceremonially consigning it to the flames or the earth.

In what I have so far said about mourning I have conflated the mourning that takes the form of private grief and the more public form of mourning which involves a ceremony to commemorate the one who has died, and perhaps also to focus on aspects of his or her life. Private grief and private mourning are just that, and as C. S. Lewis has well shown in *A Grief Observed*,[3] grief is in many ways unpredictable and uncontrollable. It tears at one's insides and exposes hollowness within. In the end, perhaps, this internal grief subsides, but maybe after several months or even years, and not without recurrences just when one felt that one was emerging from the morass of despair. Yet in the end "passionate grief" (assuming it has worked) "does not link us with the dead but cuts us off from them."

Misdirected mourning, tied up as it often is with our own feelings of loss and anger, can do the dead some kind of wrong, says Lewis. In line with Aristotle's approach to the dead body, Lewis inveighs against the Victorian practice of trying to keep the effects of the dead just as they were when they were alive. But the things of the dead were what they were when animated by the presence of the dead when alive. Now they are no more "theirs" than is the form in the coffin their body. It all amounts to a form of mummification, in Lewis's view. "They beg us to stop it," he says, and only then can we begin to see them in their own right, rather than "all foreshortened and patheticized and solemnized by my miseries."[4]

In the picture painted by Lewis, grief is terrible, unpredictable, and likely to overwhelm us again just when we think we have got past it. There may even be a twist in the tail of the working out of grief, when we look forward to a time when it will all have dissipated, but then are crushed once more by the thought that there will be a time when the loved one has ceased to matter to us in the way he or she did in the intensity of our grief. But there is something unhealthily self-centered about this, however inescapable it might be in the intensity and turmoil of unassuaged grief. If and when it has done its work, this passionate, truly other-directed grief of which Lewis speaks will cease to cling on to the illusion that the Resurrection or any sort of afterlife will mean resuming life as it was on Earth. As Lewis tells us, in *Paradiso* (Canto XXXI, 31–33) Beatrice smiles from afar off and turns not to Dante, but to the eternal fountain.[5]

Personal mourning can, as Lewis suggests, take on various forms, and lead to various conclusions, more or less helpful or even desirable. But, of its nature, it is personal. What is now called "closure" may never come, however much one mourns and grieves. Indeed, the more inward-looking this mourning is, the harder it may be to emerge from its coils. The more I am obsessed with *my* loss, the less I see the person who has been lost, and hard, even at times impossible, as it may be to reach that stage in the dying of a loved one, it is only then that grief—which never leaves us—can become livable. A public recognition of the dead may be an important stage in the journey out of one's inner torment, if only because it takes the mourner out of him- or herself and places the sadness in a public world in such a way as to manifest the way in which the sadness is something shared, not mine, but ours. It has become something public and objectively felt and marked, and in its now shared nature something more bearable for the individual who might otherwise believe he or she bore it all him- or herself, with no support or compassion. The whole phenomenon becomes more objective. In moving from a private grief to a shared sense of loss, there is a possibility of the dead one beginning to be seen in his or her own right, as Lewis advocates, rather than as a ghost haunting me alone, all foreshortened by my own miseries, as he puts it, and crushing me with its heavy miasma.

With this movement from private grief to the public world in mind, I now want to consider mourning of a more public kind. This is the mourning that reminds us that the deceased was part of a community wider than his or her immediate relations. Rooted in a wider community as the deceased was, that community is moved to mourn his or her memory in a public way. In doing this there is acknowledgment both of the individual deceased and of the place and society in which he or she lived. Consequent on this recognition of the public life of the deceased we also feel that something is missing if a person who has died is not given a public funeral or commemoration (and in Britain church funerals have to be open to the public). Why is it that a private or secretive burial, with an unmarked grave, in the old days had an air of disgrace about it, as was the case with those who had committed suicide? A pauper's funeral, without mourners or ceremony is normally seen as intolerable and intolerably sad, implying that the person who died had no support or companionship in life, or at least none when he or she died. Nowadays there may be those who do not want or say they do not want a funeral of any sort for themselves or their loved ones, but this does not invalidate the very widespread motivation which still exists today to mark a death publicly. This refusal can come to seem curmudgeonly and hurtful to those who are left, whose grief cries out for marking in a communal, ritual way.

I would suggest that the custom of marking a death publicly, whether religiously or not, arises from the opposite of what Donne intended by his often misunderstood words, that no man is an island. We do not go to someone else's funeral to be reminded that the bell tolls for each of us attending. We go to mourn the loss of someone who has played a part in the lives of all of us mourners. No man is an island, either we who attend or the person whom we are mourning, and it is for someone who was not an island to the rest of us that we are present. It is solidarity or fraternity with the deceased that our mourning articulates, which is why it is sad, even tragic, for someone to have no funeral, to be buried in an unmarked grave, or for their body simply tumbled into some communal pit or, pace the 1960s film star, for his or her body to be cast out and disposed of as simple refuse, with no grave or memorial at all.

Very many people in recent and not so recent times were accorded no respect in their death, no mourning, no memorial. From too many examples which readily come to mind, we could mention the mass, often coffin-less burials during the Great Irish Famine in the second half of the 1840s, people "disappearing" in the Gulags of the USSR and the killing fields of Cambodia, the forbidding of mourning and the planting of crops over burial plots during Mao's induced famine of 1958–61 in which thirty-eight million died, and, of course, the remains of Holocaust victims simply being bulldozed into pits at Belsen. The last case is particularly poignant because it was done not by the murderers or enemies of the victims, but by their "liberators" who felt, rightly enough, that in order to prevent the spread of typhus and other deadly diseases among those still living in a very precarious state, they had no other option. This example hits close to home for me because my wife's father was one of those tasked with this appalling duty in April 1945. The first example also has resonance for me because my great-grandfather left Ireland for Scotland at the time of the Famine, along, of course, with around one and a quarter million other emigrants. He and they left behind something like one and a quarter million dead, and a mere six and a half million still living in Ireland, out of an originally healthy population of about eight and three-quarter million at the start of the Famine in the early 1840s.

To appreciate the full horror and degradation of what we are talking about, it helps to bring cases home in a personal way, for it reminds us that what we are talking about is not numbers of anonymous, forgotten, and unknown people. We are talking about real people, with whom people like us and even close to us had connexions, real people, yes, with identities, names, and memories, but who now and even at the time of their deaths became anonymous, forgotten, and unknown. The mourning and memory which seems a natural rite in a peaceful and civilized situation is denied to all these people *en masse*. Their remains are treated with perhaps even less dignity than the actor of the 1960s recommended: he at least thought there should be a cremation of sorts. And for those who feel some connexion with those so treated, this can come to seem intolerable.

Hence a phenomenon which has been growing in recent years: a memorializing or even a re-burying of people who, for whatever reason, have been laid in unmarked mass burial sites. Thus in Ireland, to take one striking example from among many, on May 19, 2010, in Kilkenny those who had died in the workhouse in the 1840s were re-buried in solemnly consecrated ground; the burial ground in the workhouse in which they had originally been placed had never been consecrated, "a fact which would have been of great grievance and probably also a sense of shame, which perhaps explains why the existence of the cemetery had been forgotten." In fact, the very existence of the unconsecrated cemetery had only been re-discovered in 2005. The skeletal remains of those who had been buried there in pits, with their very basic coffins piled on top of each other and subsequently forgotten, were then given detailed forensic examination. Nine hundred and seventy individuals, including many children under the age of five, were identified and re-interred in a new Famine memorial garden. The re-burial ceremony included a multi-denominational religious ceremony to the memory of all who had died in the Great Famine, and "the people, whose remains now rest in the memorial garden, were given their final respectful treatment in death, which they were denied when they died about 160 years previously."[6]

Obviously there have been many more attempts in many different ways and in many parts of the world, particularly in Eastern Europe and the Balkans and in Ireland itself, to do the sort of thing that was done in Kilkenny in 2010. But taking this example to stand for so many others, I want now to consider why such commemorations and re-dedications are important, and what they might tell us about remembering the dead, specifically the unknown and often unrecorded dead who died in large-scale catastrophes and massacres. There seem to be two separate reasons: one to give the individuals concerned a belated decency in their death; the second to mark an event or succession of events of which history has somehow contrived to obliterate the memory. We have already said something about the first reason. It is fulfilling a duty owed to the dead, a duty that for whatever reason was neglected or deliberately refused. And although the Great Famine is widely known about in a general sense, as the Kilkenny case demonstrates, little is known about the hundreds of thousands of people who actually died in it, who they were, and where they were laid. But, going on from that, and taking us into the second reason for a ceremony such as that at Kilkenny, it is a mark of the way in which we living today are bound in multifarious ways to those who have gone before us. Our present is rooted in their history and their fate. Not to acknowledge this in a way diminishes and distorts the present, our present.

In an essay entitled "On the Use and Abuse of History for Life,"[7] Nietzsche makes the point that man is distinguished from the beasts by having history, by being in a sense historical, rooted in a past and with a future in mind. He then distinguishes three approaches to history: the monumental, the antiquarian, and the critical. The monumental is that which deals with great men and great events; the antiquarian is that which recovers the past for its own sake; and the critical is that by which we now come to terms with the past, in a way to overcome it. The key point in Nietzsche's essay is the use of history *for life*. I do not want to follow him very far in any of this, but his aim of history "for life" is important and his distinctions are useful. Obviously, the Kilkenny poorhouse dead are the very sort of people monumental history will pass over and, even if they were known about, ignore or dismiss. Unlike the citizens of Leningrad in the Soviet and siege eras, they did not have a Shostakovich or an Akhmatova to commemorate them (but then nor do most of those who perished unknown and unremembered). So, the Kilkenny dead belong to antiquarian history, as is graphically demonstrated by the need to conduct archaeological and forensic research to disinter not just their remains but even vestiges of their memory. But this was not done just for its own sake, to give those who were lost some belated respect and recognition, but also in order to re-appraise the past and come to a different and richer sense of the present, which is how I am seeing critical history. So, in making the effort to afford the forgotten dead the respect they were denied at the time of their death—the first reason for doing it—we fulfill the second reason, that of gaining a fuller and more concrete understanding of what we are today.

It is at this point that things can begin to get tricky. We have suggested that there is a sense in which we owe it to forgotten and improperly interred groups to accord them the respect that was denied them at their actual time of death. But this proper and pious mourning may not be easy, and it can be constrictive and negative. I have taken the Great Irish Famine as an example not just because I am myself part of its fallout, so to speak. In its day in the mid-nineteenth century and in Ireland itself, the Famine was the occasion of great bitterness. Ireland was, at the time, ruled from London, its own parliament having been abolished by the Act of Union of 1800, partly as a result of an unsuccessful anti-British uprising in 1798, which itself had followed over two centuries of killing and persecution of the Catholic Irish by the Protestant British. To put it no stronger the Famine was handled extremely badly by the rulers of the country and by many of those who owned the land. The rulers were in London and the landowners were mainly Protestants with an English background, dating back to the time of the Elizabethan and Cromwellian conquests of Ireland. While people starved in their thousands, great balls and horse racing and yachting festivals were held. During the Famine many peasants were evicted from their primitive hovels because they could not pay their rent, and these evictions were sometimes welcomed by the landlords, who saw it as a chance to reclaim the land for more productive purposes. Food was at times exported from Ireland, and there was rhetoric from British sources about the indolent Irish and a Malthusian need to cut down the population. The Poor Law was administered with great harshness. Peasants who had plots larger than a quarter of an acre were refused any sort of relief. Too often there was a doctrinaire utilitarian stress on administering relief in such a way as not to encourage begging, rather than as a desperate and humane attempt to alleviate a terrible human tragedy.

There were better sides to the story. Some landlords, clergy, and government officials worked tirelessly against the odds. Some of the few Catholic landlords behaved as rapaciously as some of their Protestant peers, while some of the best behavior came from the widely reviled absentee landlords in England. Nor was it the case that the government in London made things worse deliberately, as opposed to being influenced by heartless ideology and at times ignorance.

Nevertheless, despite the mixed and at times conflicting picture presented by the Famine, it is easy to see why the Famine generated great bitterness among the Catholics in Ireland, who had suffered persecution for centuries before that under discriminatory Penal Laws, which among other things forbade them even to educate their children. Emancipation, granting Catholics some civic rights was achieved only in 1829. Nor did the fallout from the Famine end with the Famine itself. Emigration from Ireland continued throughout the rest of the nineteenth century; by the 1890s, 40 percent of those who had been born in Ireland were living abroad, particularly in the US. The Irish diaspora is itself a big factor here. Many of those who had left Ireland, and even more their children and descendants, had their views on Ireland and Irish history colored by tales of the Famine, and were in a way stuck in an inflexible mind-set rooted to that time (now more than 170 years ago). Thus, to take just one example, in the 1990s, during the Irish Peace Process, there was an Irish website, http://www.IrishHolocaust.org, which stated that just "as no Jewish person would ever refer to the 'Jewish Oxygen Famine of 1939–45,' so no Irish person ought ever to refer to the Irish Holocaust as a famine." Interestingly, and perhaps in a way hopefully, the target of this diatribe was not just the British but also the Irish authorities of the late twentieth century, who presented the Famine in a more balanced way in their school curriculum, and the then President of Ireland, Mary Robinson, who was held by the website to be less than sufficiently driven by anti-British venom.[8]

So, the question arises as to whether the reviving of memory by something like the Kilkenny ceremony might be undesirable in stirring old bitterness and ancestral hatred. If so, should we avoid mourning of this sort, lest it reinforce and exacerbate contemporary divisions? I have taken the case of Ireland as my example here, but the question I am posing has multiple resonances. Consider, for example, what is now known as the "Bloodlands," that area of Central and Eastern Europe now comprising Latvia, Estonia, Ukraine, Lithuania, Belarus, and Poland, in which twenty million were killed between 1930 and 1950. Thirteen million were civilians and four and a half million Jews. The time scale is significant—the bloodletting started before and continued after the Second World War; but what is more significant for our purpose is that until the fall of the Berlin Wall, the memory of what happened in those places then was frozen by the Communist authorities, and even now in some of the countries concerned it is considered undesirable to refer to more than the Holocaust from that period. The reason is that the killing was often between ethnic and now national groups within the Bloodlands. The fear is that by re-awakening memories of what happened, old hatreds would be resuscitated; better on this view to let sleeping dogs lie, whether of the Armenian Genocide, the Bloodlands, or other such phenomena in Europe or elsewhere. Nonetheless, there is an enterprising group called "The European Remembrance Symposium," under the umbrella of the European Network Remembrance and Solidarity, involving impressively idealistic young people, trying to record memories from the time of the Bloodlands and elsewhere and to commemorate the forgotten dead. Are they right to do so?

To return to Nietzsche's distinction, what we are talking about here will be a critical approach to the antiquarian recovery of such memories. In Nietzsche's view the antiquarian approach is one in which one is fixed in the past, unable to move on, as with a certain sort of grief. It "buries further living," as he puts it in the third part of "Use and Abuse." What we need at this point is a critical approach to history, one in which, having learned about the past, we are enabled to break from it in order to live now and in the future. In the context of our discussion here, perhaps the most important observation Nietzsche makes at this point is that "it requires a great deal of power to be able to live and to *forget* just how much life and being unjust are one and the same." What I am suggesting is the opposite of this. It requires a great deal of power to live and *understand and accept* that life and being unjust are one and the same.

Critical history means understanding the routes by which the present has been made, no doubt deploring many of them. It does not preclude attempting to remedy some of the unjust fallout from past abuses, as far as it is in our power to do so. But it also means accepting that at every stage of human development there were abuses, injustices, and horrors of an unacceptable sort and to an unacceptable degree. We have to accept that progress away from the horrors of the past will occur only in a spirit of reconciliation and even forgiveness between the heirs and descendants on either side of whatever happened in the past. In other words, we re-bury the forgotten dead not just to accord them respect, but also in order that, having acknowledged what had happened and even in some cases, where appropriate, expressed repentance and made reparation, we then join with the ancestral enemy in moving on together. It was for this reason that in describing the Kilkenny re-burial I emphasized that the ceremony was multi-denominational. We could imagine the Catholics forgiving and the Protestants repenting, but the Catholics would have remembered that they will be forgiven only if they forgive those who trespass against them, and the Protestants that forgiveness comes only to those who are truly repentant. None of this would be possible were we ignorant of the past, and the victims of the past to which we still have living connection buried in oblivion. The memories will fester underground or remain frozen in a revengeful view of the past in such a way that there would be no possibility of mutual recognition or the ultimate accord we should all hope for. It is, of course, just that, which the IrishHolocaust.org website in their fixed and static view of the past and of their current enemies wanted to prevent.

The Bloodlands and Ireland of the Famine are very much alive even today, in the sense that they have a direct bearing on the state of things now and in our lives, even if we do not recognize it. IrishHolocaust.org recognize that, but what they do not see is that ramping up and, as most scholars attest, exaggerating an ancestral wrong cannot end it. In Nietzsche's sense, their memory is an antiquarian one in which they are locked and would lock the rest of us if they were to have their way. The memorial and the mourning are not wrong. Indeed, they are necessary, but, as they are felt and thematized by IrishHolocaust.org and all such movements, they are forms of grief transformed into unshakeable anger, from which there is no escape.

We, all of us, however we are affected by grief or painful memory, have to absorb the fact that we are no longer in the situation which elicited our grief and mourning. Whether it is public or private, and whether it was 170 or 70 years or even just months or days ago, it is no longer the case. Unlike the antiquarian approach to history, we must come, sooner or later, to recognize that it has changed, changed utterly, to paraphrase Yeats, and so must we. Part of what steers that change in a positive way is the living through the grief, recognizing and remembering what has happened and mourning accordingly, but in doing so breaking free from the psychological and social weight that would otherwise drag us down once more.

NOTES

1. By permission of the literary estate of Sir Geoffrey Hill.
2. See Aristotle, *De Anima*, ii 1, 412b10–26.

3. C. S. Lewis, *A Grief Observed* (London: Faber & Faber, 2015 [originally published 1961, under the pseudonym N. W. Clerk]).

4. The quotations from *A Grief Observed* in this and the previous paragraph are from p. 44.

5. See Lewis, *A Grief Observed*, p. 60.

6. My account of the re-burial at Kilkenny is based on Jonny Geber, "Burying the Famine Dead: Kilkenny Union Workhouse," in the magisterial *Atlas of the Great Irish Famine*, edited by John Crowley, William J. Smyth, and Mike Murphy (Cork: Cork University Press, 2012), pp. 341–48. Details of similar commemorations in Ireland can be found in the *Atlas*, pp. 620–21. My account of the Irish Famine draws heavily on the impressively detailed and well-researched articles in the *Atlas*.

7. Friedrich Nietzsche, "On the Use and Abuse of History for Life," in *Untimely Meditations*, originally published 1874. I have referred to the translation by Ian C. Johnston available at: https://la .utexas .edu/users/hcleaver/330T/350kPEENietzscheAbuseTable All .pdf.

8. See the *Atlas of the Great Irish Famine*, pp. 597–98.

BIBLIOGRAPHY

Geber, Jonny. "Burying the Famine Dead: Kilkenny Union Workhouse." In *Atlas of the Great Irish Famine*. Edited by John Crowley, William J. Smyth, and Mike Murphy. Cork: Cork University Press, 2012, pp. 341–48.

Lewis, C. S. *A Grief Observed*. London: Faber & Faber, 2015 [originally published 1961, under the pseudonym N. W. Clerk].

Nietzsche, Friedrich. "On the Use and Abuse of History for Life." In *Untimely Meditations* [originally published 1874]. Translation by Ian C. Johnston. Available at: https://la .utexas .edu/users/hcleaver/330T/350kPEENietzsche AbuseTableAll .pdf.

12

The Work of Mourning
Roger Scruton

In a significant essay entitled "Mourning and Melancholia," Freud wrote of "the work of mourning," meaning the psychic process whereby a cherished object is finally laid to rest, as it were buried in the unconscious, and the ego liberated from its grip. Until the work of mourning has been accomplished, Freud argued, new life, new loves, new engagement with the world, are all difficult if not impossible. This is the explanation, as he saw it, of the state that used to be known as melancholia—a kind of willed helplessness in which the dead lie unburied on the surface of consciousness, greeting every bid for freedom with a blank, joyless stare.

I am not, in general, persuaded by Freudian psychology. But in this matter, it seems to me, Freud was on the right lines. We lose many things in our lives. But some losses are existential losses. They take away some part of what we are. After such a loss we are in a new and unfamiliar world, wherein the support on which we had—perhaps unknowingly—depended is no longer available. The loss of a parent, especially during one's early years, is a world-changing experience, and orphans are marked for life by this. The loss of a spouse is equally traumatic, as is the loss of children, who take with them into the void all the most tender feelings of their parents.

Nevertheless, however grievous the blow, mourning is a therapy that points towards survival. Through mourning we bury the dead. But we also raise them from the dead, not as living beings, but as purified images, washed clean of their faults and transfigured by our mutual forgiveness. They are revered as they could never have been revered in life, since only this will enable us to escape from our guilt. For the first outpouring of grief is also a reproach—of the dead person for dying, and of the mourner for having survived him. Gradually, mourning takes on the form of a dialogue, in which the grieving party both seeks and offers forgiveness: let all those imperfections be forgotten, is the thought, and let us be at peace together.

But this dialogue is not easy: it involves a face-to-face encounter of a new kind, maybe after years of avoiding such a thing. There is, as psychotherapists have often pointed out, a period of anger, a bitter reproach towards the other who has let you down so completely. And this anger can take on an obsessive and exploratory character, seeking the ways in which the other's death was a secret plan, a policy decision, a plot to cast you off as a burden, just at the moment when you needed him most. Sometimes you can lay the dead person to rest only after you have killed him for a second time, like Sylvia Plath in her great poem "Daddy":

> Daddy, I have had to kill you.
> You died before I had time—
> Marble-heavy, a bag full of God . . .[1]

Mourning is a ritual, and also, in certain circumstances, a duty: and these features illustrate the claims that the dead have on us. Mourning is something that we *owe* to the dead, since the process of mutual forgiveness must be pursued until our dead no longer haunt us. The Greeks took this matter very seriously. Thus, when Odysseus visits Hades, the spirit of Elpenor, who had fallen to his death from the roof of Circe's palace, and whose body was left there in the haste to flee, appears to him first, addressing him in the following words:

> I beseech you, by all those whom you left behind, by your wife and by the father who reared you as a child, and by Telemachus your only son whom you left within your halls, that you will, sailing from the kingdom of Hades, put in with your good ship at the isle of Aeaea. And there my lord I beseech you to remember me and not to leave me there unwept and unburied, lest I should become a cause of divine wrath against you. But burn me there with all my arms and raise a mound for me by the shore of the grey sea, in memory of an unfortunate man, so that those yet to be will know the place. Do this for me, and on my tomb plant the oar that I used to pull when I was living and rowing beside my companions.[2]

Elpenor is asking for funeral rites. But he is also asking to be mourned. Do not leave me, he implores, unwept and unburied. (*Aklauton, athapton.*) In invoking Odysseus's family Elpenor conveys the sense that the duty towards him is an inextricable part of the fabric of honor and obligation by which the Greek hero conducted his life. The duty to shed tears, both personal tears and ritual tears, arises at the moment of death, and must be honored. Elpenor invokes the possibility of divine wrath; for this is a duty of piety, and until it is performed, the cosmos is shot through with a metaphysical fault.

That idea pervades the seminal play of *Antigone* by Sophocles, which concerns (among so many other things!) the conflict between the duties of piety and the duties of government. Antigone obeys the call to bury her dead brother, Polyneices, whom her uncle Creon, King of Thebes, has condemned to lie unburied outside the walls of Thebes. Antigone's obligation to mourn and to bury her brother is in her view absolute, and she proceeds inexorably to her death in fulfilling it. There is no suggestion in the play, or in Antigone's speeches, that her brother will receive any *other* benefit from her action, than lawful burial. Nevertheless, the obligation to pull the curtain across his life is absolute, and it falls on her. She owes it to him, and the world will be out of joint until she has accomplished it. It is possible that she entertains religious beliefs, according to which burial and ritual mourning are required by the soul of Polyneices, as they were required by the soul of Elpenor. But reference to those beliefs is no part of the plot. The important point, impressed on the audience by Sophocles, is that Antigone *owes* something to her dead brother, and that if she does not fulfill her obligation, it is she herself who suffers: she falls from the exalted condition of the free, heroic spirit into the pit of those contemptible beings for whom no obligation can trump the mere habit of staying alive.

Obligations of that kind are less and less acknowledged in modern societies. We are far more likely to be interested in what the deceased person owes to us by way of a legacy than what we owe to him or her in the way of mourning. Of course, we still offer funerals to our dead, though we expect them to budget for this while still alive. And we grieve for them as we must. But it is increasingly rare to raise a monument, or even to lay our dead to rest in a grave that we might subsequently visit. The habit of cremating the dead and then scattering their ashes reflects our postreligious conception of what they become by dying, namely nothing. We briefly snatch at their nothingness and then watch them fade from our empty hands. At the back of our minds is the thought that all duty ends with the life to which it was owed. The funeral rituals that surround the practice of cremation are therefore especially prone to Disneyfication, as Evelyn Waugh maliciously and hilariously shows in *The Loved One*. Since the obligation is unreal, its fulfillment becomes a kind of ritualized pretense, an opportunity for displays of kitsch emotion. And that too is therapeutic, since it casts a light back across the life that has been lost, and re-shapes it as a fake. This life and this love, it tells us, were no more real than the feelings displayed at the end of it, so let's make a pretty display of them and move on.

In behaving in that way, however, we are denying something. Those who have been truly close to us in life cannot in fact be scattered as their ashes can. They remain brooding within us, as Freud saw, waiting for the rest that we alone can offer them. This is one reason why, even in the age of cremation, we ritualize our mourning, so as to endow it with the character of an objective and public event, an imperative that falls on us all and which lifts the dead person to a new place in the community—a place of safety from which he has no will to escape. However Disneyfied, the ritual remains a moral necessity; without it we shall be haunted, as Odysseus was haunted by the ghost of Elpenor.

But ritual is not enough. We also need to mourn, and this is the difficult part, for it obliges us to tend the grave within, to revisit what we have lost and to rehearse an attachment rooted in things that cannot be changed. It requires us to come to terms with the loss, incorporating it into our future, so that what we are and what we were belong to a single continuum. By mourning we take responsibility for our loss, acknowledge it as ours, a debt to be redeemed. Not to mourn is to live at a lower level, detached from our real attachments, denying the past and the identity that grew in it. It involves, for us as much as for Antigone, a refusal to be called to account, a stepping down from interpersonal being into the world of carnal appetite. And all this is implied in the sympathy that we feel for those who mourn, who are raised like Antigone to the highest spiritual plane. Blessed are those that mourn, for they shall be comforted: so it is said in the Sermon on the Mount. Those who mourn leave the world of animal appetite behind, and reach to the realm of the gods.

Religion enables people to bear their losses, not necessarily because it promises the hope of reversing them, but rather because it encases them, surrounds them with a protective seal of ritual, as the oyster grows a pearl around the grain of sand. Whether or not religion offers consoling doctrines of the afterlife (and those of the Greeks were far from consoling), it offers us a direct way of dealing with loss, as a rite of passage in which the whole community takes part. The loss of religious belief thereby leads to an even greater loss of other and necessary states of mind—beliefs about what we owe to the dead, and about our own status as their survivors.

Loss is fundamental to the human condition. But civilizations differ in their way of accommodating it. The Upanishads exhort us to free ourselves of all attachments, to rise to that blissful state in which we can lose nothing because we possess nothing. And flowing from that exhortation is an art and a philosophy that make light of human suffering, and scorn the losses that oppress us in this world.

By contrast, Western civilization has dwelt upon loss and made it the principal theme of its art and literature. Scenes of mourning and sorrow abound in medieval painting and sculpture; our drama is rooted in tragedy and our lyric poetry takes the loss of love and the vanishing of its object as its principal theme. It is not Christianity that gave us this outlook. Virgil's *Aeneid*, ostensibly an expression of Aeneas's hope as he is god-guided to his world-transforming goal in Italy, is composed of losses. The terrible sack of Troy, the loss of his wife, the awful tale of Dido, the death of Anchises, the visit to the underworld, the ruinous conflict with Turnus—all these explore the parameters of loss, and show us that our highest hopes and loyalties lead of their own accord to tragedy.

For all that, the *Aeneid* is just as much a religious text as the Upanishads. The world of Aeneas is a world of rites and rituals, of sacred places and holy times. And Aeneas is judged by the gods, sometimes hounded by them, sometimes sustained, but at every moment accountable to them and aware of their real presence in the empirical world. It is for this reason that Aeneas can look his many losses in the face and also set them at the distance that enables him to gain from them. They come to him not as inexplicable accidents but as trials, ordeals, and judgments. He wrestles with them and overcomes them as you might overcome an opponent. And each loss adds to his inner strength, without hardening his heart.

This attitude to loss reflects the questioning and self-critical spirit of Western civilization. The Western response to loss is not to remove yourself from the world. It is to bear it *as* a loss, to mourn it, and to strive to overcome it by seeing it as a form of consecrated suffering. Religion lies at the root of that attitude. Religion enables us to bear our losses not, primarily, because it promises to offset them with some compensating gain, but because it sees them from a transcendental perspective. Judged from that perspective they appear not as meaningless afflictions but as *sacrifices*. Loss, conceived as sacrifice, becomes consecrated to something higher than itself: and in this it follows a pattern explored by René Girard in his bold theory of the violent origins of the human disposition to recognize sacred things.[3] I think that is how people can cope with the loss of children—to recognize in this loss a supreme example of the transition to another realm. Your dead child was a sacrificial offering, and is now an angel beckoning from that other sphere, sanctifying the life that you still lead in the material world. This thought is of course very crudely captured by my words. Fortunately, however, three great works of art exist that convey it completely—the medieval poem *Pearl* from the *Gawain* manuscript, Mahler's *Kindertotenlieder*, and Britten's church parable *Curlew River*.

In our civilization, therefore, religion is the force that has enabled us to bear our losses and so to face them as truly ours. The loss of religion makes real loss difficult to bear; hence people begin to flee from loss, to make light of it with Disneyfying ornaments, or to expel from themselves the feelings that make it inevitable. They do not do this in the way of the

Upanishads, which exhort us to an immense spiritual labor, whereby we free ourselves from the weight of Dharma and slowly ascend to the blessed state of Brahma. The path of renunciation presupposes, after all, that there is something to renounce. Modern people use drugs, instant excitements, and commodified sex in order to forestall both love and mourning, to arrive at the condition where renunciation is pointless since there is nothing to renounce. Renunciation of love is possible only when you have learned to love. This is why, in a society without religion, we see emerging a kind of contagious hardness of heart, an assumption on every side that there is no tragedy, no grief, no mourning, for there is nothing to mourn. There is neither love nor happiness—only fun. The loss of religion, one might suggest, is the loss of loss.

We should not let the matter rest on that pessimistic note. Western civilization has provided us with another resource, through which our losses can be understood and accepted. This resource is art. The features of Western civilization which have made loss such a central feature of our experience have also placed tragedy at the center of our literature. Our greatest works of art are meditations on loss—every kind of loss, including that of Paradise, including that of God himself. These works of art convey in imaginative form the concept that more fortunate people were able to acquire through the elementary forms of the religious life—the concept of the sacred. This is what Nietzsche had in mind, I suspect, when he wrote—shortly before going mad—that "we have art so that we may not perish of the truth."[4] The scientist may have seen through to the truth of our condition, but it is only one part of the truth. The rest of the truth—the truth of the moral life, of the human form divine, and the abiding need for sacrament—must be recovered in another way. And that, I believe, is why poets like Rilke and Eliot are so important for us. They offer us spiritual exercises through which those old concepts of the transcendental and the sacred can be rescued from their withered state and made flexible and vital, the true tendons of the inner life. And so, even in an age without faith, we can rediscover the experience of sacred things, and attain to

> A condition of complete simplicity
> (Costing not less than everything)
> And all shall be well and
> All manner of thing shall be well
> When the tongues of flame are in-folded
> Into the crowned knot of fire
> And the fire and the rose are one.[5]

The Christian reference of those final lines of *Four Quartets* is an echo only—a hearkening back to experiences that demand not belief, but only imagination, in order to confer their moral gift. But they express the condition of a soul that has ceased to mourn, not because it has fled from the work of mourning, but because it has accomplished it, and emerged in a condition of freedom, free again to love.

It is fair to say that, in the wake of the First World War, we have lived in an elegiac culture. An elegy is a way of accepting the loss of some precious thing. It rejoices in the fact that the precious thing was given. If it is sad, it is with an accepting sadness. An elegy says: this we were given, and it is gone, but we should be grateful for it, and try to live up to its memory.

We in England are very familiar with elegiac art. The First World War took away the social order, the pastoral way of life, and the noble aspirations of the English, and dumped us suddenly and brutally in the modern world. Much of our modern art and music is an invocation of things of which we are bereft. The paintings of the Nash brothers and Stanley Spencer, for example, works like the above-quoted *Four Quartets* of T. S. Eliot, the cello concerto of Elgar, the fifth symphony of Vaughan Williams, and the concerto for double string orchestra by Tippett: such works invoke our lost pastoral homeland in a spirit of tender regret. They offer us a manageable sadness, which is also an encouragement. Something of all that remains, they say: something to live up to, material to reforge and recast in a renewed attempt at living rightly. I hear this in the later works of Vaughan Williams, and especially in his *Pilgrim's Progress*. By mourning what we have lost, we also regain it, in another and transmuted form. So the elegy tells us.

I once wrote a book entitled *England: An Elegy*. I was aware when writing it that I was emphasizing the good, not the evil, that my country had stood for. But I felt entitled to do so, not merely because the good in my view outweighed the evil, but also because I was embarking on a legitimate work of mourning, just as Elgar had embarked on such a work in his cello concerto. Elegies are attempts at reconciliation and redemption, works of mourning in the sense intended by Freud. Mourning, as I have described it, is a process of reconciliation, in which the dead are retrospectively granted the right to die. Hence all funeral rites and all elegies for the dead are designed to highlight the virtues and to minimize the vices of the departed person. But what if the dead cannot be forgiven? What if their vices are an immovable obstacle to all attempts to accept them? Then mourning becomes impossible.

Germans after the war felt this about their country. The Germany that we know from art, music, and literature—the Germany of the Gothic cathedrals and the gingerbread cities, of Dürer and Grünewald, of Luther's Bible, of Goethe, Schiller, Kant and Hegel, the Germany of the Romantic poets and of the greatest continuous musical tradition that the world will ever know—that Germany had been poisoned in people's thoughts by Hitler. It would have been easier to deal with the memory of the Hitler years, if they had been imposed on Germany by some alien power which had sought to obliterate this great nation, as the Mongols obliterated the civilization centered on Baghdad, or as the Chinese are at this moment obliterating Tibet. But it was not like that. The Nazis proclaimed themselves heirs to German civilization. Hitler was not just a madman: he was an aesthete and an intellectual, like Stalin and Mao; he emphasized in all his speeches the history and achievements of the German people; he invoked the art, music, and philosophy of Germany as justifications for his cause and objects of his pride. And the Germans followed him on his path of conquest, sharing his triumphs and forced very soon to share his disastrous defeat. Although their music was not destroyed by the war, their cities—the greatest cities in Europe—were reduced to rubble, their civilian population exposed to the horrors of blanket bombing and the rapine of the Soviet Army, and the noses of the survivors rubbed in the unspeakable reality of the holocaust. Their country was destroyed, but it was impossible to mourn it.

Two psychoanalysts, the husband-and-wife pair Margarete Nielsen and Alexander Mitscherlich, reflected on this situation in a book published in 1967—*Die Unfähigkeit zu trauern*—the Inability to Mourn. The Germans could not grieve for their dead and at the same time accept the guilt that their dead had incurred. Even the heroic self-sacrifice of the German armies on the Russian front could not be given as a proof of virtue. All were guilty—guilty not only for the insane destruction of their country, but also for the crimes against humanity and civilization that had been unleashed by the Nazis. The world insisted that the Germans accept their guilt. Hence the world denied them the relief of mourning. Their dead lay unburied in their conscience, like Polyneices outside the walls of Thebes. As in the *Antigone* of Sophocles, piety called for mourning while politics forbade it.

The subsequent history illustrates what is lost when we cannot mourn. The Germans, unable to bury the corpses that lie scattered in every recess of their culture, cannot redeem their guilt. They can neither confront the past nor turn away from it. The "work of mourning" has therefore not been collectively undertaken, and as a result the Germans suffer a kind of national paralysis, a collective melancholia. Much that happens in contemporary German culture stems from this. The refusal of the churches to speak out against Islam; the propaganda of the architectural modernists against those patriots who seek to rebuild Berlin as once it was; the nihilistic musical life of Darmstadt and Donaueschingen; the fanatical commitment to the European Union, which offers transnational citizenship in the place of a purely national allegiance; and in all this the complete absence of elegiac works of art—nothing to counter the self-advertising guilt of Anselm Kiefer, the desolation of Günter Grass, or the pretentious clap-trap of Stockhausen. Germany itself has been hidden away, and can be reborn only on one condition: that mourning should begin. But mourning has been forbidden, and a deep discomfort remains.

From the same source, it seems to me, sprang the decision of Angela Merkel, accepted by a substantial number of the German people, to open the borders to refugees, in full knowledge that those refugees will not, in the foreseeable feature, either integrate into German society or in any way share the open and democratic way of life that the Germans have wished to achieve. The vast cost—administrative, social, economic, and political—of this gesture derives from guilt. But it will not assuage that guilt. However admirable the impulse that led to this gesture, it will not give the people what they really need, which is the belief in Germany's right to take its place in the community of nations. Until the work of mourning has taken its course, that place will be no more than a dream. And meanwhile the unpurged guilt of Germany remains.

NOTES

1. Sylvia Plath, "Daddy," in *Collected Poems* (New York: HarperCollins, 1992).
2. Homer, *The Odyssey*, Book XI, II, 66–78.
3. René Girard, *La violence et le sacré* (Paris: Grasset, 1972).
4. The remark is collected in the posthumous collection known as *The Will to Power*. See Erich Heller, *The Importance of Nietzsche: Ten Essays* (Chicago: University of Chicago Press, 1988), chap. 9.
5. T. S. Eliot, "Little Gidding," in *Four Quartets* (London: Faber and Faber, 1963).

BIBLIOGRAPHY

Eliot, T. S. "Little Gidding." In *Four Quartets*. London: Faber and Faber, 1963.
Girard, René. *La violence et le sacré*. Paris: Grasset, 1972.
Heller, Erich. *The Importance of Nietzsche: Ten Essays*. Chicago: University of Chicago Press, 1988.
Plath, Sylvia. "Daddy." In *Collected Poems*. New York: HarperCollins, 1992.

13

Sidgwick's Dilemma

Lesley Chamberlain

At the end of a long philosophical career Henry Sidgwick (1834–1900) found that there was no reason for human beings to be moral. He hesitated over whether to make his findings public. He wrote:

> Hence the whole system of our beliefs in the intrinsic reasonableness of conduct must fall, without a hypothesis unverifiable by experience reconciling the Individual with the Universal Reason, without a belief, in some form or other, that the moral order which we see imperfectly realized in this actual world is yet actually perfect. If we reject this belief, we may perhaps still find in the non-moral universe an adequate object for the Speculative Reason, capable of being in some sense ultimately understood. But the Cosmos of Duty is thus really reduced to a Chaos: and the prolonged effort of the human intellect to frame a perfect ideal of rational conduct is seen to have been foredoomed to inevitable failure.[1]

Along with Sidgwick's latest biographer, Bart Schultz, I take this to be a "Death of God" moment.[2]

Perhaps the reason why Sidgwick's crisis has not been described in quite such dramatic terms was that he was not really a believer. As John Maynard Keynes, who played golf with Sidgwick, said: "he never did anything but wonder whether Christianity was true, proving that it wasn't and hoping that it was."[3] Sidgwick worried about the gap at the heart of his thinking, but as Keynes also observed, he lacked intensity. Chaos loomed, the wages of virtue might be dust, but Sidgwick did not go through spiritual agony. There was no intimate dark night of the soul. Further, he thought if he could have evidence of life after death, this would resolve the matter. Bernard Williams, perhaps in this respect, described Sidgwick as "innocent."[4] The most personal worry he confessed to was hypocrisy. He felt that someone as skeptical as him ought not to be teaching ethics.

Schultz tells us that Sidgwick detected "a moment of monumental significance for Western civilization, a potential cataclysm" in his intimation of chaos.[5] But Sidgwick's at best theistic position was entirely socialized into a concern for the protected social fabric of England. A Dostoevsky-like utterance, "if there is no God then all is permitted," might damage the philosophical heart of an England at the height of its worldly power.

Schultz was right to mention but not to press the Nietzschean parallel. The 1870s and 1880s did witness this extraordinary outburst of loss of faith across different Christian cultures in and on the edge of the West, but national philosophical and spiritual habits had an overriding influence on the intensity with which this loss was expressed. Between Dostoevsky and Nietzsche and Sidgwick there is no comparison. Sidgwick mourned the death of God because his good order of things was the empire. Dostoevsky flirted with what metaphysical anarchy would permit in the dark hearts of human individuals corrupted by centuries of political brutality. Nietzsche, meanwhile, a great inward German, expressed the loss of God with unparalleled personal intensity. He was the madman who had lost God and was still looking for him, when no one else cared.

> THE MADMAN—Have you not heard of that madman who lit a lantern in the bright morning hours, ran to the market place, and cried incessantly: "I seek God! I seek God!"—As many of those who did not believe in God were standing around just then, he provoked much laughter. Has he got lost? asked one. Did he lose his way like a child? asked another. Or is he hiding? Is he afraid of us? Has he gone on a voyage? emigrated?—Thus they yelled and laughed.
>
> The madman jumped into their midst and pierced them with his eyes. "Whither is God?" he cried; "I will tell you. *We have killed him*—you and I. All of us are his murderers. But how did we do this? How could we drink up the sea? Who gave us the sponge to wipe away the entire horizon? What were we doing when we unchained this earth from its sun? Whither is it moving now? Whither are we moving? Away from all suns? Are we not plunging continually? Backward, sideward, forward, in all directions? Is there still any up or down? Are we not straying, as through an infinite nothing? Do we not feel the breath of empty space? Has it not become colder? Is not night continually closing in on us? Do we not need to light lanterns in the morning? Do we hear nothing as yet of the noise of the gravediggers who are burying God? Do we smell nothing as yet of the divine decomposition? Gods, too, decompose. God is dead. God remains dead. And we have killed him.
>
> "How shall we comfort ourselves, the murderers of all murderers? What was holiest and mightiest of all that the world has yet owned has bled to

death under our knives: who will wipe this blood off us? What water is there for us to clean ourselves? What festivals of atonement, what sacred games shall we have to invent? Is not the greatness of this deed too great for us? Must we ourselves not become gods simply to appear worthy of it? There has never been a greater deed; and whoever is born after us—for the sake of this deed he will belong to a higher history than all history hitherto."[6]

And yet, of course, besides this magnificent outpouring of metaphysical sorrow, there was a problem for sober philosophy. With his lifelong concern to justify duty as a morally superior pursuit to individual happiness, the supposedly utilitarian Sidgwick veered constantly towards the Kantian imperative, but just could not anchor himself there. Given utilitarianism's inability to capture the voluntary impulse, moral philosophy itself seemed dead in the water.

Nietzsche thought so at least. In his multi-layered passage in *The Gay Science*, he kills off the entire Socratic moral tradition, when, unlike Socrates going down to the Piraeus to observe the festival and define virtue by means of agreeable conversation, *Nietzsche's* madman goes down to the marketplace only to find a jeering public. Not only is human thought no longer tethered to reason, but the earth itself has become unhinged, and the only way an individual who sees nothing but spiritual incoherence can survive is to become a god himself, thus to create his own order of superabundant substitutes for the old faith.

To repeat, there is nothing approaching this position, I think, in the English tradition, as a visceral experience of the condition of moral philosophy, still closely tied to theology, towards the end of the nineteenth century.

But here I want to consider two attenuated British responses to the Death of God within philosophy, and while neither of them proposes that we should continue to mourn, they provide strikingly different reasons as to why we should not. Further, because they both respond to Sidgwick, they suggest an especially interesting comparison with each other.

The two figures in question are Alasdair MacIntyre and Bernard Williams. I describe their responses as attenuated both because they were written a full century after Nietzsche and because neither announced his intention as such. MacIntyre's *After Virtue* was published in 1981 and Williams's *Ethics and the Limits of Philosophy* in 1985. Coincidentally, both men were the same age, born in 1929, and these books were their greatest works, respectively.

Let me start with what both thinkers had to say about Sidgwick's dilemma: whether to confess to the chaos he had found in the place of the divinely assured good order of things.[7]

MacIntyre's sympathy could hardly be for a perplexed member of the late-Victorian intellectual elite aghast at his social responsibility.

MacIntyre was a Marxist when he first encountered Sidgwick and remained throughout his career a post-Marxist optimist about human nature. But MacIntyre felt very keenly the loss of a metaphysical guarantee of moral being, and this led to him letting the elitist Sidgwick off the hook:

> No philosopher expressed the moral situation of nineteenth-century England—and to some extent we are all still in the nineteenth century—better than Henry Sidgwick. Sidgwick is a touching figure whose defects are usually the defects of his age. He was preoccupied with the loss of his own Christian faith in a way that is foreign to us. His moral psychology is crude because the psychology of his time was crude.[8]

The books central to MacIntyre's career—from the Riddell Lectures of 1964, published three years later as *Secularization and Moral Change*, to *A Short History of Ethics* (1966), from which I am quoting here, to *After Virtue*—constructed an extraordinary scenario to make palpable that loss of Christian faith that Sidgwick endured, and to try to explain and see beyond it.

Contemporary fear of "a nuclear holocaust"[9] helped generate in MacIntyre an imagined secular event equivalent to the Death of God. The preface to *After Virtue* referred to a "moral calamity" and the opening chapter referred repeatedly to a "catastrophe" in which the whole order of meaning which underpinned the moral life of a society, and a country, had been wiped out. The verb "lament" was not misplaced. The task of the present age was to reconstruct a meaningful order piecemeal, with the enormous difficulty that the terms rescued from the past had lost their context and were lifeless. The catastrophe, he told us, was only belatedly shadowed by philosophy. The actual disaster was the change in British society resulting from industrialization and urbanization. These had generated antagonistic classes where there was once community and set the false religion of liberal individualism in motion. Now Sidgwick was no working-class hero, but MacIntyre admired him because his feeling for the catastrophe was social, and his crisis reflected the decline of religious authority in society as a consequence of those profound economic shifts. Though he labored under enormous social regret, it was not MacIntyre's own psychology to mourn. Nor, unlike Nietzsche, whose individualism he despised, was MacIntyre prone to giving the catastrophe personal expression. He was by nature and conviction a social builder, and rebuilder, along Marxist-influenced lines. He wrote in the closing pages of *After Virtue* that like Marx, he was an optimist but the way ahead—evidently the best way would be communitarian, or at least communal—would not be easy.

MacIntyre was and is an Idealist, passionately in search of re-enchantment through a marriage of ideologies that retain faith in human moral potential. His first book, written at the age of twenty-three, was *Marxism and Christianity*. In the 1968 preface, he claimed to have become skeptical of that early goal, finding the modern church inadequate and the worldly instantiations of Marxism a travesty, but his career seems founded upon that search in a general sense.[10] A few years after the first publication of *After Virtue*, MacIntyre became a Thomist and accepted that the teleology of human action flowed from a metaphysical foundation in the nature of the human person.[11] He remains an ardent critic of liberal individualism.

On the Christian side he would like to live in a world in which his preoccupation with losing his faith and finding it again would not be foreign to us, but part of the ongoing spiritual reconstruction of everyday living. It would not be a matter of ongoing mourning, but rather of taking seriously Sidgwick's touching and foundational dilemma.

Bernard Williams, whose career ran in extraordinary parallel to MacIntyre's, took a very different path. At first glance he seems intensely scornful of Sidgwick, lambasting the latter's "Government House utilitarianism" as craven, stuffy, and shallow.[12] The old man's esoteric morality, keeping secret what could not without too great a political risk be disclosed to the simple people, belonged to an obsolete colonialism. Williams, in other words, set himself up not as an Idealist but as a fearless 1960s social liberal in opposition to the late-Victorian hypocrite.

And yet *Ethics and the Limits of Philosophy*, a reprise of Sidgwick's dilemma, becomes Williams's own quietly impassioned answer to the Death of God. It is a great book, in which the reference to Nietzsche comes rightly before the reference to Sidgwick. Already in the third chapter, Williams tells us: "Nietzsche's saying, God is dead, can be taken to mean we should now treat God as a dead person; we should allocate his legacies and try to write an honest biography of him."[13] One wonders, had Williams been a writer, whether he would not have tried to write that story. (He did, incidentally, see his rival MacIntyre as a writer of intellectual history, not a philosopher. The life of God was a story and now there were contending new tales to try to explain humanity's shifting moral potential.[14])

One might also say that mourning is not appropriate for Williams because God died a hundred years ago. To mourn would be neurotic— Freud would say that—and a sign of some other disturbance in any subject fixated on a catastrophe so far in the past.

Coming back to the reprise of Sidgwick's dilemma. Who will tell the story of the demise of moral philosophy as an absolute code of morality, from which we can deduce all obligation and blame? Measuring himself implicitly against Sidgwick and with Nietzsche, Williams sees himself as having been Nietzschean dynamite in the profession. He is not afraid to say repeatedly that no rational certainty is available in ethics, such that philosophy could build a tenable theory upon it. For Williams, the death of God coincides with and co-names the death of philosophy as being capable of delivering ethical theory. This is his argument, and it is effective. For the kind of thinker Sidgwick was, when ethical theory ran parallel to a belief in God, this thinking was "transcendental to life, existing in a space quite outside the practice it is supposed to regulate or justify." The past motivations for this may have been "very metaphysical and general, lying for instance in the idea that we consider the world as it really is only when we see it from the outside, *sub specie aeternitatis*. Some of the rational dignity ascribed to trying to see the ethical world from that point of view seems to derive from such conception of objectivity."[15]

Meanwhile, the story Williams is telling, in a suppressed way, but as a reflection of his mature belief that real stories tend to undo the theoretical philosopher's examples, entails "showing up . . . attitudes [incorporated in philosophical arguments] as resting on myths, [on] falsehoods about what people are like."[16] As society has become more and more self-reflective as to what people are really like, there is that need to "[re]allocate God's legacies." This is Williams's project.

The story intertwines with the theory. In chapter 6, Williams must say what was wrong with Sidgwick's and indeed Kant's intuitionism. To this end, he charges that this model of intuition in ethics "failed to explain how an eternal truth could provide a practical consideration."[17] The practical life is too complex to be accounted for by simplifications from on high.

Williams's text also wraps itself around a vision of future possibilities. He mentions transparency as a modern ideal of how society should function, implicitly in contrast with Sidgwick's elitism. Liberals and non-liberals will agree with him, he feels. Appealing to "any who retain radical hopes born of the Enlightenment and those who do not," Williams notes that: "Many Marxist theories embody versions of this [transparency], in the aim for a society that can do without false consciousness."[18]

So, there is ground on which our two eminent twentieth-century British moral philosophers after the Death of God can meet, and one can see Williams is indeed working on the same problems as MacIntyre, namely the problem of moral authority, of Marxism as a rival and/or replacement for Christianity, and, in respect of competition between these two, looking towards a new openness that would be the best outcome, in a Hegelian fashion, subsuming both. Sidgwick was a masochist who proceeded with "a certain dry relish" to close down the diversity we now work with.[19] Since Sidgwick's time, who we are has become much more complex.

Therefore "The aim of ethical thought" is "to help us construct a world that will be *our* [my emphasis, LC] world, one in which we have a social, cultural and personal life."[20]

One can hear a strong allusion to Nietzsche here, as Williams answers the Death of God: "Our [ethical] arguments have to be grounded in a human point of view; they cannot be derived from a point of view that is no one's point of view at all."[21] Williams insists on a Nietzschean complication of the human, which does not fall under a single definition. He reaches the emphatically un-Socratic conclusion, moreover, that reflection can destroy ethical knowledge.[22] The surprisingly sympathetic allusion here is surely to Heidegger, and it might also embrace the anti-individualistic communitarian ambitions of MacIntyre. It is because reflection can indeed destroy ethical knowledge that certain thinkers try to legitimate the return of a simpler god-fearing society in our complex times. Our way of seeing things has indeed brought about *Entzauberung*, and the Left should understand the Right here, without condoning extremism.

I will not set out Williams's project any further here. I would only add something which, in his original remark on Sidgwick, MacIntyre also feared: namely that with the death of God, there are psychological states perhaps lost to us forever. Future generations will not know, from mere words, what it was like for a person to lose their faith. At the heart of *Secularization and Moral Change*, MacIntyre writes: "We cannot do with Christianity in the modern world, but often cannot do without it either, because we have no other vocabulary in which to raise certain kinds of questions."[23] In this way, we are unable "to respond to the facts of death."[24] "This is one of the great cultural and social gaps in our lives."[25] He is not calling for a revival of hell-mongering, but "the fact is that contemporary Christianity says *nothing* about death."[26] Williams is attuned to this too when he notes in passing that the notion of grace will become unintelligible. Philosophy will have left a record of what it was to judge people for their actions, but no one except a Christian within that past value system will know the effect of believing in God's forgiveness of saints and sinners alike.

In the story of the re-allocation of God's legacies, the teller would help us understand these feelings, and they might indeed be emotional possibilities, within our dialogue with ourselves, that we would want to mourn. But who can this teller be? How do we write a history of emotions that are no longer felt, or have such different names that it is difficult or impossible to recognize them as also having a past context? There are feelings no longer felt, and presumably they are like the dried-up twig that evolution has passed by; and who saves dried-up twigs when the main body of the plant is raging?

In fact, in a neglected work also of the 1980s, the psychologist Anthony Storr observed something of the parallel death of solitude with the death of God. He evoked solitude as making possible a certain inwardness and intensity which might be named by some as a relationship with God, or a friendship with Jesus. Such a relationship was felt to surpass all others. The person who befriended God was less demanding of and reliant upon his actual human relationships and may even have lacked them. Such a person often felt himself, herself, to be more creative in that silently comforted inwardness. This complex of beliefs linking God, solitude, and creativity belonged to what seems now to have been a past way of being human.[27]

Historically, friendship and love were another answer to Sidgwick's fear of moral chaos. The Bloomsbury Group, bolstered by G. E. Moore's *Principia Ethica*, were sure that the emotional quality of subjective experience would be enough to compensate for the lack of a metaphysically ordained, objective, order of goodness.[28] And, just to retain the symmetry of the post-God picture, it might well be said that there was something sub-Nietzschean about the Bloomsberries' eager discovery of moral individualism, or amoralism, and something still Sidgwickian about them in that their freedom was reserved for their social class.

Williams, although not free from its spirit, did not find this answer sufficient. As for MacIntyre, he was not impressed by Keynes representing the Bloomsbury attitude,[29] and when the cult of human love worked its way forward into liberal theology in the 1960s, he found it "vacuous."[30]

One chapter of the story of After God might then become the tale of the rise of an obsession with human relationships accompanied by a fall-off of spiritual intensity.[31] Latterly, if I can speak for an imagined MacIntyre here, that chapter would recount the commodification even of friendship, which we see all around us in the post-industrial, digitalized world, and the story of a new kind of hypocrisy alleging that all shall be well.

But MacIntyre cannot tell the whole story because he has returned to the church, and I have mainly confined myself to Bernard Williams whose landmark work *Ethics and the Limits of Philosophy* sets out the After God situation with a sober optimism. One value on which both Williams and MacIntyre agree is the shape of a whole life. MacIntyre finds the prospect of how to exercise judgment upon it difficult because "We are uncertain what it is to live well or badly." He needs God to judge. Compare this with Williams's insistence that a possible future ethics (not a morality, but a way of answering ourselves as to our own moral possibilities) will be confidently concerned with that shape, besides bringing the same confidence to truth and truthfulness.

NOTES

1. Henry Sidgwick, *Methods of Ethics* (London: Macmillan, 1874), p. 473.
2. Bart Schultz, *Henry Sidgwick, Eye of the Universe: An Intellectual Biography* (Cambridge: Cambridge University Press, 2007).
3. Roy Forbes Harrod, *The Life of John Maynard Keynes* (London: Macmillan, 1951), p. 135.
4. Bernard Williams, *Morality: An Introduction to Ethics* (Cambridge: Cambridge University Press, 2012), p. 97.
5. Schultz, *Henry Sidgwick*, p. 3.
6. Friedrich Nietzsche, *The Gay Science*, trans. by Walter Kaufmann (New York: Vintage, 1974), Book Three, §125, pp. 181–82.
7. It is curious to note that Sidgwick and Nietzsche both died in 1900.
8. Alasdair MacIntyre, *A Short History of Ethics* (New York: Macmillan, 1966), p. 243. In *Secularization and Social Change* (London: Oxford University Press, 1967), p. 37, MacIntyre noted that "Sidgwick agonized over whether he could continue conscientiously to hold his Cambridge fellowship given his religious doubts whereas Keynes an intellectual generation later could put aside any social worries about unbelief. Keynes was certain as to the falsity of Christianity and this replaced doubt. For Sidgwick there was an agonizing doubt as a way of life in which the connection between the Christian religion and the actual choices that men have to make in their moral and social lives had become remote."
9. Alasdair MacIntyre, *After Virtue* (Notre Dame: University of Notre Dame Press, 1981), pp. 1–5.
10. For his disappointment with Christianity, cf.: "Christianity confronted with the secular life of the post-Industrial Revolution society has in fact found it impossible to lend meaning to that life or to enable people to understand and find justifications for living out its characteristic forms" (MacIntyre, *Secularization and Social Change*, pp. 66–67). For his still rather awkwardly hedged disillusion with Communism, see the closing pages of *After Virtue*.
11. Alasdair MacIntyre, *After Virtue*, 3rd edition (Notre Dame: University of Notre Dame Press, 2007), p. xi.
12. Bernard Williams, *Ethics and the Limits of Philosophy* (Cambridge, MA: Harvard University Press, 1985), pp. 120–22. Keynes also said that Sidgwick was "suffocated by respectability." But compare this with a later part of the text, in which Williams says of past societies: "They may not have been wrong in thinking that their social order was necessary for them. It is rather the way in which they saw it as necessary—as religiously or metaphysically necessary—that we cannot now accept"; Williams, *Ethics*, p. 165. The 1982 article on Sidgwick (in *Making Sense of Humanity*) concentrates on demolishing his utilitarianism but has a politeness about it that makes it less interesting; see Bernard Williams, *Making Sense of Humanity and Other Philosophical Papers, 1982–1993* (Cambridge: Cambridge University Press, 1995).
13. Williams, *Ethics*, p. 33.
14. Bernard Williams, *Essays and Reviews, 1959–2002* (Princeton: Princeton University Press, 2004), pp. 184–86, pp. 283–88.

15. Williams, *Ethics*, p. 111.
16. Williams, *Ethics*, p. 71.
17. Williams, *Ethics*, p. 94.
18. Williams, *Ethics*, p. 101.
19. Williams, *Ethics*, p. 109.
20. Williams, *Ethics*, p. 111.
21. Williams, *Ethics*, p. 132.
22. Williams, *Ethics*, p. 147, p. 166.
23. MacIntyre, *Secularization and Social Change*, p. 69.
24. Ibid.
25. Ibid.
26. Ibid.
27. Anthony Storr, *Solitude* (London: Flamingo, 1988), p. 2, p. 32, and *passim*.
28. In fact, Sidgwick had toyed with the same idea and the Sidgwick specialist is not impressed by Moore's originality.
29. See above note 8.
30. MacIntyre, *Secularization and Social Change*, p. 71.
31. It might be said that the Bloomsberries lacked spiritual intensity above all. They had no curiosity as to what it might mean for a man to lose God, to feel he had killed him. Or perhaps they could only muster intensity and feel loss in their friendships, and in their sexual passions. Recall Keynes's judgment of Sidgwick above.

BIBLIOGRAPHY

Harrod, Roy Forbes. *The Life of John Maynard Keynes*. London: Macmillan, 1951.

MacIntyre, Alasdair. *A Short History of Ethics*. New York: Macmillan, 1966.

MacIntyre, Alasdair. *Secularization and Social Change*. London: Oxford University Press, 1967.

MacIntyre, Alasdair. *After Virtue*. Notre Dame: University of Notre Dame Press, 1981.

MacIntyre, Alasdair. *After Virtue*, 3rd edition. Notre Dame: University of Notre Dame Press, 2007.

Nietzsche, Friedrich. *The Gay Science*. Translated by Walter Kaufmann. New York: Vintage, 1974.

Schultz, Bart. *Henry Sidgwick, Eye of the Universe: An Intellectual Biography*. Cambridge: Cambridge University Press, 2007.

Sidgwick, Henry. *Methods of Ethics*. London: Macmillan, 1874.

Storr, Anthony. *Solitude*. London: Flamingo, 1988.

Williams, Bernard. *Essays and Reviews, 1959–2002*. Princeton: Princeton University Press, 2004.

Williams, Bernard. *Ethics and the Limits of Philosophy*. Cambridge, MA: Harvard University Press, 1985.

Williams, Bernard. *Making Sense of Humanity and Other Philosophical Papers, 1982–1993*. Cambridge: Cambridge University Press, 1995.

Williams, Bernard. *Morality: An Introduction to Ethics*. Cambridge: Cambridge University Press, 2012.

14

"Israel but the Grave..."
The Art and Architecture of Mourning
Alexander Stoddart

How do we approach the homes of the dead? In the burial grounds in and around our towns and cities, and those on the outskirts of villages and sometimes in more remote locations, we find ourselves intruders and come to question what it is we seek among the mossy stones and prosaic inscriptions. Some people enter these places in a spirit of adventure, usually in company, smiling in determination; the excursion is a challenge and they march quickly, looking around. Others are tending their loved ones and go immediately to their plot to change the flowers in a business-like way. Still others are after the architecture and sculpture, since we make special provision, and a different manner of accommodation, for the dead, whose bodily needs are much reduced.

Graveyards and their tombs, like funerals, are not for the dead but for the living. In them we set up mute embassies which we fancy serve as points of contact between ourselves, who are bound to the phenomenal world, and those whose phenomenal being has ceased—to become part of a realm beyond it, and concerning which little can be said. In this communicative endeavor we are doomed to fail, and the silence roars on. Yet it is of interest that it is precisely with works of art that we seek to make this contact, except if we are engaging the services of a medium. At funerals we find ourselves tearful as the poetry commences, or perhaps on account of some sudden music. Why should this be the "cue" for weeping? The following essay tries to outline some of the impressions I have received over a lifetime of visiting burial sites ancient and modern, tombs, civic amenities such as crematoria, war graves, animal graveyards, and then the mighty Victorian facilities laid down in the height of the Hygienic

Cemetery Movement of the first half of the nineteenth century. My personal fascination with the habitations of the dead begins with a childhood experience of the impressive Glasgow Necropolis; and it was an experience from afar, and fleeting.

The Necropolis is a compendium. In this great Victorian City of the Dead, we can discover any number of the famed sepulchral forms used as architectural and sculptural gestures, available since antiquity, with which to address the dead and to console the living. The first section will offer a brief history of the site, from its location beside the original cell of the City's Patron Saint (Mungo) up to its purchase by the Merchant House of Glasgow in the early nineteenth century, and will linger a little on its "golden age" of tomb and memorial design in the middle years of the nineteenth century. The second section will look at some of the individual testimonial forms common in this cemetery as in others. The third section will ruminate on matters arising from the contemplation and company of tombs, gravestones, and monuments. The final section will look at the question of the enduring tomb form, as a fane long surpassing the lifetimes of the two or three generations which are likely to mourn at its side. I will focus on Classicism as the architectural style I believe to be best suited for the purpose of housing the dead. This is because, I will argue, Classicism embodies those aspects of our relationship with the dead that are most difficult to represent, and for that reason the most disturbing. This is evidenced both by the tremendous edifice of the Glasgow Necropolis, and the curious place it and other such monuments to the dead have amid the world of the living.

Glasgow's legendary origin centers around the story of a young holy man named Mungo (or Kentigern, to give him his Celtic name). Having conceived out of wedlock, his mother Thenew (or Theneva, or Denw) was, like Danae in Greek legend, sealed within a corracle and sent out to sea from the East Lothian coast. The rough vessel floated north and eastwards up the Firth of Forth, to land at Culross in Fife where an old monk named Serf took in the desperate young woman. There the child was born and brought up to the monastic life and, on reaching his twenties, embarked upon his significant hero-journey (as such figures must, from Siegfried to Snow White), driving an ox-drawn plow westwards across Scotland's central belt.

The team ground to a halt at the confluence of the River Clyde and its tributary, the Molendinar burn. Here, beneath a rocky hill, Mungo set up his Cell and began to minister to the local inhabitants, already Christian but bordering the resolutely pagan Strathclyde Britons to the south and west. By the Middle Ages the Cathedral had been built upon what is almost certainly the Saint's burial place, and a celebrated sepulchre erected there, full of gold and color, and attended by a pilgrim presence, day and night, singing hymns of praise while circling the shrine (see Figure 14.1). Today only the foundations of this fane can be seen, in the Cathedral crypt, for the Reformation had passed through and, although the iconoclasts were relatively lenient with Glasgow's church, some things had to go. Glasgow kept a fond memory of Mungo alive through subsequent centuries, and also honored his mother, whose name *Thenew* became masculinized as *Enoch* and was used to name a city square and a railway station.

Figure 14.1. Glasgow Cathedral seen from Glasgow Necropolis, with the Bridge of Sighs linking the two. *Author's own records.*

The stories of Mungo in Glasgow set the foundation for the city's unique *pastorale*; a strong sense of *rus in urbe* which is often overlooked due to the predominant mercantile and industrial narratives promoted in the last century, and in the political activism and stylish social profiling of recent decades. And it was on that very rocky hill rising behind the Cathedral of Glasgow that one of the finest expressions of that generous, picturesque *instinct to enchant* appeared, with the erection, by the Merchants' House of the city in 1825, of a towering monument to the Reformer John Knox (c.1514–1572)—who must, ironically, stand as a major tutelary deity

Figure 14.2. The crest of the Glasgow Necropolis, with statues of John Knox and Charles Tennant of St. Rollox. *Author's own records.*

of Weberian "disenchantment." A Doric column of the utmost severity serves to support the colossal figure of Scotland's most famous iconoclast, the particular architectural order being well chosen as indicative of the proud "primitivism" of the Reformation project; Doric for the Old Testament, the "primitive hut" order, the order of Revolt, among other connotations (see Figure 14.2).

But beneath this stark memorial there grew a bosky landscape at the lower levels and, during the decades to follow, an assembly of sepulchral buildings of the most striking variety and exotic flare, to form the famous Glasgow Necropolis, thought by some to be the finest "City of the Dead" in the British Isles. It had all been the plan of the Merchants' House, following on from the limited development of the hill as a formal park, then as a fully appointed and designed burial ground.

By 1832, everything was ready for the first interment—and that happens to have been of a Jew, one Joseph Levi, a jeweler. The tiny Jewish community in Glasgow had made an early purchase of land within the Necropolis plan, so that, integrated but secluded, its people might have a place to rest. The awkward site, a steeply sloping triangle at the extreme north of the park, on the lowest level adjacent to the old Molendinar's water course, is graced with a baroque entrance assembly of arch and column, designed by John Bryce. The column, of indeterminate order, is said to derive from Absalom's Pillar in Jerusalem, but bears very little resemblance to any archaeological remains to be found today in the Kidron Valley. Hebrew characters convey the rhetorical Mi Kamoka Adonai (Who is like you, o Lord?) at the top of the pillar shaft, and similar inscriptions, some with dates using the Jewish calendar, complete the enchanting air of sequestered piety around this often-overlooked cultural treasure. And then there is something modern; a full inscription of a poem of around 1814 by Byron, drawn from his collection entitled *Hebrew Melodies*:

> Oh! Weep for those that wept by Babel's stream,
> Whose shrines are desolate, whose land a dream;
> Weep for the harp of Judah's broken shell;
> Mourn—where their God hath dwelt the godless dwell!
>
> And where shall Israel lave her bleeding feet?
> And when shall Zion's songs again seem sweet?
> And Judah's melody once more rejoice
> The hearts that leaped before its heavenly voice?
>
> Tribes of the wandering foot and weary breast,
> How shall ye flee away and be at rest!
> The wild-dove hath her nest, the fox his cave,
> Mankind their country—Israel but the grave![1]

Figure 14.3. The Jews' Enclosure, Glasgow Necropolis. *Author's own records.*

Today the entire inscription is eroded away—apart from the faintest trace of the last line. I can remember when it was all legible (see Figure 14. 3).

The Jews' Enclosure, as it is known, sets the formal tone of the Necropolis, as it developed during the mid-nineteenth century. Its architectural components are worth studying, even though these are far from typical of the Classical canon used elsewhere in the grounds, together with some distinguished instances of Gothic, Romanesque, and even Islamic forms. Possibly, the use of an exaggerated Baroque for the entrance arch is significant; the manner, by the time the Enclosure was being built, was becoming distinctly old-fashioned and associated with some early eighteenth-century sepulchral structures immediately adjacent to the Cathedral. The adoption of this waning style might well be simply the habit of the architect (who has other works in the Baroque on the Necropolis), yet it is for us to muse upon the effect, irrespective of the intentions driving it. The furnishings of cemeteries are seldom well documented, and we are left in a distinct hermeneutic position when we come to assess them. We interpret, because we do not understand. My own view is that the Baroque appears here owing to an established idea, at the time, of the "exoticism" of the Jews, as a people known as "Oriental," whose being is more in the past than the present. Thus, the Jews' Enclosure is invested with a distinct air of sadness, quite different from the scrubbed effects in the large modern Jewish cemeteries in the southern outskirts of Glasgow, where the city's prosperous Jewish communities now locate.

The Golden Age of the Glasgow Necropolis must be placed in the middle of the nineteenth century, when its reputation not only as a burial site, but also as a monumental feature became fixed and famous. Interments from afar became normal, and also monuments erected to people buried elsewhere, so that, to take an example from later in that central period (1882), we find the Fifth President of the Royal Scottish Academy, the painter Sir Daniel MacNee (1810–1882) commemorated here, with the tragic story of his entire family's pre-deceasing, despite his being buried in the Dean Cemetery in Edinburgh.[2] The colonial dimension is ubiquitous, as would be expected in this high Imperial city, and the major industrialists, traders, literary figures, academics, and clergy of the West of Scotland gain monumental notice. It would seem that there is less mourning on this hill, and more celebratory recognition. And so there is a bifurcation between the formal (perceptual) quality of the Necropolis, which is firmly in the solemn funerary mode, and the more presentational side, which conveys the concept of Glasgow's civic and national greatness.

A key feature of the architecture here, and generally in the western tradition of tomb design, is the recourse to the forms of Greek Classicism, which in Scotland rose to perfection in the earlier nineteenth century. Why would this style become the most efficient idiom with which to commemorate the dead? I have come to the conclusion, as a lifelong devotee of this very style in art and architecture, that this is because, like the dead themselves, Classicism is a dead style. If we announce this idea in contemporary society, we should expect the company to laugh like a drain. Why on earth would one, dedicating his entire life and work to this cultural inheritance, suddenly declare the whole shooting-match to be over before it began, and the very option one aims to defend *not alive*?

To understand this, it is best to approach the matter from the position of Classicism's enemy—which is of course Modernism, or Contemporism, as it is best to describe current trends in the art and design world. Think how often a modernist architect will extend respect towards the Gothic style, where he cannot abide the stoa and its columns, or the pediment with its crowning *akroterion*. He will eschew the entire corpus of Roman architecture—except for the arch (or "arc" as he likes to call it)—and many a work of musical cacophony will have the arch form attributed to it. The arch is respectable, where the trabeated arrangement (the post-and-lintel system) is deeply suspect. These aversions and indulgences derive, in my opinion, not from associations in the outer world (Empire, capitalism, slave-owning, the comfortable complacencies of *Country Life*, and so on), but extend into that outer world (*the* world) from qualities intrinsic to and inherent in the simple shapes themselves, and the various means whereby they combine to defy gravity in the built structure.

Now, as it is customary in traditional mourning to abstain from sports, pub-crawling, wenching, and all the more thrilling and moronic of human endeavors, we find that with the donning of the black armband we are expected to reduce our frequency and volume of *movement* as a key provision. In this way we pay our respects to the dead in a flattering spirit of imitation (for these ones have reduced their action to a zero, if we discount the slow shiftings and nudgings of the bacterial investment in the remaining cadaver). As we "weep for those who wept," so we pause for those who have stopped. Therefore, when we come to make architectural provision for those who have terminally arrested, it is only appropriate that the least dynamically active of architectonic systems be embraced for the purpose, and the trabeated system provides just that solution. The lintel sits, dead and dull, on the equally gormless posts, the thrusts involved going in a straight direction plumb to the very center of the Earth, to collide at an infinitesimal point lost among the Empire State Building-sized crystals that geologists think pack together in Hell. In this way the dynamics of Classical architecture are very simple (if not entirely absent) and this relative stillness makes the style fit for the absolutely still. Modernism, which has never done well in the field of tomb architecture, is a style most effectively pathologized as a period reaction, dedicated to movement, thrust on a horizontal plane, and affirmative of the will-to-live—all of which make it both philistine . . . and dangerous. We can call it by its 1920s names as "Rationalism" or "Futurism," and would not be mistaken to associate it with Fascism, as the historical record attests.[3]

The Gothic style, on the other hand, while admirable and amazingly complex, is indulged by vitalist modernists who, despite its unbreakable association with religion, find that it appeals through its high and dynamic engineering. It is a style that expresses *thrust*, and all its features, exposed for the world to see, serve to assist in the operation of this engine. The flying buttress (we remember that early flight dements people like Le Corbusier into thinking the flying machine an example for all architects to follow) is seductive in its very nomenclature, as it thunders downwards under its masonry pile-up to counter the lateral spread of its roof-tonnage, exposed to present what the resolutely romantic-Classical Glaswegian architect Alexander Thomson (1817–1875) would call "a wilderness of slates." All such exposure, all this demonstrationism, is what makes the Gothic a worldly style. It results in an agitated arrangement when employed in tomb design. This must surely be why, when horrors and ghost stories are being told, and the cinema projects pictures of The Undead, and aimless teenagers pour out into city centers of a Saturday with the desire to stand out in the festival of mutual display—in short, when the life-force is most fully and uncannily on show—we always find the word *Gothic* near-to-hand. Accordingly, Ruskin advises that there ought always to be "something wolfish" in the best Gothic.[4]

Then there is the arch. Now Thomson, mentioned above, had no illusions about this form and discussed it in his Haldane Lectures, delivered to the architecture students in Glasgow during the 1860s.[5] He declared the arch morally despicable, known (of course) to the Greeks but kept hidden in basements and out-of-the-way shanties and hovels. His reasoning was primarily associative; the cruelest people of antiquity (the Romans) made for themselves a veritable festival of the arch in the Colosseum in Rome, where slaughter was the recurrent activity. But for Thomson also something *in* the arch signals moral turpitude, and he finds the clue in the Hindu saying, "The arch never sleeps . . ." This refers to the tortuous reality of the fact that an arch stands up precisely because it is always falling down. This truth, paradoxical in the extreme and thus highly appealing to those who are dialectically inclined (viz. Hegelians, Marxists, and socialists of all stripes), renders the arch a perpetual revolution (rising being the thesis, falling the antithesis, the abiding arch the synthesis).[6] It fairly seduces, for it is really a thought-trick, like Rousseau's "The People, one day, will have to be forced to be free," or the Leninist "dictatorship of the Proletariat," or the especially mischievous slogan from the Parisian *soixante-huitards* "be reasonable!—demand the impossible" (see Figure 14.4).

Thus, to those who are sensitive to such forms of agonizing turbulence, the arch will quite naturally offend. In Glasgow, one crosses over the culverted Molendinar burn to reach the Necropolis by means of a high and most elegant single-span bridge. Symbolically, I interpret this (although

Figure 14.4. The Bridge of Sighs, linking the Cathedral with the Necropolis. *Author's own records.*

it cannot have been originally intended, yet I persist, for it suits my argument so to do) as a final representation of the quintessential condition of the World (fighting) as one leaves it to enter the realm of the Departed Ones, where trabeation is the norm, and peace.

Thomson's critique of the arch is so closely paralleled in the quite extensive analysis of architecture by his German senior contemporary, the philosopher Arthur Schopenhauer (1788–1860), that we wonder if the two had read each other's works on the subject. In *The World as Will and Representation*, the "Sage of Frankfurt" makes an early assessment to the effect that architecture is above all the expression of the nature of the metaphysical Will's lowest objectification, gravity, along with "cohesion, rigidity, hardness, those universal qualities of stone, those first, simplest, and dullest visibilities of the will, the fundamental bass-notes of nature"; and further, "Even at this low stage of the will's objectivity we see its [the will's] inner nature revealing itself in discord; for, properly speaking, the conflict between gravity and rigidity is the sole aesthetic material of architecture; its problem is to make this conflict appear with perfect distinctness in many different ways."[7]

Schopenhauer is concerned to point out that this gravity/rigidity contest is "so openly and naively displayed by ancient (Greek) architecture," whereas in the Gothic the reduction of the load, in contrast with the bearing portion, serves to obscure this very conflict: "Whereas in ancient architecture the tendency and pressure from above downwards are represented and exhibited, just as well as those from below upwards, in Gothic architecture the latter decidedly predominate."[8] In this way, instead of Classicism's "truce" between bearing and borne, we see in the Gothic a triumph of the one side—namely the supporting element. Thus, the Gothic presents a conquest, and this is at the expense of any strong sense of a terminal upper body (the soffit generally presenting a net of further groins, finishing in a multitude of points). The building is a countdown to take-off. The appeal of this dynamic profile is its high vitalism, an expression of unleashed ambition in the vertical. Modernism has a similar ambition, but on the horizontal; we find that both excite, in different measure, a certain personality type; to put it bluntly, that type which has no patience with ideas of quietism or renunciation, which likes to "punch the air" of a Sunday afternoon, or extend its dominion over tracts of neighboring land, usually steppe, with local authorities highly complicit.

Any effective architecture of mourning will of necessity have to embrace the restrictive fact that the interior of the completed structure will, like the Pyramids' inexplicable chambers and passages, be designed to bask in endless darkness, unvisited by the Quick and unobserved by the Dead. In Classical design we will always be ready to admit that the interiors of such buildings are less effective and arresting than those of the Gothic (Schopenhauer also observes this fact), and that the true being of the building consists in its exterior, public face.[9] Is this attributable to the normality of *al fresco* civic life in the southern lands, or is it an expression of a certain moral and ethical disposition to hold in esteem the public and communitarian side of human existence, and thus to design for the enrichment of the shared experience?

It is certainly the case that in antiquity whole sectors of cities were, on the street side, similar to those found in the historic quarters of many cities in the Arab countries; that is, presenting a drab vernacular exterior of stucco and whitewash in which a door will open to a glorious and "paradisiacal" interior in the form of an *atrium* or courtyard.[10] Yet in the great civic centers it is clearly the case that a deliberate public exposure of particularly temple architecture was critical to attain. The very plan of the Athenian Acropolis II (the Acropolis of Pericles) is such that the buildings set upon the flattened rock, as seen from the entrance at the Propyleon, take account both of religious and historically significant and non-negotiable sites (notably that of the Erechtheon) while setting out the Parthenon and other structures according to the three-quarter-view principle, obtaining a powerful aesthetic effect. Where the Gothic entices us in with promises of participation in vertical victory and also with saturated color effects in the stained-glass windows, and while Modernism likewise draws us irresistibly indoors to escape the full-blown brutality of its typical exterior aspect, there is less in Classical architecture to recommend much tarrying and we always feel on gaining the outside prospect once more that we have come into the authentic company of the structure.[11]

Hence, in a sepulchre or mausoleum in the Classical style, the *forbidden* nature of the interior (common to all such accommodations) is suitably met in formal, even symbolic terms; the occupants are singularly heedless and needless of stimulating effects. We might also consider, in this regard, how the ancients are said to have imagined the state of being dead—that the light is low, the skies dull above the Fields of Asphodel, and the spiritual atmosphere heavy and melancholy. As the philosopher says, in the interior of ancient buildings (i.e., Grecian or modern neo-Classical structures) "the flat ceiling always retains something depressing and prosaic."[12]

In the Necropolis of Glasgow there are many dull interiors of this sort. One can glimpse them where the design has included a cast-iron screen or gate. In general, these interiors are dementingly dull, and one cannot gaze for longer than a few seconds therein. This is exactly how we approach the contemplation of death itself, in everyday life. Our attention span is miniscule. We might then conclude that, in tomb design, Classicism promulgates a truth (*the* truth) about life and death; that it is truly the "Style of the Dead"—and as such liable to endless attacks and furious denials by those for whom the truth is positively dreaded; life-affirmers, sentimentalists, activists, and ideologists.

I said that my first experience of Glasgow Necropolis was in childhood; fleeting and from afar. In my childhood, my parents would visit relations in the east of Scotland from time to time, and the journey took us past Glasgow Cathedral, there being no city bypass option in the middle of the last century. Behind the Cathedral rose the sparkling profile of the Necropolis's assembly, and there would be a palpable silence in the car when this feature was drawing near. My father, who was a diligent commentator on every effect to be observed on this or any other car journey, always remained quite silent in the face of this astounding composition which, from my perspective of a six-year-old or so, seemed inexplicable. The Cathedral would be mentioned—but as for the entity behind it . . . no comment. And somehow, I too knew not to say anything, despite my spiraling curiosity. Then came a day when, on the same journey at that point, traffic lights arrested the vehicle, so we were stuck in full view of this taboo thing. In the pause I ventured to make a comment, roughly along the following lines: "It looks like a pile of chess pieces . . ." At this, my father expressed quite serious annoyance, turning sharply in his seat with a grim expression on his face—and so the journey carried on with that classic, family-of-four tension we know to make Christmas, New Year, and Summer Holidays so very special. I knew not to comment on this thereafter, and then the bypass was laid in, so we were spared the trauma. I found out all about the Necropolis later, when I became a teenager and bent upon perplexing my dear parents to the extreme of my ability, as one must.

The little awkwardness that day introduced me to a lifetime of appalled wonderment at the world's adolescent excruciation when faced with the dead and their things. That "first amazement" has served to indicate to me above all the cause of Classical art and design's great struggle in the world, from the earliest times, through the Dark Ages, the Bonfire of the Vanities, the savage Reformation, the sometimes terribly ignorant era called the Enlightenment to today's cultural environment, which proclaims constant vibrancy, a "moving on" ethics and aesthetics, and which might be better described as "contemporal" than "contemporary," as it sees its mission to be founded in the trivial fact of being the current fashion. Although this most recent development rejects the ambition of the previous era to ascertain the objective truth (truth being a-temporal is a bad subject for contemporal art), it nonetheless, somewhat paradoxically, embraces the faith that the "conjecture/refutation" basis of all proper science can be applied to works of art and architecture.

Faced with places like the Necropolis, which mock vibrancy by being an embassy to the terminally still, people therefore must adopt strategies of coping, and this gives rise to fascinating and predictable antics. In the first place there is the questing enthusiasm of the graveyard connoisseur. He visits in groups and is positively expletive in his appreciative responses. Shortly he will write a brief article for the newsletter, focusing on the various eccentricities to be found in the biographies of those interred—and the interest is primarily biographical. Others seek out ascendency and historical significance, while the frequency of pop music video-makers, drama, and dance groups deserves attention. Before an Egyptian-style tomb in the upper zone of the Necropolis, I once witnessed something like this taking place and was affrighted to hear a young lady directing the jigging company to "put on your evilest face!" She wasn't smiling. A burial ground like this will attract summer drinkers and drug users, and sometimes bandits lurk in ambuscade. I have never been so frightened of the dead as of the living in such places—as indeed in all places (see Figure 14.5).

The will to live takes great offense at the presence of the dead amid its own predominant species-rush, and thus seeks to disrupt the resting-places of those who no longer compete in that race. Frequently love matches are consummated in graveyards, and here we drive close to the metaphysical imperatives that surround the procreative impulse. There is no better context in which conception might occur for, on the principle of *chiaroscuro*, against a backdrop of Classical memorials, all "noble decay and calm grandeur," the monstrous activity of copulation sings out like a Royal Fanfare. Mother Nature herself encourages her indentured servants, striving for their lives against the current of oblivion in which they

Figure 14.5. Granite Egyptianizing tomb, Glasgow Necropolis. *Author's own records.*

find themselves. And their (always male) offspring can be relied upon, in their adolescence, to invade the place of their conception to topple a few of those very stones that witnessed their sorry advent. The activity of such hapless breeders functions as a futile attempt to refute the terminal truth of existence. But there are minor exceptions. In one of the vaults in Glasgow, perhaps forty-five years ago, a tramp had made a home for himself, his bedding tidily arranged under that very "depressing and prosaic" ceiling. He seemed to me to be a respectable person; this was long before Glasgow Necropolis came back into public knowledge and was still in disgrace in that most insensitive decade known in infamy as "the 1970s."

This essay, which I feel it is only humane to draw to a close, omits in the end to say anything of the sadness, the *grief*, of mourning as it might manifest in the form of the stones we use to commemorate the dead. In truth, I see not the slightest sign of sadness, or mourning, in any monument I know—but perhaps this is because of my professional involvement in such works, which is fraught with contracts, deadlines, official obstructionism, stupid and sentimental ideas from various quarters, all managed against the general backdrop of *the Struggle against Kitsch* which is the fated, life-long ordeal of all those who dip their toes into Classicism's oceanic stream. Thus, I find that a monument, mausoleum, or tombstone can stand vigil over the dead, but in the attitude of a sentry; one would never speak to it, nor rely in any way upon its power to comfort. For this, and for our tears, we turn to ourselves as we appear in our fellow men and women, for no *stele* can embrace. Yet if the proportions are correct, if there is some "justice" in the contract binding load and support, if there is a kind of *chastity* in the demeanor of the marker—then there we can at least find some consolation, for the pain of bereavement is primarily that of being thrust suddenly into an unaccustomed asymmetry. This is why tomb architecture (as in the architecture of the hearth) is resolutely symmetrical. (And we note that the chimney piece is the other great bugbear of the Modernist designer. How does one possibly accommodate the china dogs?) We turn to art, in its widest sense, for support and comfort. We turn to Modernist art, in its widest sense, for aggravation and distress, which is to say—for *action*.

For action—and also for *creation*. You will find, if you listen carefully in the right circles, that Classical architects and artists (the latter make a vanishingly small community) seldom like to mention the c-word, *creativity*. They think it vulgar and dread that shortly they will be asked to account for how they "approach the creative process . . ." Those who are religiously literate will find a sub-blasphemy in the expression, and those who are Scottish will object that the verb "to create" means to stir up trouble. And this aversion (to the "creativity" nuisance) explains why such designers retain their loyalty to the consolational symmetry mentioned above as the opposite spiritual state to grieving bereavement. We know that astrophysicists are increasingly fielding the awkward and perennial question of what preceded, or at least caused, the "Big Bang" by postulating a "spontaneous asymmetry" from which all *Creation* began (the Old Testament supplies a comprehensive illustrative and mythological account of the whole thing). Perhaps creativity and the uniquely anti-symmetrical design ethos (and ethics) of Modernism exist in an alliance; that the instinct to wreck the symmetrical is in origin a homage to the primal event of becoming, and a hymn of praise to the Creator God. If this were true, then the jutting, piercing, thrusting, rasping, cutting, slicing, disrupting, and challenging characteristics of architectural (and social, political, and moral) Modernism are in fact expressions of god-fearing piety, where those who cleave unto the "handed" forms of tombs and hearths are the true seditionaries. And this could be why they are mob-hounded. Never forget that if you are concerned that your cloth cap is making you seem old before your time, you can always wear it at a jaunty angle, which will result in a fetching, raffish, and in fact *naughty* appearance. It fairly gives a fellow a new lease of life.

NOTES

1. Lord Byron, "Oh! Weep for Those," in *Hebrew Melodies, the Complete Works in One Volume* (Paris: Baudry's European Library, 1857), pp. 281–82.

2. The handsome obelisk is decorated on its base with a bronze *basso-relievo* in the late style of John Mossman (1817–1890), Glasgow's preeminent sculptor and architectural decorator. His family had essentially built the Necropolis, starting with his father, William the Elder (1793–1851), who had moved to Glasgow in 1830 from Edinburgh, enticed by the developments on this very site and the architectural boom elsewhere in the city.

3. Italy embraces Futurism as a perfect corollary to its embrace of Fascism, where Germany's endeavors in Classical design arise *despite* her National Socialism in the Third Reich. Hitler's love of the music (not the thinking, but the music) of Richard Wagner is equally anomalous; no typical Nazi wants to sit through six hours of glacial, legless music dedicated to a stupefied, if pure, Fool and a festering spear-wound. He wants *oompah*, just as modern Nazis crave *heavy metal*.

4. See John Ruskin, *The Stones of Venice*, Vol. II (London: George Allen & Sons, 1908), Chap. VI, §VIII.

5. See Alexander Thomson, *The Light of Truth and Beauty: The Lectures of Alexander "Greek" Thomson, Architect, 1817–1875*, ed. Gavin Stamp (Glasgow: Alexander Thomson Society, 1999), pp. 172–73.

6. For the origin of this idea in Hegel and his followers see the transcripts of Hegel's lectures on aesthetics: *Philosophie der Kunst oder Ästhetik. Nach Hegel.*

Im Sommer 1826. Mitschrift Friedrich Carl Hermann Victor von Kehler, eds. A. Gethmann-Siefert and B. Collenberg-Plotnikov (Munich: Wilhelm Fink Verlag, 2004), pp. 170–71.

7. Arthur Schopenhauer, *The World as Will and Representation*, Vol. 1 (New York: Dover, 1966), Third Book, The World as Will and Representation Second Aspect, §43, p. 368.

8. Arthur Schopenhauer, *The World as Will and Representation*, Vol. 2 (New York: Dover, 1966), Supplements to the Third Book, Chap. XXXV, p. 590.

9. Schopenhauer, *The World as Will*, pp. 591–92.

10. Norbert Schoenauer, for example, argues quite persuasively for the existence of a pervasive "oriental" inward-facing house type that was only gradually superseded by the "occidental" outward-facing house type from the late Middle Ages onwards—the inward-facing model remaining dominant in many parts of the world right up until the collapse of street-based urbanism in the mid-twentieth century. See Norbert Schoenauer, *6,000 Years of Housing*, revised and expanded edition (New York: W.W. Norton, 2000).

11. Because Modernist architecture admits of no adornment or decoration, and is concerned to breach the divide between exterior and interior with great sheets of toughened glass, a further seduction consists in the opportunity to the visitor to *become himself* the proxy for the startling sculptural and decorative effects all civilized people expect of their buildings. In consequence, with the occupants effectively "showcased" within these sterile pavilions, they serve to satisfy an exhibitionist egoism characteristic of so many of the stylish and beautiful people to be found posing within.

12. The ancient sense of the Realm of the Dead is wonderfully and faithfully conveyed in the film by Ridley Scott entitled *Gladiator* (2000) during the final scenes of the protagonist's decease (this might be due to the film's writer, William Nicholson, since he uses almost exactly the same characterization of the afterlife in a children's book he wrote earlier in his career). The *oeuvre* of the Swiss painter Arnold Bocklin (1827–1901) is largely devoted to the representation of this clammy weather and I cannot doubt that Scott and his designers were fully aware of Bocklin's reliable testimony in this regard.

BIBLIOGRAPHY

Lord Byron. "Oh! Weep for Those." In *Hebrew Melodies, the Complete Works in One Volume*. Paris: Baudry's European Library, 1857.

Philosophie der Kunst oder Ästhetik. Nach Hegel. Im Sommer 1826. Mitschrift Friedrich Carl Hermann Victor von Kehler. Edited by A. Gethmann-Siefert and B. Collenberg-Plotnikov. Munich: Wilhelm Fink Verlag, 2004.

Ruskin, John. *The Stones of Venice*, Volume II. London: George Allen & Sons, 1908.

Schoenauer, Norbert. *6,000 Years of Housing*. Revised and expanded edition. New York: W.W. Norton, 2000.

Schopenhauer, Arthur. *The World as Will and Representation*, Volume 1. New York: Dover, 1966.

Schopenhauer, Arthur. *The World as Will and Representation*, Volume 2. New York: Dover, 1966.

Thomson, Alexander. *The Light of Truth and Beauty: The Lectures of Alexander "Greek" Thomson, Architect, 1817–1875*. Edited by Gavin Stamp. Glasgow: Alexander Thomson Society, 1999.

15

The Difficult Art of Outliving

Raymond Tallis

If philosophy has an ultimate purpose, it must be to help us to live well, or at least better, individually and together. One of its defining activities is cultivating or prolonging puzzlement, even astonishment, in order to awaken us to the fathomless mystery of our lives. If philosophy seems to be defined by problems, this is because these are its typical way of pinching ourselves awake, making us aware that our lives seem ordinary and straightforward only because we are such strange creatures. Alas, those problems sometimes cut loose from their roots in wonder and surprise and shrivel to technical issues. The philosophical conversation becomes a boundless desert of arguments, counter-arguments, and counter-counter-arguments. Our gaze on the world is blurred by a sandstorm of footnotes.

And so, I welcome this initiative of Humane Philosophy and am honored to be part of it. It is, I believe, committed to reminding us of what philosophy is, or should be, about, and to reunite the art, the discipline, the craft with some of the richest and most profound conversations humanity has had with itself about its own nature. A truly humane philosophy is suspicious of the recent scientific pretensions of philosophers, and of the idea that the discipline should take its cue—ontologically, metaphysically, and even ethically—from science; and the connected notion that it is not possible to philosophize except by setting aside the ox cart of one's native language, and one's imagination for the Harley Davidson of formal logic and a zone purified of imagination and intuition.

In the *Apology* Socrates is attributed the view, by his ventriloquist Plato, that the aim of philosophy should be to teach one not so much how to live as how to *die*. He was echoed by Cicero: "to philosophize is to learn how to die."[1]

This needs qualification. As a doctor who has witnessed many deaths, I think philosophy has very little to offer once the process of dying gets under way. Socrates himself was famously able to think on a snowy battlefield and Wittgenstein had some of his deepest thoughts after his prostate cancer had proved to be no longer amenable to treatment. Generally, however, philosophy has little to offer us in the spaces defined by pain, breathlessness, incontinence, helplessness, nausea, or confusion.

So, while philosophy as we understand it in the Western tradition has little to say to us on our death bed, might it nevertheless help to teach us about death. Or enhance our awareness of our finitude notwithstanding that our days have for most of our life no visible boundary. If so, at its most profound, the philosophy committed to the art of living is inseparable from sharpening our awareness of dying.

Martin Heidegger contrasted authentic "being-towards-death" with inauthentic being that is lost in the "they" with its unreflecting acceptance of a public consciousness—of what we as "they" think—expressed in gassing or *gerede*. He is perhaps not the most inspiring example, given that he was at least an initially willing fellow-traveler with one of the wickedest regimes in history and turned a willfully blind eye to the Holocaust. A more compelling witness perhaps is Montaigne—who took Cicero's aphorism as the title of an essay—whose essays express an early phenomenological approach to philosophy. "Let us banish the strangeness of death," he said, "let us practise it, accustom ourselves to it, never having anything so often present in our minds than death: let us always keep the image of death [. . .] in full view."[2] Behind this is, I suspect, the belief expressed by E. M. Forster, that while "Death destroys a man; the idea of death saves him."[3]

Saves him? Talk of salvation exaggerates the power of just thinking about death. It seems a bit more convincing in a lecture theater in broad daylight, surrounded by one's fellows, than it does in solitary insomnia at 3:00 a.m., when the ticking of the bedroom clock suggests an insatiable mandible attached to a mindless universe, defoliating the world. Even so, to live to the full, one must be constantly aware of the transience of things; and import death life's dateless—and indeed dataless—night, into a Thursday afternoon.

The traditional preoccupations of philosophy—the nature of reality (the stuff of the world, the nature of space and time), the origin and limits of our knowledge, the place of the mind in the cosmos—serve to highlight through its mystery the life that death cancels.

All of this is preliminary because my talk—a response to the advertised theme of the meeting, mourning—is about something between the art of living and the art of dying; namely the art of *out*living. And I am going to return to the question of philosophy at the very end. My comments are not merely preliminary: they are also prolegomenal. Because in my talk I am not going to *do* philosophy but describe a challenge which philosophy should confront if it is going to do its work of assisting us to flourish through enhancing our awareness of the mystery of life which is tragic as well as fathomless. I have to confess that when I began writing this talk, I thought I knew what I was going to say. Now, having written it, I am less sure of my destination, except insofar as I have not arrived at it. But that's confidential.

When we think of mourning, mourning for that we have loved and outlived, we quite properly focus on bereavement, and I will come to that in a while. But first I want to examine the more general intertwining of life and death. It is so pervasive I shall simply pick up a few trailing threads.

Your speaker, at the age of sixty-nine, is a freak of longevity. He has exceeded the life expectancy of most humans over most of history. And his story is consequently one of many modes of outliving. The most obvious are his parents, his grandparents, uncles and aunts, teachers, many colleagues, friends and enemies, heroes he worshipped and villains he abhorred and vilified. But he has also outlived periods of his life, projects that consumed him, enthusiasms and passions: so many sloughed off skins. He has lost his childhood, boyhood, youth, middle age, and the youth of old age. He has outlived his career, the childhood of his children, and seen them too outlive preoccupations, hopes, dreams. He is a dozen kinds of emeritus.

As he has aged, so he has lost possibility: there is less and less open future and more and more determinate past. His life has become more precisely defined—by a process of pruning conducted by secateurs with more heads than hydra: *omnis determinatio est negatio*. His choices have closed off the open future of his youth and lock in or pathway dependency means that he has arrived at a place from which he cannot go backwards. Seen in that light, the CV is less a list of achievements than the building blocks of the prison constructed out of decisions and accidents. Even so, he has been lucky. Very lucky. Absurdly lucky. He is, after all, largely intact.

Of all his outlivings, the most profound is the outliving of his earlier selves. His forty-year-old self was a remote descendent of his ten-year-old self. And the teenager would scarcely recognize the elderly gentleman catching surprised sight of himself in a mirror and would probably not be on speaking terms with him. Co-evolving with his selves are the successive worlds—of beloved or familiar or just ordinary places, of offices, of circles of friends, acquaintances, and colleagues—imperceptibly or abruptly coming to an end.

The vector is often hidden by the cyclical nature of his life: the regular renewals of the yearly round, the weekly timetable, the Saturday morning football with the children, successive Christmases, and the annual holiday. Hidden or not, behind accumulation and growth, there is a counterpoint of loss. The knowledge that life at its most abundant is mixed with death: the flowers of spring wither, their work done; the wrappings from dehiscent buds litter the woodland floor. Our lives are the summer before dark, the hours before nightfall. If we fail to notice this, it is because at our moments of transition, we are looking forward, looking past them, and this sustains us until the final phase when we lose the alibi and the obligations of the future.

The underlying story of growing that is growing away, of gain that is loss, becomes evident at certain moments of transition; as when for example we move out of the family home, gaining freedom but losing our childhood, or when we take our own child to school for the first time and start the process by which we cease for them to be all and everything. The child who was utterly dependent on you grows up to be an adult who has a world of his own from which he communicates with yours. At such moments we experience moods in which we outlivers seem exiles from a lost paradise. A. E. Housman caught this beautifully:

> Into my heart an air that kills
> From yon far country blows;
> What are those blue remembered hills,
> What spires, what farms are those?
>
> That is the land of lost content,
> I see it shining plain.
> The happy highways where I went
> And cannot come again.[4]

Now old, we wake at 3 a.m. and remember the sunlit days on the beach with the children and cry with anguish Villon's immortal lines: "Where are the snows of yesteryear?"

Even if we adopt a Whiggish view of our own history—confirmed by looking at old photographs that show us as raw, unformed, and with a ridiculous haircut—we know that after we have left our childhood—and lost a seemingly boundless future—living and losing, living and outliving, are inseparable. Thus, the source of the elective sadness, the white melancholy, the sweetness of mourning for the past simply because it was past; beautiful because bygone and beyond recall. Each outliving moves us perceptibly or imperceptibly closer to death after which it will be others who will do the outliving and on whose fidelity to our memory we shall rely for our continuing existence.

But it is time to turn to the non-elective, unbeautiful sadness: the crushing grief of bereavement, of a catastrophic loss that ransacks one's life and fills what is left with a miserable hunger for that which has been lost. In what follows, I draw on a grief imagined for myself and the closely observed grief of a good friend who, three years on from the sudden loss of his wife, is not much further on: he remains close to the calamitous moment when she came into the room and said, "I have a terrible headache" and their forty-year conversation came to an end.

He turns to her to smile, and her face is not there to receive it. He thinks of something he must tell her, but she has nothing to hear it by. He is tormented by dreams in which she is trying to get hold of him by phone. He returns from traveling to what was *their* home and he is now the sole owner. In consequence every space—behind the front door, in the kitchen, in the bathroom, in the bedroom, in the unshared bed, in every cupboard where her unoccupied clothes are, the row of dresses uninhabited—is hung with a Not that evacuates meaning from what he sees, hears, says, thinks, owns. Because there is no remission, her death seems at times stubbornness, an unending silence, an eternally averted gaze, an infinite sulk. Her death is everywhere, in everything, not least in the eyes of acquaintances who reflect back to him his status as a widower. It no longer matters whether he walks to the right or the left because all places are equidistant from the non-existent place where she is still alive. Julian Barnes described this in *Levels of Life* as being comparable to losing a limb or an organ.[5] My friend, a doctor, corrects him: what he has lost is the interstitial tissue that bounded him together as a coherent entity.

Bereavement is 24/7. Can things go on like this? Sooner or later, someone is going to say, "It is time to let go, time to move on." The work of grief has been done. Wipe your eyes, look away from the world that is lost to the world that remains. Of course, keep those many anniversaries and the special moments and the little box in which the memories are stored. Cultivate for her sake the friendships of those who knew her. But now is the time to look to the future.

What good, decent, humane sense! It is what the Queen Gertrude, his mother, counseled Hamlet, chiding him for what she deems the excess of his mourning over his dead father.

> Do not for ever with thy vailéd lids
> Seek for thy noble father in the dust.
> Thou know 'tis common: all that lives must die,
> Passing through nature to eternity.[6]

Gertrude's motives for urging good cheer are, of course, impure. Even so, we recognize the sentiment behind the message. At some stage we must "get over" bereavement and resume our lives. This is the difficult art of outliving.

But there are barriers. "Moving on" seems like a betrayal. Indeed, several betrayals. It is self-betrayal. It is to embrace the outliving of something—that togetherness—that filled the vessel of one's days. "I will get over you" says that at a certain level there is something essential in me that is outside or beyond our relationship, something that was left intact when you went, out of which I can build a new story, a new life, a new self. It is a self-betrayal to assign the relationship to a past that is past; to say, "You will matter less." Miss Havisham's refusal to remove the wedding dress she was wearing when she was jilted at the altar, leaving the wedding breakfast and the wedding cake on the table, having the clock stopped at the moment when she received the letter, is an expression of a profound fidelity to herself.

In such a state of mourning, any continuation of ordinary life, even that which is necessary to get from day to day washed, fed, sheltered, in communication with others, seems almost impious: that he should devote himself to trivia in the vicinity of the gigantic fact of her absence, that he should be pushing a shopping trolley while she is dissolving in the rain. Survivor guilt permeates the continuation of the long, detailed littleness of daily life after he has failed to save, and can no longer help, her.

How, then, to remember and not to be paralyzed by memory; to know the size of another's death without being diminished by it; to feel the loss but not to be eaten from within by it; to pay tribute to the past without mortgaging the future? There is, it seems, no right path between the commemoration of mourning and "moving on," giving the dead their due, their life in one's own life, and yet being able to continue the ordinary, necessarily local, even trivial, patterns of thought and action that daily living requires.

Mourning refuses to say of the past that it is merely the past and that, being the past, it is less real than the present. Or to say that the loss is a temporary setback. It will not collude with the indifference of the world, of the crowd, of the stranger, of the material universe, in pronouncing the insignificance of all that was significant, that mattering is transient. At the heart of love, after all, is the implicit declaration "You are irreplaceable; you are inseparable from what I am; the days we share are my life; when you went you took my life with you." Moving on is an acceptance that nothing, however much it matters, matters in the end, that all things will pass, and it will be as if they had never been. The continuation of the pain, conversely, is a tribute to the reality and depth of the relationship.

We try different ways of giving ourselves permission to "move on." We do so for the sake of others in our lives: to remain a fully engaged parent of our children, sharing with their joys and sorrows; to put on a brave face for our friends and to become again the genial companion that we once were; and to resume the projects in which we and others invested so much. We may even find permission in the imagined wishes of the one whom we mourn. "She would have wished me to find happiness."

There is an example in a beautiful, because honest, letter from Charles Dickens to his younger sister Letitia who had just lost her husband of twenty-five years, that begins with his saying, "I do not preach consolation because I am unwilling to preach at any time, and know my own weakness too well."[7] Acknowledging that "the disturbed mind and affections [. . .] seldom calm without an intervening time of confusion and trouble," he advises Letitia, "In a determined effort to settle the thoughts, to parcel out the day, to find occupation regularly or to make it, to be up and doing something, are chiefly to be found in the mere mechanical means which must come to the aid of the best mental efforts."[8] Thus, occupational therapy. And he also adds that, while it is impossible to be sure, "our prolonged grief for the beloved dead may grieve them in their unknown abiding-place, and give them trouble."[9]

This is on the edge of the consoling thought that the departed beloved is still in some sense alive, beyond our grieving memory, in another and better world where, as we see so often on park benches memorializing the dead, the deceased and the bereaved will be reunited. Such hope is movingly expressed in Bishop King's "An Exequy to His Matchless Never to Be Forgotten Friend"—his beloved wife. He imagines how each day will bring him nearer to her. Every hour is "a step towards thee":

> But Hark! My pulse, like a soft drum,
> Beats my approach, tells thee I come.[10]

There is no such consolation for infidels like your speaker. I cannot entirely follow Gertrude in her remonstration with Hamlet. While all that lives must die, its passage through nature leads not to eternity but to nothing. A pyramid of ashes truly is the final state of RT and those he has loved and lost. To think otherwise seems like magic thinking.

And there is another difficulty that makes mourning inescapable. It is captured by the melancholic diarist H. F. Amiel in a penetrating observation: "All that is necessary, providential—in short, *unimputable*—I could bear, I think, with some strength of mind. But responsibility mortally envenoms grief."[11] Those who are bereaved find a multitude of ways of feeling guilty that prevents them from moving on because their guilt travels with them.

There are obvious sources of guilt. Time and again, as a doctor, I had to reassure grieving relatives that they were not responsible for the patient's death; that it would have made no difference if they had noticed something earlier, acted sooner, called the ambulance more quickly. There is the guilt, perhaps justified, at not having treated the deceased more thoughtfully, more kindly; at betrayals and even infidelities, or a selfishness that took the other one for granted and failed to admit, acknowledge, or realize their full reality. It is hard not to regret the preoccupations, duties, ambitions, achievements which opened up spaces in which each could forget the other for such stretches of time. Just in virtue of being so often in different places, in the world, in a city, in a room, their togetherness was an intermittence of being apart, something both took for granted and accepted as entirely normal—which it was. No one, after all, has achieved anything significant without turning their back on those closest to them for long periods of time. And there was, it seemed, an entirely innocent and necessary infidelity built into the very structure of the relationship: the multiplicity of the friends, colleagues, confidants, relations, the pressure of imperatives that divided and diluted the presence of each to the other. We are dis-tracted, drawn apart from those closest to us, by the obligation to deliver on our obligations.

One version of this guilt is described with exquisite precision in the agony of Thomas Hardy's beautiful and disturbing *Poems 1912–13* written after the sudden death of his wife. He had been estranged from her and did not appreciate that she was seriously ill. In *The Going* remorse is mixed with something close to resentment that she had not warned him of her death. The last day was like any other:

> Why did you give no hint that night
> That quickly after tomorrow's dawn,
> And calmly, as if indifferent quite,
> You would close your term here, up and be gone
> Where I could not follow
> With wing of swallow
> To gain one glimpse of you ever anon![12]

His regret that they had not revisited the early days of their marriage when they were in love is bitter indeed:

> Why, then, latterly did we not speak,
> Did we not think of those days long dead,
> And ere your vanishing strive to seek
> That time's renewal?[13]

He is crushed by knowledge of missed opportunity:

> O you could not know
> That such a swift fleeing
> No soul foreseeing—
> Not even I—would undo me so![14]

There is regret for the small and large acts of unkindness and irritability and moments of indifference and anger. Of being busy and in his case dissatisfied.

But there is a realization of an apartness that goes deeper than this. That the other can die—can be alone, unaccompanied, in this the most profound change that takes her into an unreachable solitude—seems proof of the degree to which we are "enisl'd" in the sea of life as Matthew Arnold put it and how "we mortal millions live alone."[15] This was echoed by Schubert in his diary: "People imagine they can reach one another, but in reality they only pass one another by. O misery for one who realizes this! March 27, 1824."[16]

Bereavement is a brutal way of reinforcing awareness of the extent to which we live alone. The permanent separation by the greatest of all distances—that between life and death—highlights the separateness that checkers all togetherness even in the closest and most fulfilled relationship. Behind it is the fundamental truth—no less profound for being a truism—that we are continuously ourselves, and only intermittently with our closest intimate. What the other knows immediately about herself is often for us a matter of guesswork or the subject of inquiry. We do not know even what it was like for the lost one to be in our company and how and to what extent our distinct co-presences were congruent, given the frequent and necessary divergence of preoccupations, duties, projects, anxieties, viewpoints, sensations, and a final journey that has to be taken alone. The other's voice and comforting hand can touch the suffering, the fear, the bewilderment only superficially, and the destination—where the deceased are deserted even by their own bodies—is beyond even solitude. If she can die when he lives, if we are now separated by the most profound of differences, and forever, how deep did "we" go?

And there is something else at work. Thomas Hardy again—a memory of a happy moment in his childhood:

> *The Self-Unseeing*
> Here is the ancient floor,
> Footworn and hollowed and thin,
> Here was the former door,
> Where the dead feet walked in.
>
> She sat here in her chair,
> Smiling into the fire;
> He who played stood there,
> Bowing it higher and higher.
>
> Childlike, I danced in a dream;
> Blessings emblazoned that day;

> Everything glowed with a gleam;
> Yet we were looking away![17]

"Yet we were looking away"—looking outward, looking forward, looking backward—looking anywhere but here; being anywhere but here. And there are so many modes nowadays of looking away, of losing our togetherness in the weightless element of elsewhere, the boundless worlds of electronic media.

Hardy's child's "looking away" is a poignant example of something woven into the very fabric of time and shared time or togethering. And mourning our loss, we dwell on the extent to which we failed to be entirely present in what we had before we lost it.

Thus "grief mortally envenomed." Those who mourn may feel solitary because their sorrow is not shared by, or not at least felt as intensely and continuously by, those who would support them. Our friends have their own lives to get on with, and, when the time comes, their own mourning to do, their own memories and regrets to come to terms with. Mourners may remember with regret how, in the past, they have not mourned the many others whom others have mourned. The circle of those whom they value and miss is tightly drawn. To be bereaved is to be reminded that one is part of the heartlessness of the world: we cared a lot for some, a little for some more, and nothing for the overwhelming majority. Mournable deaths are vastly outnumbered by those that are beyond the reach of our capacity or inclination to mourn.

Sustenance may come from public rituals of mourning, but there is sometimes the feeling that the event has hollows near its heart; that it is too general; that it shares something of the Remembrance Service when we assert that "we remember them" though in our two minutes or more, we do not even begin to define who the remembered are, never mind give them even the fleeting posthumous life of being remembered for what they were. There is a sense that the performance of sorrow tinges the careful, the calculated tact, of kindly friends who may consequently be revealed as imperfect strangers in whose consciousness one lives a very intermittent life, and in whose minds there is a portrait one would not recognize. This is another way in which mourning highlights our state of being enisled, rooted in the truth that we are continuously aware of ourselves and only intermittently in the presence of others and even more intermittently aware of what they are thinking, feeling, and needing, and scarcely able to respond to those thoughts, feelings, and needs. The widow's weeds and the black arm band request special treatment but cannot requisition imagination, empathy, or true co-presence.

And, finally, as a mourner, you are made aware of the fragility of your own life. The other's death is a prelude to your own. Whose turn will it be next to be taken out to be shot? To lose the beloved is the largest step towards the inevitable loss of everything—one's life, one's world, and one's self. Hamlet's protracted mourning—he "Hath that within which passeth show"[18]—is not therefore pathological, a suitable case for cognitive behavioral therapy, whatever Gertrude has to say.

Even so, life has to continue. Here is Claudius:

> 'Tis sweet and commendable in your nature, Hamlet,
> To give these mourning duties to your father,
> But you must know your father lost a father,
> That father lost, lost his—and the survivor bound
> In filial obligation for some term
> To do obsequious sorrow. But to persevere
> In obstinate condolement is a course
> Of impious stubbornness, 'tis unmanly grief,
> It shows a will most incorrect to heaven [. . .]
>   Fie! 'Tis a fault to heaven,
> A fault against the dead, a fault to nature,
> To reason most absurd, whose common theme
> Is death of fathers, and who still hath cried
> From the first corse till he that died today,
> "This must be so."[19]

The message, articulated with increasing impatience—get over it, move on, if everyone behaved like you, life would grind to a halt—is of course poisoned by the fact that we know that Claudius, the murderer of Hamlet's father, is ordering Hamlet to "get over" his, Claudius's—own crime. But it is one we recognize: others who wish us to recover from our loss may not only be acknowledging that living would be impossible if it was entirely caught up in outliving but also have needs of their own.

Our friends perhaps grow tired of our grief, wish we would remove the black band round our life, would talk about something else than unbearable loss. The shallows of ordinary conversation prefer gossip and good cheer: death is too dark and too big, like a shark in a warm rock pool where our children play with their toys. This is reflected in the feeling sometimes experienced by those who grieve that others might wish to avoid them. A woman I knew described the experience as being the psychological equivalent of suttee—where the widow is immolated along with her husband on the funeral pyre. Or, more gently, where the topic of the loss is to be avoided. Julian Barnes observed—in his memoir of his own bereavement—how friends pretended not to hear when he mentioned his deceased wife's name.[20] The grief-stricken encounter the monstrous indifference of everyday life in which everyone's troubles are their own, the necessary heartlessness at the heart of ordinary life which "must go on."

At any rate, there is an implicit statute of limitations on the grief of loss. There is a certain amount of what Freud called "the work" of mourning to be done. It is a process of disinvestment of the self in the lost beloved. At its heart is a retraining of habits of expectation, of reference, of self-location; a withdrawal from a version of oneself. Killing the pain of loss seems to diminish, half-kill that which one has lost; to cease to miss seems to dismiss; and—because the other and oneself were so inseparably intertwined—to commit at least partial suicide. It is to collude with the loss and make it complete; even to suggest that the past was a kind of dream and the present nightmare a passage to an updated reality.

Sooner or later, life continues and extends beyond and outside the spaces occupied by loss. Absence, the not, the no-longer occupy shrinking territory. The period when he talked to her (except in his imagination) starts to recede, displaced by the hours, days, weeks, months, years in which he has talked *about* her, and the beloved is more often she, or "your mother," or "my late wife" than "thou."

If at length the bereaved give themselves permission to flourish again, it is in part because there are others who deserve their attention; in descending order of importance, children, other relatives, colleagues, and friends. The initial, necessarily outward show of recovery gradually permeates inwards and becomes more than a show. The therapy of occupation and preoccupation does its subtle work, most effective if least noticed. There will of course be catastrophic relapses—when the coat is hung up and the door closes on an empty and silent house, its spaces packed with evidence of the world they had created between them, when places are visited alone that had been visited together—but the direction of travel has been set.

Thus, the work of mourning. And what do philosophers have to say that might help us? Is there anything that they could address to our future bereaved selves that those selves would not read with contempt? What advice do they have regarding the art of outliving? The earliest preserved sentence of Western philosophy—owing to Anaximander—tells us the score. Gertrude's "common condition of humanity" is the common condition of all beings:

> Where things have their origin, there they must also pass away according to necessity, for they must pay the penalty and be judged for their injustice, according to the ordinance of time.[21]

This is more than saying, "That in virtue of which stuff happens, stuff must also unhappen, so that everything which passes towards must pass away." More than asserting that particulars have no right to be, and if they have come into being, must redeem their original sin of contingency by ceasing to be. It says, according to Heidegger's interpretation, that what is present is *a-dikon*—unjust or etymologically out of joint. Time itself is out of joint. The present "is a lingering that escapes both a coming to and a going away." Lingering is "an insurrection [. . .] on behalf of sheer endurance."[22] An endurance that Hardy's "looking away" undermines. This offers little comfort. It does, however, underline the extraordinary privilege of being, of being-there, and most importantly of being-there-together.

Jump forward half a millennium to a more predictable port of call—to Lucretius, *De Rerum Natura* and the reason for not fearing death. We have had non-existence before we were born, he says, and remember nothing of it. We should not fear returning to this state. And we do not live to experience our own death. The argument is of course deeply flawed because it overlooks the non-equivalence of being non-existent (which feels, knows, and anticipates nothing) and anticipating non-existence. The asymmetry, the non-equivalence, is underlined when we outlive those whom we have loved.

Even if Lucretius helped us to come to terms with mortality, it would have nothing to say about outliving. First of all, the death of the beloved is one we do experience. But secondly, there is no consolation in thinking that, since you lived happily without your beloved in the years before you met her, you could just as well live happily without her again. After all, you have become what you are at least through your love for the one you have lost. You are the story of your life and that story is shared in its most important part with the story of the life that is lost. To live without her is to live without yourself—or a great part of yourself. The love that continues without its object feels that it is reaching into a void.

The interface between philosophy, therapy, and preaching that is exemplified in the Stoic tradition scarcely assists those who love life and whose love of live is inextricably caught up with the love of another. Spinoza's belief that, insofar as we are rational, we ought to value equally the past, present, and future does little to assuage sorrow. And the Spinozist Einstein's letter to the widow of his friend Michele Besso makes one shudder:

> Now Besso has departed from this strange world a little ahead of me. That means nothing. People like us, who believe in physics, know that the distinction between past, present, and future is only a stubbornly persistent illusion.[23]

There is little comfort to be had from such thoughts. Stoic and other prescriptions, consoling in theory, are useless in the face of howling reality.

The truly wise Dr. Johnson reflects this in *Rasselas*, the allegorical novel he wrote at high speed in great grief after the death of his mother, aiming thereby to pay for her funeral. Rasselas, in his journey to seek happiness, is impressed by a philosopher preaching Stoic values. He is cautioned by Imlac his mentor: "Be not too hasty to trust, or to admire, the teachers of morality: they discourse like angels but they live like men."[24] As he soon discovers, when in due course he visits the philosopher. He finds him in a darkened house poleaxed by the death of his own daughter, discovering the emptiness of his philosophy: "What comfort, said the mourner, can truth and reason afford me? Of what effect are they now, but to tell me, that my daughter will not be restored?"[25]

We have all our words and attitudes ready in advance and then find that, when they are needed, the words are drained of meaning and the attitudes are not possible. The grand generalizations of philosophy do not reach into those interstices of life where we encounter our losses and mourn. As Yeats put it: "Man is in love and loves what vanishes, what more is there to say?"[26]

Even so, a life without unreasonable love, without the special meaning each might have in another's eyes—however little objective legitimacy it has—would be a life empty of human meaning. And a universe underpinned by a God who (notwithstanding the evidence) cares for the fall of a sparrow as much as for the one whose loss you fear above all, whose love is evenly distributed over His creation (and the current 7,900,000,000 needy souls) is as comfortless as one in which no one is cared for. A world in which no one mattered especially to anyone else—that each, careless of his own life, should be careless of others' lives—would be a bleak place. Without unreasonable love, binding the days each to each, life would break down into a succession of moments. A utilitarianism, guided by a felicific calculus, that valued all equally would be at once admirable and chilling and, ultimately, by separating actions from affections, would pave the way for societies in which a loveless tyranny flourishes under the flag of universal beneficence and justice.

Our hold on life is frail, much of living is a long succession of farewells small and large, with and without ceremony—and our grasp on its moments weak. We always, as Rilke said in his *Duino Elegies*,

> retain the attitude
> of someone who's departing [. . .]
> we live our lives, for ever taking leave.[27]

Slipping through our own fingers, we lose those who share our lives. As we get older, we are increasingly outlivers, until we ourselves are numbered among the lost. We have to find a seemingly impossible path that embraces the future without betraying the past, finding new meanings while not turning one's back on what was once new and meant everything.

What is to be done? In the Kingdom of Means we fight to postpone death, knowing that in the eyes of eternity the difference between being still-born and dying as an octogenarian is scarcely perceptible. In the Kingdom of Contemplation, we cultivate a pre-emptive mourning by a foreseeing and foresuffering that helps us rejoice in what has not yet been taken from us. Which brings me back to the beginning of my talk—to Forster, and Montaigne—and to philosophy.

And philosophy? Philosophy with its wonderful problems to pinch ourselves awake brings its true value: not consolation but astonishment and untaking the taken for granted. This, of course, falls far short of the detachment from persons, places, and things that would protect us from mourning. It is a love not of wisdom—who, after all, is wise?—but a special kind of love of the world—a respect for its mystery, possibly for its tragedy, and certainly for its complexity. This is philosophy at its best. Truly humane philosophy.

If, then, there is an art of outliving, it must be inseparable from that aspect of the art of living expressed perfectly by Shakespeare, speaking this time in his own voice: "To love that well, which thou must leave ere long." Philosophy worthy of the name—beyond the technicalities, the polemics, the scholarship—might, by unpeeling our gaze, assist the "loving well" that may help us better to negotiate the ordeal of outliving the places, ways of life, and the people we have loved.

NOTES

1. Marcus Tullius Cicero, *Tusculan Disputations*, trans. Alan E. Douglas (Warminster: Aris & Phillips, 1985), Book I, 31.
2. Michel de Montaigne, *The Complete Essays*, ed. Michael Screech (London: Penguin, 1991), Book I, §29, p. 96.
3. E. M. Forster, *Howards End* (London: Penguin, 2000), p. 237.
4. A. E. Housman, *A Shropshire Lad* (New York: Dover Thrift Editions, 1990), p. 27.
5. Julian Barnes, *Levels of Life* (London: Vintage Books, 2014).
6. William Shakespeare, *Hamlet* (London: Penguin, 2001), Act I, scene ii.
7. Charles Dickens, *The Letters of Charles Dickens, Volume 2*, ed. Mamie Dickens and Georgina Hogarth (Frankfurt: Outlook Verlag, 2020), p. 136.
8. Ibid.
9. Ibid.
10. Henry King, "An Exequy to His Matchless Never to Be Forgotten Friend," in *The New Oxford Book of Seventeenth Century Verse*, ed. A. Fowler (Oxford: Oxford University Press, 1992), 288–90.

11. Henri Frédéric Amiel, *Amiel's Journal, Volume 1*, trans. Mrs. Humphry Ward (London: Macmillan & Co., 1885), p. 16.

12. Thomas Hardy, "The Going," in *Satires of Circumstance: Lyrics and Reveries with Miscellaneous Pieces* (London: Macmillan and Co., Limited, 1914), pp. 95–96.

13. Ibid.

14. Ibid.

15. Matthew Arnold, "To Marguerite—Continued," in *The Poetry of Matthew Arnold*, ed. Kenneth Allott (London: Longman Norton, 1965).

16. Franz Schubert, cited by David Schroeder, *Our Schubert: His Enduring Legacy* (Lanham, MD: Scarecrow Press, 2009), p. 113.

17. Thomas Hardy, "The Self-Unseeing," in *Poems of the Past and the Present* (London: Macmillan and Co., Limited, 1919), pp. 441–42.

18. Shakespeare, *Hamlet*, Act I, scene ii.

19. Ibid.

20. Barnes, *Levels of Life*.

21. "The Anaximander Fragment," in Martin Heidegger, *Early Greek Thinking*, trans. David Farrell Krell and Frank A. Capuzzi (New York: Harper & Row, 1984), p. 13.

22. Ibid., p. 43.

23. Albert Einstein, "Letter to Michele Besso, July 29th, 1953," in *Albert Einstein–Michele Besso Correspondence 1903–1955*, ed. P. Speziali (Paris: Hermann, 1972).

24. Samuel Johnson, *Rasselas* (Philadelphia: Willis P. Hazard, 1856), Chap. 18.

25. Ibid., p. 37.

26. W. B. Yeats, "Nineteen Hundred Nineteen," in *The Tower* (London: Penguin, 2018).

27. Rainer Maria Rilke, *Duino Elegies*, trans. Steven Cohn (Manchester: Carcanet, 1989).

BIBLIOGRAPHY

Amiel, Henri Frédéric. *Amiel's Journal, Volume 1*. Translated by Mrs. Humphry Ward. London: Macmillan & Co., 1885.

Arnold, Matthew. "To Marguerite—Continued." In *The Poetry of Matthew Arnold*. Edited by Kenneth Allott. London: Longman Norton, 1965.

Barnes, Julian. *Levels of Life*. London: Vintage Books, 2014.

Cicero, Marcus Tullius. *Tusculan Disputations*. Translated by Alan E. Douglas. Warminster: Aris & Phillips, 1985.

Dickens, Charles. *The Letters of Charles Dickens, Volume 2*. Edited by Mamie Dickens and Georgina Hogarth. Frankfurt: Outlook Verlag, 2020.

Einstein, Albert. "Letter to Michele Besso, July 29th, 1953." In *Albert Einstein–Michele Besso Correspondence 1903–1955*. Edited by P. Speziali. Paris: Hermann, 1972.

Forster, E. M. *Howards End*. London: Penguin, 2000.

Hardy, Thomas. "The Going." In *Satires of Circumstance: Lyrics and Reveries with Miscellaneous Pieces*. London: Macmillan and Co., Limited, 1914.

Hardy, Thomas. "The Self-Unseeing." In *Poems of the Past and the Present*. London: Macmillan and Co., Limited, 1919.

Heidegger, Martin. *Early Greek Thinking*. Translated by David Farrell Krell and Frank A. Capuzzi. New York: Harper & Row, 1984.

Housman, A. E. *A Shropshire Lad*. New York: Dover Thrift Editions, 1990.

Johnson, Samuel. *Rasselas*. Philadelphia: Willis P. Hazard, 1856.

King, Henry. "An Exequy to His Matchless Never to Be Forgotten Friend." In *The New Oxford Book of Seventeenth Century Verse*. Edited by Alastair Fowler. Oxford: Oxford University Press, 1992), pp. 288–90.

Montaigne, Michel de. *The Complete Essays*. Edited by Michael Screech. London: Penguin, 1991.

Rilke, Rainer Maria. *Duino Elegies*. Translated by Steven Cohn. Manchester: Carcanet, 1989.

Schroeder, David. *Our Schubert: His Enduring Legacy*. Lanham, MD: Scarecrow Press, 2009.

Shakespeare, William. *Hamlet*. London: Penguin, 2001.

Yeats, W. B. "Nineteen Hundred Nineteen." In *The Tower*. London: Penguin, 2018.

Index

Abortion, 58, 71n5, 73n45.
  See also God (Judeo-Christian)
Absalom's Pillar (Jerusalem), 207
Achilles, 173
Act of Union, (1800) 178
Adam, 23–25, 31n6, 68
  Fall and 23–25, 31n6
  sins of 36
Adams, M., 32n13
Aeneas, 187
Afterlife, 3, 22, 26, 28, 60, 156, 186, 219n12
Ainsworth, M. 111–12
Akhmatova, A. 178
Alternative Service Book, 35
Amiel, H.F., 227
Anaximander, 232
Anchises, 187
Antigone, 81, 185–86
Anxiety, 43, 45–46, 50, 110, 113, 115, 129n8, 134, 229
Aquinas, Thomas, 24–25, 31n8, 34, 36–38, 67
  Commentary on the Book of Job, 36–37
  Summa Theologiae, 24–25, 31n8.
  See also evil

architecture, sepulchral
  Baroque, 207, 209
  Classical, 6, 204, 208–217, 218n3
  Gothic, 209–211, 213–14
  Roman, 210
  Romanesque, 209
Arendt, H., 84–85, 87
  "radical evil" and, 84–87
Aristotle, 34, 67, 102n4, 173–74
Armenia, genocide and, 180
Arnold, M., 229
Aron, A., 137–39
Aron, E., 137–39
Ars Moriendi (treatises), 38
Aspasia, 82, 93–94, 102
Athens, 82, 93, 102, 214
  Acropolis, 214
  Erechtheon, 214
  Parthenon, 214
  Propyleon, 214
  resurrection and, 82–83
atrium (architectural feature), 214
attachment, 133–36, 144n4, 152, 186
attachment behaviors, 110
attachment, patterns of, 111–14
  bereavement and, 113

239

attachment, theory of, 110
Augustine, 31n8

Babits, M.,
    The Book of Jonah, 89
Baghdad, 190
Balkans, the, 177
Barnes, E., 25
Barnes, J., 94–95, 100, 225, 231
    Levels of Life, 94, 225
Beck, F., 109
    Diary of a Widow, 109
Belarus, 179
Belsen, 176
Benjamin, W., 77, 79.
    See also melancholy
bereavement, 4–5, 38, 97, 108, 110,
        114–15, 120–21, 127, 151–52, 154,
        165, 167, 217–218, 223, 225–26,
        231
    antidepressants, and 115
    anxiolytics and, 115
    brain, changes in, 109
    closure and, 127
    depression and, 132
    disabling effects of, 110, 114
    disorientation and, 110–11
    dual process and, 108
    emotional turmoil and, 108
    existential nature of, 121–22
    faith and, 113–14
    loss orientation and, 108, 110–11
    private, 149
    psychology of, 107
    public, 149
    restoration orientation and, 108, 110
    searching for the dead and, 109
    solitary life and, 229
    support and, 107
    therapy and, 114–15.
    See also attachment, patterns of *and*
        isolation
Berlin, 190
Berlin Wall, 180
Besso, M., 233
Bible, 61, 189
    Acts, 24

Epistle to the Colossians, 29
Gospels and, 80, 83, 128
infertility and, 61
Isaiah, 48
Job, 46–47, 49
John, 22, 29
Lamentations, 23
Luke, 4, 128
Matthew, 83
New Testament, 22, 24, 29, 47, 83,
    164
Old Testament, 17n5, 39, 47, 207,
    218
Psalms, 4, 83, 129
Revelation, 21
Romans, 26, 29
Sermon on the Mount, 186
Wisdom, 35
Big Bang, 218
Binyon, L., 127
    'For the Fallen,' 127
'Bloodlands' (WWII), 179–81
Bloomsbury Group, the, 200
Book of Common Prayer, the, 35, 173
Boswell, J. 7, 13
Bowlby, J., 109–111, 152
Brahma, 188
brain, 8, 109
Braulio of Saragossa, 44
Britten, B., 187
    Curlew River, 187
Bryce, J., 207
burial, 34–35, 39–40, 48–49, 77, 82,
        172–73, 175–77, 185, 203–204,
        207, 209, 216
    re-burial and, 177, 181, 182n6.
    See also cremation *and* graveyards
burial grounds. *See* graveyards
Byron, G.G., 207
    Hebrew Melodies, 207–208

Cambodia, killing fields of, 176
Catholic Office of the Dead. *See* Office
    of the Dead, Catholic
cemeteries *See* graveyards
Centre for the Art of Dying Well, The
    (St Mary's University), 38

Ceres, 80–81
Chicago Disability Pride Parade, 25
China, 190
Chloroform, 115
Cholbi, M., 135–37, 140, 143.
    See also grief *and* loss
Christ, 22, 24, 26, 28–30, 31n6, 34–35,
        37–38, 46, 48–49, 64, 68–69, 83,
        87, 157, 172, 200
    boulesis and, 37
    crucifixion of, 22, 29, 42, 48, 128
    death of, 43
    incarnate, 22, 28–30, 31n6, 69
    God and, 28
    Paschal Mystery of, 42
    Passing Over, 49
    Passion of, 37
    Persephone, myth of and, 81
    Resurrection of, 37, 41–43
    Sacrifice of, 36, 42, 48–50
    solidarity with, 49
    thelesis and, 37
Christianity
    baptism and, 34, 41–42
    community and, 64, 157
    doctrine and, 20, 23, 26–30, 33, 49
    Eucharist and, 34, 48
    faith, loss of, 195–96
    importance of, 199
    Mass and, 34, 39–40, 42, 49
    redemption and, 3
    Roman Catholic, 33–34
    theology and, 22
    truth of, 193.
    See also afterlife *and* Creation, the
        and Cross, the *and* death *and*
        God (Judeo-Christian)
        and liturgies *and* Office of the
        Dead, Catholic *and* prayer
Christmas, 122, 215
Chrysostom, John, 24
Cicero, 222
Circe, 184
Claudian (Claudius Claudianus, poet),
        80
    The Rape of Proserpina, 80–81
Claudius (*Hamlet*), 231

Clyde R., 204
Cognitive Behavior Therapy (CBT),
        114–15, 231.
    See also bereavement
Communism, 180
concentration camps, 3, 86
Conran, Fr., 114
Consciousness, 8, 10, 122, 124, 140,
        183, 198, 222, 230.
    See also nothingness
Continuing Bonds theory, 150–52
Corinthian War, 82
coronavirus (COVID-19) pandemic, 4,
        40, 119, 127, 155, 164–65.
    See also funerals
Creation, the 20–23, 25, 67–68, 73n45,
        87, 218, 234
cremation, 40, 176, 185–86
Creon, 81–82, 172, 185
Cross, the, 45, 48, 69
Cruse Bereavement Care, 115
crying, 107–110, 112

Danae, 204
Dante (Durante degli Alighieri), 4,
        17n3, 121, 174
    Paradiso, 174
Daoism, 1
Dark Ages, the, 215
Darmstadt, 190
Darwin, C., 108–109, 133
    The Descent of Man, 108
    *The Expression of the Emotions in
        Man and Animals*, 108.
    See also grief
Dastur, F., 78
Davidman, J., 141
dead, relationship with, 134, 136–40,
        142–43, 152–53, 175–76, 185
death, 1–4, 6–7, 10–16, 33–42, 44–49,
        61, 63, 65, 68–69, 79–83, 86,
        88–89, 94, 97–98, 109, 111, 113,
        122, 134, 136, 139–42, 149, 153–
        54, 156, 158–59, 161–63, 171–73,
        175, 177–78, 184–85, 193, 195,
        198, 214, 222–31, 233–35
    anger and, 44, 49

awfulness of, 15, 18n8
brain and, 8
children and, 151, 187
as derailment, 172
disruption and, 1, 139
as divine will, 34–35, 37–38
as evil, 3, 35–36, 49
as existential fact, 78
fear of, 233
forgotten, 176–78
Mass and, 43
meaning of, context for, 114
philosophy and, 83, 222
unfinished business and, 43
unmourned, 5.
See also God (Judeo-Christian) and nothingness and prayer
Demeter See Ceres
Depression, 4, 77, 80–81, 88, 112–13, 115, 129, 132, 134, 144n6.
See also bereavement
Derrida, J., 77–80, 84
deutero-truths, 160
Devil, the, 84
Dharma, 188
Diagnostic and Statistical Manual of Mental Disorders (DSM-5), 132, 144n6
DSM-4, 144n6
Dickens, C., 227.
See also Havisham, Miss (Great Expectations)
Dickens, L., 227
Dido, 187
Dies irae, 45, 48, 172.
Disenfranchised Grief theory See grief
Disneyfication, 185–87.
dividuality See personhood
Dominican Order, 35
Donaueschingen, 190
Donne, J., 156–57, 175
Dostoevsky, F., 19, 194
dual process, the. See bereavement
Duffy, E., 35
Dunn, J., 164
Dürer, A., 189
Durkheim, E., 77

Edinburgh, 209
 Dean Cemetery, 209
ego 78–79, 86, 100, 131, 183.
See also grief and melancholy
Einstein, A., 233
elegies, 189
Eleusis, 82
Elgar, E., 189
Eliot, T.S., 188
Four Quartets, 188–89
Elizabeth (biblical figure), 62
Elpenor, 184–86
Emmaus, 128
emotion, 10, 110, 113–14, 153–55, 160, 165–66, 185.
See also bereavement
empathy, 97, 142–43, 230.
See also Stein, E.
Empire State Building, 210
England, 35, 40–41, 122, 179, 189, 194–96.
See also funerals
Enoch, 205
Epicurus, 144n2
Erikson, E., 159.
See also generativity
Estonia, 179
ethics, 3, 194, 198, 200, 215, 218
European Network Remembrance and Solidarity, 180
European Remembrance Symposium, 180
European Union (EU), 190
evil, 3, 19–21, 23, 25–27, 29–30, 35–36, 49, 68, 81, 84–87, 189
Aquinas and, 36.
See also Arendt, H. and death
Exultet, the, 23–25, 31n6.
See also felix culpa

Fackenheim, E., 85
Fall, the, 20–25, 27, 29–30, 32n14, 67.
See also Adam
Famine, Irish, 176–79
background to, 178–79
diaspora and, 179
Fascism, 210

felix culpa, 23–27, 29–30, 31n6
Fields of Asphodel, 214
Final Commendation, 40–41
fittingness, 103n7
fMRI (functional Magnetic Resonance Imaging) technology, 109
Forster, E.M., 222, 235
Francis, St, 171
Frankfurt, H., 103n6
Frankl, V., 85
Freud, S., 77, 79–80, 82, 100, 102n4, 111, 114, 131–34, 136, 138–39, 143–44, 152, 160, 186, 197, 232
   'Mourning and Melancholia,' 100, 114, 131, 151, 183.
   See also melancholy *and* mourning
Fuchs, T., 137–40, 143
   identification/representation and, 137, 143.
   See also grief
funerals, 33–35, 39–44, 50, 82–83, 150, 162, 165, 172–73, 175–76, 184–85, 189, 203, 231, 234
   Athenian funeral speech and, 93
   children and, 44
   coronavirus (COVID-19) and, 41
   England and, 40, 175
   Maori Tangi and, 114
   Order of Christian Funerals, 41–42.
   See also grief *and* liturgies
Futurism, 210, 218n3

generativity, 159–60
Germany, 158, 189–91
   melancholy and, 190
   mourning and, 191
Gertrude (*Hamlet*), 225, 227, 231–32
Gethsemane, 37–38
Girard, R., 187
Glasgow, 204–205, 209, 211, 217
   Bridge of Sighs, 205f, 212f
   Cathedral of, 205f, 206, 209, 212f, 215
   Jewish community of, 207
   Jews' Enclosure, 208, 208f, 209
   Merchants House of, 204, 206–207

Necropolis of, 6, 204, 206f, 207–209, 212f, 214–16, 216f, 217, 218n2
Patron Saint of. *See* Mungo (Patron Saint of Glasgow)
tomb design and, 204.
See also architecture, sepulchral
God (Judeo-Christian), 3, 16, 19–23, 25, 28–31, 33–38, 41–43, 45–48, 58, 61, 63–70, 85, 87– 88, 113, 154, 158, 171, 184, 188, 194, 200, 218, 234
   abortion and, 73n45
   'After God,' 200
   anger toward, 44
   as Author of Life, 47
   conscious, 85
   death and, 36
   death of, 194–99
   feminism and, 65–67
   forgiveness and, 43
   friendship and 33, 36, 48
   gestational models and, 65–66, 68, 70
   Holocaust and, 85
   love and, 20, 29–30, 33–34, 36, 42–44, 46, 67–68
   perfection of, 66, 68
   pregnancy and, 65, 67–68
   self-emptying and, 67, 87–88
   as triune, 28, 33
   uncaring, 234
   unconscious, 85
   will of, 35–38.
   See also Holy Spirit *and* Christ *and* suffering
Goethe, J.W. von, 189
good life, the, 94–96
goodness, 20–21, 66, 68, 87–88, 129, 200
Gorer, G., 150–51.
Gospels *See* Bible
Grass, G., 191
graveyards, 40, 64, 177, 203–204, 207, 209, 216
grief
   ambiguity of, 137
   anger and, 44–45, 174

'bargaining' and, 43
Christian, 3
culture and, 114, 138, 143
'de-presentifying' (Fuchs) and, 137
Disenfranchised Grief theory, 150–51
ego and, 136
endless, 96–102
ethnic differences and, 1
existential nature of, 121–22
funerals and, 34, 39–40
as goal-seeking emotion, 109–110
'grief muscles' (Darwin) and, 108
human identity (Cholbi) and, 135
investment in (Cholbi), 135
loss and, 95, 98–99
love and, 97, 100, 107
ontological framework of, 68
pain and, 101, 124, 135, 217
pervasive nature of, 122, 124–25
phenomenology and, 137, 140
'presentifying' (Fuchs) and, 137
private, 5, 174–75, 181
process of, 40, 49, 115, 138
profound, 95
Prolonged Grief Disorder, 113
public, 181
psychology of, 107
resolution of, 136
self-knowledge and, 135
taxonomy of (Lindemann), 132
transformations and, 137
typologies of, 150
uncontrollable, 174
vulnerability and, 96
virtue and, 94.
  See also God (Judeo-Christian) *and* Lewis, C.S. *and* mourning *and* pregnancy loss
Grünewald, M., 189
guilt, 20, 57, 183, 190–91, 227–28.
  See also survivors
Gulags (USSR), 176
Gurus, 157–58

Hades, 48, 81, 184
Haldane Lectures, 211

Hamlet (individual), 225, 227, 231
Hannah (biblical figure), 62
Happiness, 38, 93–94, 101, 120–21, 123, 131, 188, 195, 227, 234
Hardy, T., 125–26, 228–30, 232
  'At Castle Boterel,' 125
  Poems, 1912–13 228
  'The Going,' 228
  'The Self Unseeing,' 229
Harley Davidson, 221
Havisham, Miss, (*Great Expectations*) 226
health, mental, 132.
  See also depression
Heaven, 20–21, 27–28, 34, 42, 44, 48, 60, 82, 172, 231
Hector, 173
Hegel, G.W.F., 189, 198, 211
Heidegger, M., 123, 129n8, 172, 199, 222, 232
  Sein zum Tode, 172
Hertz, R., 138
Hezekiah, 48
Hill, G., 171–72
Hitler, A., 190, 218n3
holocaust, nuclear, 196
Holocaust, the, 85, 176, 179–80, 190, 222.
  See also God (Judeo-Christian)
Holy Spirit, 83
Homer, 80, 172
  Iliad, 172
hope, 2–3, 36, 41–42
Horace, 4, 121
Horatius. *See* Horace
Housman, A.E., 4, 122–23, 224
Hume, D., 2–3, 7–9, 13–14
  Hume's Argument, 10–11
  Hume's Challenge, 10–14, 16–17, 17n3.
  See also nothingness
Hygienic Cemetery Movement, 203–204

injustice, 96, 99, 180, 232
  anger and, 96, 99
intentionality, 78–80, 83, 86, 89.

See also mourning *and*
    phenomenology
Ireland, 176–78
    Peace Process and, 179.
    See also Famine, Irish
IrishHolocaust.org website, 179, 181
Islam, 154, 190, 209
isolation, 119, 126
    as form of bereavement, 120
    effects on humans and, 119–20.
    See also mourning
Italy, 187

Jerusalem, 48, 164, 207
Jesus. *See* Christ
Job, 20, 36, 38, 46–48, 54n97
John Damascene (John of Damascus), 37
Johnson, S. (Dr. Johnson), 2, 7–8, 14, 144n2, 234
    Rasselas, 234.
    See also nothingness
Jonas, H., 85
Gottesbegriff nach Auschwitz, 85
Jones, S., 61, 64, 69–70
Judaism, 20, 77, 207, 209
    Talmudic tradition and, 158
Jupiter, 81

Kabbalah, 87.
    See also tzimtzum
Kaddish, 85
Kant, I., 84–85, 87, 189, 195, 198
Keats, J., 4, 122
kenosis, 87–88.
Kentigern. *See* Mungo (Patron Saint of Glasgow)
Keynes, J.M., 193, 200
Kidron Valley, 207
Kiefer, A., 191
Kierkegaard, S., 133–35, 137, 142–44
    'The Works of Love,' 133
Kilkenny, 176–79, 181
King, H., 227
    An Exequy to His Matchless Never to be Forgotten Friend, 227
Kingma, E., 61, 66, 68

Knox, J., 206, 206f
Konstanz Minster, 64
Korsgaard, C., 135
Kübler-Ross, E., 40

Last Day, the, 43, 46–47
Latvia, 179
Lauds, 39, 44, 46–49, 52n55
Lazarus, 48, 172
Lear, J., 102n4, 104n20
Le Corbusier, C.-E. J., 211
Leningrad, 178
Leninism, 211
Levi, J., 207
Levinas, E., 78, 84
Lewis, C.S., 141, 143, 174–75
    A Grief Observed, 174
    experience of grief and, 141
Lindemann, E., 114, 132
    'The Symptomatology of Acute Grief,' 114
Lindemann, H., 68
Lithuania, 179
liturgies, 3, 35–36, 38–42, 44–45, 124–25
    Funeral Liturgy, 34–35, 41, 43–44, 49–50
    Funeral Mass, 39, 41, 46, 48, 52n57
    "Gelasian" Sacramentary, 35
    Liturgia Horarum, 35
    Liturgy of the Dead (general), 34–35, 37, 39, 45, 48–49, 50n1
    medieval, 35, 42, 45, 48–50
    New Liturgy, 3
    Old Liturgy, 3
    Ordo Exsequiarum, 35, 41–42, 44, 52n6
    post-Tridentine, 35
    Requiem Mass, 41, 45, 48, 52n58, 172–73
    Rituale Romanum, 34–35, 44, 50, 52n56, 54n104
    Roman Catholic Liturgies of the Dead, 33–34
    Sarum Use, 48, 50.
    See also Dies irae and *Exultet*, the
living well. *See* good life, the
Locke, J., 18n7

London, 178–79
loss, 1–6, 4, 36, 40, 62–63, 67, 79–81,
    86, 88, 94–101, 107, 110, 112–15,
    119–28, 131–43, 150–52, 154, 159–
    61, 163, 165, 174–75, 183, 186–87,
    189, 194, 196, 224–26, 230–32, 234
  academic, 150–51
  culture and, 150
  disruption and, 136
  existential, 183
  experience of, 135
  faith and, 194, 196
  human identity and (Cholbi), 135,
    143
  loss orientation, 108, 110–11
  religion, importance of and, 186–88
  severity and, 139
  shock of, 134
  theology of, 2
  Uncommon Losses theory, 150–51
  virtue and, 96
  vulnerability and, 96, 143
  Western civilization and, 186–88.
  See also grief *and* mourning *and*
    pregnancy loss
loss orientation. *See* bereavement *and*
  loss
Löwith, K., 84
  The Meaning in History, 84
Lucretius, 17n3, 233
  De Rerum Natura, 233
Luria, I., 87
Luther, M., 69, 189.
LXX. *See* Septuagint

MacIntyre, A., 6, 102n5, 195–97,
    199–200
  After Virtue, 195–96
  A Short History of Ethics, 196
  Marxism and Christianity, 197
  Secularization and Moral Change, 196,
    199
MacNee, D., 209
Mahler, G., 187
  Kindertotenlieder, 187
Manley Hopkins, G., 4, 123–25
  'Spring and Fall,' 123

Mao, 176, 190
Maori 114.
  See also funerals
Maori Tangi. *See* funerals
Marriott, M., 157
Marušić, B., 103n9, 104n21
Marxism, 196–98, 211
Mary, 64, 172
Mass. *See* Christianity
Matins, 39, 44, 46–47, 49
  Matins of the Dead, 46–47, 50
McCabe, H., 38
Meincke, A.S., 69
melancholy, 77, 79–82, 85, 88, 183, 214,
    224
  Benjamin and, 79
  ego and, 79
  Freud and, 79, 82, 100, 144n4, 183.
  See also Germany
Melanesia, 157
Merkel, A., 191
Merleau-Ponty, M., 141
  'style' and, 141
Michael, St, 48
Miscarriage. *See* pregnancy loss
Misery, 20, 119, 121, 229
Mitscherlich, A., 190
  Die Unfähigkeit zu trauern, 190.
  See also Nielsen, M.
Modernism, 210, 213–14, 218, 219n11
Molendinar Burn, 207
Moller, D., 97–98, 101, 104nn13–14,
    104n19
Moltmann, J., 69
Mongols, 190
Montaigne, M. de, 222, 235
Moore, G.E., 200
  Principia Ethica, 200
Mormons, 155
mortality, 126, 149, 151, 165, 233
mourning,
  avoidance of, 93–94
  blessedness and, 83
  comfort and, 83
  communities and, 2
  cultural aspects of, 2
  decay and, 88

denial of, 176
despair and, 129
as dialogue, 184
as duty, 184–85
existential nature of, 121–22, 183
formality of, 40, 124–25
Freud and, 79–81, 100, 114, 131, 136, 144n4, 151, 183
friends and, 153
goal of, 143
healing and, 88, 125, 127
intentionality and, 79–80, 84
isolation and, 120
knowledge and, 150
loss and, 96–97, 131
love and, 95–97, 126, 134
meanings, range of, 77
mentor/mentee relationship and, 149, 152–53, 156, 158–65
moving on and, 226–27
Neolithic burials and, 173
Old Testament and, 39
orations and, 83
phenomenology and, 78
philosophy and, 77
private, 174, 181
as problem, 21, 29–30
process of, 5, 131–34
prohibition of, 81–82
psychology of, 107, 132–33
public, 2, 149, 181
purpose of, 143
reciprocation and, 134
reconciliation and, 189
refusive analysis of, 87–89
renewal and, 81, 88
resolution/closure and, 131, 138, 174
rituals, ritualized acts of, 124, 126, 184, 186, 230
self-knowledge and (Cholbi), 135–36
self-renovation and, 88
solitary nature of, 230
supportive, 64
as therapy, 183
as transitional state, 100
unmourning, 81, 84, 86
value and, 100
virtue and, 94
"work of" (Freud), 80–81, 85, 100, 131–34, 136–37, 183, 189–91, 232. *See also* Germany
Mungo (Patron Saint of Glasgow), 204, 206
legend of, 204–205
music, 126–27, 189–90, 203, 216, 218n3

Na'aman, O., 103n9
Nash, J., 189
Nash, P., 189
National Health Service, 164
Nazis, 5, 190
Neoplatonism, 67–68, 87
Nielsen, M., 190
Die Unfähigkeit zu trauern, 190
Nietzsche, F., 121, 177–78, 180, 188, 194–200
The Gay Science, 195
'The Use and Abuse of History for Life,' 177–78
nothingness
awfulness and, 12–15, 17, 17n5
consciousness and, 10
death and, 9
future (post-death), 8–16
Hume and, 7–11
infinity of, 8, 12–13
Johnson and, 9
past (pre-birth), 8–14

O'Donnell, K., 63
Odysseus, 184, 186
Office of Readings, 44. *See also* Matins
Office of the Dead, Catholic, 3, 34–35, 39–40, 44
Medieval forms of, 44–45, 49. *See also* liturgies
Olympias, 24
Order for the Burial of the Dead, 173
Order of St. John of Jerusalem, 164
outliving, 111, 223–26, 231–33, 235

pain, 3, 7, 24, 27, 64, 94, 100, 115, 120, 123–28, 131, 134–35, 137, 217, 222, 226, 232
   love and, 94, 100.
   See also grief
panentheism, 68
Paradise, 48, 188
Parry, H., 126–27
   Songs of Farewell, 126–27
Paul (Apostle), 24, 26, 29, 37, 73n45, 88, 160.
   See also Bible
Pearl, The (poem), 187
Peloponnesian War, 82
Pericles, 82, 214
Persephone, myth of, 80–82
   resurrection and, 81.
   See also Christ
personhood, 153, 157, 164
   dividual/dividuality, 5, 156, 163, 165
   individual, 5, 156
Peter, 35
phenomenology, 2, 4, 10, 78, 86
   apocalyptic, 86–89
   intentionality and, 78
   material, 78
   transcendental, 78, 86.
   See also mourning
philosophy, Christian, 57–59, 63–69, 70.
   See also pregnancy loss
philosophy, humane, 221, 235
philosophy, role of, 221–23, 232–35
piety, 5, 133, 185, 190, 207, 218
Piraeus, 195
Plath, S., 184
   'Daddy,' 184
Plato, 77, 82–83, 93, 101–102, 221
   Apology, 221
   Menexenus, 77, 80, 82, 93, 95
Platonism, 1, 67
poetry, 39, 80, 126–27, 187, 203
Poland, 179
Polyneices, 81, 185, 190
Poor Law, the, 179
Popper, K., 84

Open Society and Its Enemies, 84
prayer, 34, 38, 43–46, 48–50, 86
   death and, 43, 45
   Sarum prayer, 44
pregnancy, 3, 57–58, 60, 62, 66, 68–69
   emptying, feeling of, 62–63
   metaphysics of, 66, 70
   postpartum and, 62
   potential for miscarriage and, 62.
   See also abortion *and* God (Judeo-Christian) *and* pregnancy loss
pregnancy loss, 3, 57–60, 62–64, 66, 68
   afterlife and, 60
   Christian philosophy and, 58–59, 62–66, 68, 70
   grief and, 58, 70
   miscarriage and, 57–58, 61–63, 66, 69, 71n3
   ritual and, 63, 70
   stillbirth and, 61, 69
   theology of, 60, 63
Preston-Roedder E., 104n14
Preston-Roedder R., 104n14.
Proserpina. *See* Persephone, myth of
punishment, 36, 119
Purgatory, 34, 44, 48, 50, 53n74
Pyramids, 213

Rachel (biblical figure), 62
Rasselas, 234
Ratcliffe, M., 140–43
Rationalism, 210.
redemption. *See* Christianity
Reformation, the, 205–207, 215
refusivum sui, principle of, 86–89.
   See also mourning
regret, 98, 101, 121, 171, 189, 196, 228–30
Reiheld, A., 62
relationships, personal, 2, 60, 94, 98, 110, 133–38, 140–43, 151, 153, 158–59, 166, 228
   love and 110–13.
   See also dead, relationship with
Requiem Mass. *See* liturgies
restoration orientation. *See* bereavement

resurrection, 3, 22, 26, 34, 42–44, 47–48, 88, 174.
   See also Athens and Christ and Persephone
Rilke, R.M., 188, 234
   Duino Elegies, 234
Robinson, M., 179
Roman Missal, 37
Rome, 211
   Colosseum, 211
Ruskin, J., 211

salvation, 36–38, 44, 87, 222
Sarah (biblical figure), 62
Sartre, J.-P., 139, 142
Schiller, F., 189
Schopenhauer, A., 213
   The World as Will and Representation, 213
Schubert, F., 229
Schultz, B., 193–94
Schut, H., 108, 114
Scotland, 161, 176, 204, 207, 209, 215, 217
scripture, Hebrew, 83
Scrutton, T. (A.P.), 63–64
Scuro, J., 62–63, 65–68
self-control, 1
self-criticism, 187
self-improvement, 135
selfishness, 124, 127, 228
self-knowledge, 135–36, 152–53.
   See also grief and mourning
self, sense of, 139, 142
self-sufficiency, 1, 94, 101–102, 102n5
self, true, 21, 26–29, 30
Septuagint, 83
Shakespeare, W., 235
Shostakovich, D., 178
Sidgwick, H., 5, 193–200
sin, 25, 43, 46
   original, 20.
   See also Adam
Socrates, 82–83, 93, 172, 195, 199, 221–22
solipsism, 139–40, 143
Son of Saul (dir. Nemes, 2015), 85–86

Sophocles, 80–82, 172, 185, 190
   Antigone, 80–82, 172, 185, 190.
   See also Antigone
sorrow, 4, 23, 25, 47, 83–84, 86, 89, 102, 121, 124, 127–28, 186, 195, 230–31, 233
soul, human, 33, 36, 43–46, 48, 120, 124, 153, 157, 185, 189, 193, 228
Sparta, 82
Spencer, S., 189
Spinoza, B., 233
Stalin, 190
Stein, E., 142–43
   On the Problem of Empathy, 142–43
St. John Ambulance UK, 164–65
Stockhausen, K., 191
Stoicism, 233–34
Storr, A., 200
Stroebe, M.S., 108
suffering, 19–25, 27, 29–30, 31n6, 36, 38, 46–48, 99, 115, 119, 126, 186–87, 229
   God and, 28, 36–37
survival, 1, 4, 14, 25, 109, 153, 183
survivors, 186, 190, 231
   guilt and, 226

Teiresias, 81
Tennant, C., 206f
Tennyson, A., 122–23
   In Memoriam, 122
Thebes, 81, 185, 190
Theneva. See Thenew
Thenew, 204–205.
   See also Enoch
theology, Trinitarian, 58, 69–70
therapy, 115, 132, 183, 232–33
therapy, emotive, 114–15.
   See also bereavement and Cognitive Behavior Therapy (CBT)
therapy, occupational, 227
therapy, problem-focused, 114–15.
   See also bereavement
Thomas (biblical figure), 22, 64
Thomism, 197
Thomson, A., 211, 213
Threlfall, K., 164–65

Tibet, 190
Tippet, M., 189
Tolstoy, L., 131
　Anna Karenina, 131
trauma, 3, 5, 60, 98, 113, 183, 215
Triano, S., 25
Trinity, the, 28, 69–70.
　See also theology, Trinitarian
Troy, 173, 187
Tubman, H., 21–23, 26
typhus, 176
tzimtzum, 85, 87–88

Ukraine, 179
Uncommon Losses theory. *See* loss
Upanishads, 186–88
Utrecht, University of, 108, 114

value(s), 11, 28, 32, 95, 103n8, 104n13, 109, 114, 126–27, 135–36, 140, 152, 154, 156, 199–200, 230, 233, 235
　beliefs and, 155
　ideas and, 153–55, 157
　identities and, 153–55
　recognition of, 2, 4, 11, 96–102, 104n13, 104n19
　shared, 154
Vatican II, 35
Vaughan Williams, R., 189
　Pilgrim's Progress, 189
Vespers, 39, 44, 47, 49, 52n55
　Vespers of the Dead, 46

Victoria, Queen, 115
Vietnam War, 173
Villon, F., 224
Virgil, 187
　Aeneid, 187
virtue, 24, 28, 37, 82, 94–101, 190, 193, 195, 228, 232.
　See also grief *and* loss *and* mourning

Wagner, R., 218n3
Waugh, E., 185
　The Loved One, 185
Weber, M., 156, 207
warfare, 128.
　See also World War I *and* World War II
Wiesel, E., 85
will, free, 32n14
will, human, 37–38
Williams, B., 194–95, 197–200
　Ethics and the Limits of Philosophy, 195, 197, 200
Wittgenstein, L., 222
world, assumptive, 108, 110
World War I, 114, 189
World War II, 3, 114, 180

Yancey, H., 69
Yeats, W.B., 181, 234

Zeus. *See* Jupiter

About the Contributors

Lesley Chamberlain is a novelist, critic, journalist, travel writer, and historian of Russian and German culture. She has written for the *Independent*, *Times Literary Supplement*, *LA Times*, *Wall Street Journal*, and *Prospect* magazine. She is the author of *Nietzsche in Turin* (Picador, 1996), *Motherland: A Philosophical History of Russia* (Atlantic Books, 2004), *A Shoe Story: Van Gogh, the Philosophers and the West* (Harbour Books, 2014), and, more recently, *Street Life and Morals: German Philosophy in Hitler's Lifetime* (Reaktion Books, 2021) and *Rilke: The Last Inward Man* (Pushkin Press, 2022).

John Cottingham is Professor Emeritus of Philosophy at the University of Reading, and an Honorary Fellow of St John's College, Oxford. Cottingham has served as editor of the journal *Ratio*, president of the Aristotelian Society, of the British Society for the Philosophy of Religion, of the Mind Association and as Chairman of the British Society for the History of Philosophy. He published over thirty books, the most recent of which include *Philosophy of Religion: Towards a More Humane Approach* (Cambridge, 2014), *How to Believe* (Bloomsbury, 2015), and *In Search of the Soul* (Princeton University Press, 2020).

Richard Conrad OP is the former Vice-Regent of Studies at Blackfriars Hall, University of Oxford, and Director of the Aquinas Institute from 2014 to 2020. He is a member of the Faculty of Theology, University of Oxford. He teaches dogmatic and sacramental theology in the Studium, and at the Maryvale Institute, Birmingham, where for ten years he directed an MA in Catholic Theology. He is also external examiner for the BA in Fundamental Catholic Theology taken by students of St Mary's College, Oscott, and an examiner for the BTh and MTh degrees of the University of Oxford.

Douglas J. Davies is a Welsh Anglican theologian, anthropologist, and academic, specializing in the history, theology, and sociology of death. He is Professor in the Study of Religion at the University of Durham. His fields of expertise also include anthropology, the study of religion, the rituals and beliefs surrounding funerary rites and cremation around the globe, Mormonism and Mormon studies. He is Fellow of the Academy of Social Sciences (FAcSS), Fellow of the Learned Society of Wales (FLSW), of the national academy of Wales, and Fellow of the British Academy (FBA).

Matt Dougherty received a PhD in philosophy at University of Cambridge in 2019. He is a University Assistant at the University of Vienna, working primarily in Ethics, the History of Philosophy, and Philosophy of Mind. He was previously Lecturer in Philosophy in the Faculty of Philosophy, University of Cambridge, and Blackfriars Hall and Studium, University of Oxford, as well as Instructor in Philosophy at Virginia Tech. He is especially interested in the idea that ethical virtue is a kind of skill, an idea discussed in ancient as well as contemporary virtue ethics. Dougherty has published research in the *Journal for the History of Analytical Philosophy, Journal of Ethics and Social Philosophy*, and *Inquiry*.

Amber L. Griffioen is Residential Fellow at the Center for Philosophy of Religion, University of Notre Dame. From 2010 to 2019 she was Margarete von Wrangell Fellow and Lecturer in Philosophy at the University of Konstanz in Germany. Her published work includes *Religious Experience* (Cambridge, 2021), *The Irrational Project: Toward a Different Understanding of Self-Deception* (Iowa Research Online, 2010), as well as research papers in journals including the *European Journal for Philosophy of Religion, Journal of Analytic Theology*, and *American Catholic Philosophical Quarterly*. In addition to her published work on religious faith and experience, the religious imagination, and medieval mysticism, she also works on issues in Philosophy of Emotion and Agency, Islamic Philosophy, and Philosophy of Sport.

Cathy Mason is Assistant Professor in Philosophy at the Central European University. Her previous positions include: Leverhulme Early Career Fellow at the University of Cambridge, Stipendiary Lecturer in Philosophy at Wadham College at the University of Oxford, and tutor in Ethics, Political Philosophy, and Aesthetics at the University of Birmingham. She completed her PhD at Trinity College, Cambridge in 2019. Her research is primarily in ethics and moral epistemology, and she is also interested in Iris Murdoch's philosophical work. She has worked on some of the particular virtues (love, hope, humility) and their connection to moral knowledge. She teaches philosophy modules in value theory: moral philosophy, ethics, practical ethics, theory of politics, and aesthetics.

Balázs M. Mezei is Professor of Philosophy at Pázmány Péter Catholic University, Hungary, where he is the chair of the Philosophy Department and Director of the Doctoral School of Political Philosophy. He was a visiting scholar at the University of Notre Dame, Georgetown University, Loyola University in Maryland, the Institute for Human Sciences in Vienna, the Husserl Archives in Leuven, the Kirk Center for Cultural Renewal, and other institutions. He is vice-president of the Hungarian Society for the Study of Religion. He has widely published on the philosophy of religion, phenomenology, and literary criticism. He is the author of *Religion and Revelation after Auschwitz* (Bloomsbury, 2013), the two-volume *Philosophy of Religion* (Szent István Társulat, 2005), *Radical Revelation* (Bloomsbury 2019), and, with Barry Smith, *The Four Phases of Philosophy* (Rodopoi, 1998). He is also the co-editor of the *The Oxford Handbook of Divine Revelation* (OUP, 2021).

Anthony O'Hear OBE is Professor of Philosophy at the University of Buckingham and Head of the Department of Education. He is also the Honorary Director of the Royal Institute of Philosophy, and Editor of the journal *Philosophy*. He previously served as Government Advisor on Education and Teacher Training. He was made an Officer of the Order of the British Empire by Queen Elizabeth II for services to education in January 2018. He has written on philosophy of science, philosophy of religion, aesthetics and culture, political philosophy, and ethics. His publications include *Plato's Children* (Gordon Square, 2005), *Philosophy in the New Century* (Continuum, 2001), *After Progress* (Bloomsbury, 1999), *Beyond Evolution: Human Nature and the Limits of Evolutionary Explanation* (Clarendon Press, 1997), and *Introduction to the Philosophy of Science* (Oxford University Press, 1989).

Colin Murray Parkes OBE is emeritus of Royal London Hospital Medical College, and Emeritus Consultant Psychiatrist to St Christopher's Hospice, Sydenham. He is a member of the editorial board of *Bereavement Care and Mortality*, and Advisory Editor on several journals concerned with hospice, palliative care, and bereavement. He was made an Officer of the Order of the British Empire by Queen Elizabeth II for his services to bereaved people in June 1996. He worked for thirteen years with John

Bowlby at the Tavistock Institute of Human Relations. Recently his work has focused on traumatic bereavements (with special reference to violent deaths, armed conflict, and the cycle of violence) and on the roots in the attachments of childhood of the psychiatric problems that can follow the loss of attachments in adult life.

Sir Roger Scruton FBA, FRSL was a writer and philosopher who wrote over fifty books on philosophy, art, music, politics, literature, culture, sexuality, and religion, as well as novels and two operas. His involvement in the underground universities in the communist states in Central Europe and active support of dissidents was recognized with the First of June Prize from the Czech city of Plzeň, the Czech Republic's Medal of Merit (First Class) presented by President Václav Havel, the Grand Cross of the Order of Merit of the Republic of Poland, and the Silver Cross of the Order of Merit of the Republic of Hungary.

Mikołaj Sławkowski-Rode is Assistant Professor at the Department for Philosophy of Culture at the Faculty of Philosophy, University of Warsaw, as well as Research Fellow, and tutor in Philosophy at Blackfriars Hall, University of Oxford, and an Associate of the Ian Ramsey Centre for Science and Religion at the University of Oxford. His interests include philosophy of culture, phenomenology, joint attention, and philosophy of mind. He is also a founding member of the Humane Philosophy Society and organizer of the Humane Philosophy Project (www.humanephilosophy.com).

Alexander Stoddart FRSE is Sculptor in Ordinary to Her Majesty the Queen in Scotland, and Honorary Professor at the University of the West of Scotland. He works primarily on figurative sculpture in clay within the neoclassical tradition. Stoddart is best known for his civic monuments, including statues of David Hume and Adam Smith, philosophers during the Scottish Enlightenment, on the Royal Mile in Edinburgh, as well as of James Clerk Maxwell, William Henry Playfair, and John Witherspoon. In 2008 he was appointed the Queen's Sculptor in Ordinary in Scotland. In 2012 he was elected a Fellow of the Royal Society of Edinburgh. Stoddart has written extensively on the philosophy of aesthetics and published many articles. He broadcasts regularly on radio and television.

Eleonore Stump is Robert J. Henle Professor of Philosophy at Saint Louis University, where she has taught since 1992. She taught at Oberlin College, Virginia Polytechnic Institute and State University, and University of Notre Dame. Currently, she also holds secondary or honorary appointments at Wuhan University, the University of St Andrews, and Australian

Catholic University. She has published extensively in medieval philosophy, philosophy of religion, and contemporary metaphysics. Her books include her major study *Aquinas* (Routledge, 2003), her extensive treatment of the problem of evil, *Wandering in Darkness: Narrative and the Problem of Suffering* (OUP, 2010), and her recent *Atonement* (OUP, 2018). Among the named lectureships she has given are the Gifford Lectures (Aberdeen, 2003), the Wilde Lectures (Oxford, 2006), the Stewart Lectures (Princeton, 2009), and the Stanton Lectures (Cambridge, 2018).

Raymond Tallis FMedSci FRCP FRSA is emeritus of the University of Manchester. Philosopher, poet, novelist, cultural critic, and a retired medical physician and clinical neuroscientist. He specialized in geriatrics, and served on several UK commissions on medical care of the aged and was an editor or major contributor to two key textbooks in the field, *The Clinical Neurology of Old Age* (Wiley–Blackwell, 1989) and *Textbook of Geriatric Medicine and Gerontology* (Churchill Livingstone, 1992). He has published over two hundred articles in leading journals such as *Nature*, *Medicine*, and *Lancet*. Among many prizes, he was awarded the Lord Cohen Gold Medal for Research into Ageing. He played a key part in developing guidelines for the care of stroke patients in the UK. From 2011 to 2014 he was Chair, Healthcare Professionals for Assisted Dying (HPAD). He was a member of the Council of Royal College of Physicians between 2016 and 2019. He is a member of the criteria-setting group for the UK Research Excellence Framework 2021 in philosophy.

Jerry Valberg is former Senior Lecturer of Philosophy at University College London where he devoted the majority of his academic career. He works primarily in the fields of epistemology and metaphysics. His writings are also concerned with consciousness, identity, and the problems of perception. His notable contributions to philosophy include the personal horizon concept. He is the author of *Dream, Death, and the Self* (Princeton, 2007) and *The Puzzle of Experience* (OUP, 1992).

www.ingramcontent.com/pod-product-compliance
Lightning Source LLC
Chambersburg PA
CBHW070028010526
44117CB00011B/1746